CUBA:
The Disaster of Castro's Revolution

CUBA:
The Disaster of Castro's Revolution

Andres J. Solares

ISBN: 978-1-64945-402-7   (Paperback Edition)
ISBN: 978-1-64945-403-4   (Hardcover Edition)
ISBN: 978-1-64945-408-9   (E-book Edition)

Book Ordering Information

Phone Number: 347-901-4929 or 347-901-4920
Email: info@globalsummithouse.com
Global Summit House
www.globalsummithouse.com

Printed in the United States of America

CONTENTS

Dedication

I dedicate this book to my wife Adriana and to our children Andres Jr, Odette and Daniel as well as to our grandchildren and family.

PROLOGUE

I was twelve years old when the rebel army of Fidel Castro and his bearded men entered on Havana in January 1959. Like most people in Cuba at that time, I could not imagine how far the consequences of this event were going to impact our lives, and even less that, sixty years later, we would still be dealing with the same main characters and events of that so-called revolution.

I came from a modest Cuban family. My father worked in a store in Havana and my mother was a housewife. I was their only son.

When President Batista left Cuba and Fidel Castro and his people formed their new government, I was starting high school at the Institute of Havana, a public high school, after finishing my primary education in one of the best private schools that existed at that time in Havana.

Until 1959, my family had been a very coherent entity, with close ties between us and my aunts, uncles, cousins, and even second cousins. No matter what ideas or economic status the different members of it had, we knew that we always could count with them and vice versa. This somehow innocent institution was going soon to suffer the brutal impact of the new order established by Castro's policies.

I had witnessed, like everybody in Cuba, all the main events that started to change the normal path of life of our society during the two years previous to the fall of Batista's regime. There were air force planes that flew over Havana at night, coming from operations against Castro's forces in other provinces; there was the noise of bombs exploding almost every night in Havana; there were people who collected money for the revolution; there was also the impact of the images shown by the press, like those of the death of the President of the Student Federation of Havana University, Jose A. Echevarria, killed by the police after reading a manifesto in a radio station or those of the assassination by the revolutionaries of Blanco Rico, an army coronel, in the middle of Havana and also those of the attack to the presidential palace—those were crude images that became very difficult to forget. It was a time that was full of news and rumors.

At the high school, we all got used to the interruption of classes, when somebody linked to the revolution called for a strike, or when the students innocently exploded some little flasks called stinking bombs, which were sold to be used as a joke in a store called the House of Tricks and became a favorite for those wishing to interrupt classes to go home early in the name of the revolution.

My parents had never been involved in politics, and other than some advice to be careful, I did not get much input from them on what was happening or the way they saw it. In any case, I felt that they had some sympathy for the revolution.

Like most of the people in Cuba, we had friends and relatives who were members of the national army and the government and also among the people who were sympathizers of the revolution.

As children, we dealt with all of them the same, but as time passed, we started to feel that there was something different affecting those in Batista's side, and we could feel the first waves of fright for what could happen if the revolution won.

I could also see how members of my family were taking more radical sides in that process, which was gradually involving the Cuban society.

A couple of years after Castro's forces entered Havana, I saw how some members of my family and also the families of some of my closest friends started to migrate to the United States while other relatives and friends decided to remain in Cuba, but clearly, they were not happy either with the new order and a result some of them ended going to prison for their opposition to Castro.

In the meantime, other members of my family, including my parents, became sympathizers of the new regime.

I was too young and did not have any political knowledge that could help me to understand well the process Cuba was experiencing, and due to this, I followed my parents and became attracted by the slogans of the revolution, which indicated that Cuba needed a big political and administrative change, even when, perhaps due to my private school background, I had reserves about the whole process, something that spontaneously limited my degree of compromise with it.

Looking backward, I realize how difficult it was for me to avoid the attraction of those slogans of the revolution, which were being promoted by a barrage of political propaganda.

During the first decade of Castro's rule, I took part in some activities organized by the government for young people, the main one being a Literacy Campaign in which I went to live with a family of farmers in a rural area of Holguin, a large city of Oriente Province, where I taught some people the basic elements of reading and writing in 1961. I could not realize at that time that the whole campaign was something used as a tool for indoctrination by the new communist government.

I started my studies of civil engineering at the University of Havana a couple of years later, and I was lucky to receive classes from some good civil engineers who had remained in Cuba, many of whom regularly criticized, in their close circle of friends, many aspects of Castro's policies, having differences with his plans and ideas, and this left a deep influence on my views.

I remember the main events of the revolution during those years, and I witnessed how Castro gradually assumed his absolute powers, as well as the growing number of disparate actions taken by his government.

I was also able to carry on many technical studies in my field, which allowed me to travel most of the island, learning firsthand about many things that other students had no idea were happening, which gave me a contrasting view between the government propaganda and the real situation of the island and the disaster the revolution was creating.

It was a bit unusual during those days for a young student of engineering to be interested in cultural and economic matters like I was, and this brought me to meet some prominent Cuban researchers and intellectuals, many of whom were also critical of Castro's policies, and this again gave me a broader perspective about the process that was going on, which, otherwise, I might have never had.

By the time I was finishing my career, UNESCO was implementing a program to assist the University of Havana in the development of some fields of engineering, and this included a number of scholarships. One scholarship was in the field of maritime transport and ports, which was the one in which I was specializing, and a short time after my graduation, I received a scholarship to go to the University of Wales, in Great Britain, to carry on post-graduate studies. During this time my family had to remain in Cuba.

In Britain, I was able to work under the guidance of some of the best academic authorities in my field in the world, and thanks to that I acquired not only a lot of new knowledge, but also a better understanding of Cuban problems.

After my return to Cuba, I tried unsuccessfully to promote a number of changes in the way the administration of ports and transport was done, and I became openly critical about the overall policies of Castro's government. Given my lecturing position, this caused that I clashed with Castro personally, as well as with other people in the government.

Obviously, thanks to the studies I had carried on, I could see clearly how the erroneous policies of the government were bringing chaos in all aspects of Cuban life and how the general conditions of the country were quickly deteriorating, and I felt that it was a moral duty to try to do something about it.

I assumed a more and more critical approach of every aspect of the revolution, and at some point, I arrived at the conclusion that it was necessary to develop new ways to deal with the problems I was experiencing. I tried then to introduce some changes in the way the students and teachers of the university dealt with the problems of our society.

My ideas apparently created some conflicts, which were discussed at high levels of the government, and as a result, I was separated from the University of Havana, after a meeting with the then Cuban president, Osvaldo Dorticos.

My position in Cuba became complicated, and at that point, the University of Wales recommended that I continued my PhD studies, and after going through numerous obstacles, I could go back to Britain, where I started doing an important piece of research in my field while I was also appointed coordinator of the Center of Research on Maritime Transport.

Apparently, Castro's people did not like what I was doing at the university, and as a result, when I went to Cuba during my vacations, they abruptly interrupted my studies and prohibited me back to Britain, even when there were protests from the British authorities due to this.

I was then forced to go back to work in my field in Cuba, but soon my views on numerous matters continued creating problems for me.

In 1975, I tried to create an independent union of port workers and engineers, which caused me to be brought to the headquarters of the secret services where I was informed that this kind of activities were prohibited and that I was going to have serious problems if I continued with my ideas.

For several years, I devoted to work in my profession, dealing with the project management of some large construction projects that were in process at a time in which Cuba was receiving large subsidies and I also tried by my own to carry on research on the different aspects of the construction industry.

With help from some colleagues, I was allowed to lecture again some post-graduate courses on management of the national economy and investments, which were rather successful, in 1980. However, when I was preparing a second version of those courses, I learned that they had been cancelled, apparently because the government was not prepared to accept more discussions on the problems that existed in the national economy, something that I was doing regularly in my classes, with the support of all sorts of data and statistics.

Since it was obvious to me that something had to be done in regard to the disparate policies that were being implemented in our country, I tried then to create a new democratic political party in Cuba, the Cuban Revolutionary Party, which pretended to follow-up of the one created by our national hero, Jose Marti, to fight for Cuba's independence against Spain, which had the same name.

I attempted the creation of the new party based on the pseudo constitution implanted by Castro, which established that Cubans had the right to request to the National Assembly the legal inscription of a political party, if this was supported by ten thousand signatures.

I started contacting and enrolling people for the above, after preparing the documents to collect the signatures required and also wrote several letters to different international personalities requesting their support for what I was doing. However, I was soon going to learn that, no matter what the paper says, the real meaning of the wording of Castro's constitution was subject to his own interpretation!

One night, on December 22, 1981, while I was at home with my family, a group of officers of the secret police knocked on my door with an order to search my house, which they turned upside down.

They found and took with them a big pile of papers related to what I was doing and all sorts of other documents, and I was taken from my home under custody, in front of my wife and children, bringing me once again to the headquarters of the secret services, where this time I was kept detained and under continuing interrogation by several officers for several months, until a cause against me was open.

Initially, I was accused of trying to promote a rebellion and I was transferred to La Cabaña prison in Havana, not before they sent me for few days, without my family's knowledge, to an infamous ward reserved for the most dangerous common assassins, which still exists at the National Psychiatric Hospital in Havana, something that, I later learned, was a regular practice used by the torturers of the secret service to try to intimidate people.

I was kept at La Cabaña, an old Spanish fortress and prison built in the sixteen century, which was still active as a prison at that time, for more than a year, waiting for the formal accusation against me and my trial.

At my trial, I was accused by the government prosecutor of all sorts of wrong attitudes against the revolution, which were ratified by a long intervention of the Secret Police officer in charge of my cause. My attorney, whom I met for the first time at the trial, was allowed then to say few things to very cautiously try to defend my innocence.

When I was finally allowed to say something, I asked the panel of four judges why I was prosecuted, because I had not violated any law and I also considered that I was a good citizen and a decent person, on top of being a successful professional.

I expressed my view that I had not violated any law for trying to collect signatures to request the recognition of the new political party, because this was legal and as I said before, according to the Constitution, something that had been briefly ratified by my attorney, who, by the way, had been a classmate of Castro at the School of Law of Havana University.

After a brief interchange with the judges, I told them that, in my view, I should not be there in front of them because, in any case, it was the government of Castro the one that really deserved to stand on trial because of its widespread corruption, bad administration and its repression of the Cuban people. This, of course, sealed by luck.

Obviously, in a country where judges for political causes are regularly selected among the most corrupt and opportunistic, as well as for their unconditional support of the government and their lack of scruples, they considered that I was wrong and I was sentenced to eight years in prison, changing my cause from "rebellion" to "enemy propaganda." That term length was the maximum prescribed by Castro's criminal code for that kind of "crime."

Some decades later, with knowledge of the international press and support from abroad, other people in Cuba tried to create a political party, and Castro changed his approach to deal with them. They were this time allowed by the secret services to collect their signatures as established by law and to present their application to the National Assembly, and they were not punished for this, but the National Assembly ignored their petition and never processed nor responded to it. Nobody was, this time, brought to prison for this but some years later their leader was killed in a fabricated accident.

I spent six and a half years in Castro's political prison, some of them in isolation cells because, on top of my sentence, I was falsely accused later of promoting trouble at each of the two prisons I was sent.

My attorney, Aramis Taboada, who also taught at the University of Havana, was sent to prison some time later, accused of something irrelevant, and he died there in strange circumstances.

During the time I was in prison, my wife managed to inform my family in the United States about my situation, and my cousins Rosa and Julio Soy, who lived in New York and Tomas Alvarez, who lived in Miami, contacted my Prof. Alistair Couper and Heather Gordon, a good friend in Britain, who presented my case to Amnesty International, which started a campaign for my freedom. This campaign was soon joined by America's Watch and different newspapers, radio, and television stations and by people and organizations around the world, including the Cuban American Foundation and other organizations in Miami.

In Washington, Of Human Rights and its director, Frank Calzon, with help from the students of Georgetown and Harvard Universities, worked very hard to develop their own campaign for my freedom and this brought many members of Congress to express also their support, passing a bill asking for my freedom.

I was selected as Prisoner of the World by Amnesty International and my case was presented to the World Conference of Human Rights of United Nations, which took place in Geneva in 1987.

Senators Edward Kennedy and Robert Dole joined forces to write a letter to Castro asking for my liberation, following similar requests from other political organizations, newspapers, and figures in Britain and other countries in Europe and all this took me out of the isolation cell where I was with a small group of political prisoners and I was then moved with the rest of the prisoners. After some months, time in which I could recover from the time spent in isolation, I was liberated and brought directly by the secret service to Havana airport, where I met my family and we came all together to the United States.

During the time I stayed in prison, I was allowed to see my wife two hours every six months and my children two hours every twelve months. I could see my mother only two hours around Mother's Day, but through three metal meshes that existed between prisoners and visitors. I could not even touch her! I could not see my father during all those years. My mother, who, as I said before, had believed in the revolution, had a heart attack and passed away while I was in prison.

During those six and a half years, my family experienced all sorts of pressures and humiliations, and my children were discriminated at their schools due to my situation as political prisoner.

My oldest son, Andres Jr., was not allowed to continue his studies at the university, and when I was about to be liberated, officers of the secret service brought him in secret, without informing my wife, to the house of a neighbor, who was a colonel of the secret services, where they proposed to him that if he stayed in Cuba, not coming with the rest of the family to the United States, they were going to give a scholarship to him and that he was going to be allowed to keep the house of my parents.

My wife, Adriana, who is an architect, was kept isolated in a corner at her job at the Institute of Physical Planning in Havana after she refused to abandon me. She became an activist within the movement of human rights and was followed everywhere she went by the secret services. She distributed my letters and denounces, which I gave to her during our sporadic visits or sent to her through other people, containing the lists of names of those prisoners who were ill or received abusive treatment, going to the foreign embassies in Havana and to the authorities of the church in Cuba. Many people who had been our friends and neighbors turned their backs on her in our neighborhood, at our children schools, in her workplace, and everywhere.

A political prison provides a good learning. I could learn firsthand there the facts of the repression established by Castro, and I feel proud of having found the courage to denounce the conditions in which so many people were kept and also of having confronted Castro with my actions.

After my arrival in the United States, I went to Geneva with other former political prisoners to denounce Castro's repression and to intercede in front of Leone Sene, the functionary of United Nations, who was for some time in charge of the case of human rights in Cuba, for the freedom of all the other political prisoners, who were still in prison, and this diplomat helped to achieve the liberation of a large number of them.

During all these years, since we came to the United States, I have continued studying Cuban problems and I have written articles and papers on these matters.

I believe, after reading numerous books on Cuba, that perhaps this book will be useful for many people to understand a little better its that reality.

The barrage of continued propaganda produced by Castro in five decades has managed to create a false image, unfortunately accepted as a whole or in part by many people in the world, regarding the Cuban revolution, which is contradicted by the real facts.

Behind this elaborated false image, there are a number of misguiding concepts, repeated once and again, which pretended to hide the cruel criminal record of his regime. The facts and events described in this book show how many essential aspects of the Cuban revolution have been manipulated.

There are many books written on Castro and his so-called revolution and I have not pretended to describe once again every aspect of Castro's regime. The main objective of this book is to give an account of the main aspects of the disaster created in Cuba by Castro and his followers, including his brother Raul, who followed him in charge of his regime after his death. Thus, this mentioned disaster becomes the main character of the book, and going through it, I have tried to explain the situation in which Cuba is at the present and the alternatives for its future. It is important to notice that Fidel Castro may be dead, but his regime has survived in essence under his brother Raul's rule and his followers.

This is a book on ideas, which argues Castro's concepts from a different perspective than the one presented by the official propaganda and many other books that defend or justify in one way or another his regime. It shows that, instead of bringing improvements to Cuba, Castro brought the worst disaster our country has experienced. It is not only a material disaster, but a moral, cultural, and economic catastrophe.

The book also describes how Castro's system has entered a final stage of decomposition, which hopefully will finally leave way for the Cuban people to start rebuilding our country.

I don't know how long it will take for this barbaric regime to disappear into the night of history, but I can see that it is already an agonizing entity.

There is not a single aspect of it that we can identify with success under an impartial analysis, and I sincerely hope that the agony of this disaster does not take long.

I hope that our arguments on Castro's ideas and concepts, which have been followed by his brother Raul Castro after his passing, can make people reflect on these matters and allow them to find the truth by themselves. I sincerely hope that those who honor me with its reading find this book interesting.

I would like to express my gratitude to my friends Roberto Rodriguez and Roberto Nuñez as well as to other friends for their assistance in finding the photos to illustrate the destruction of Havana, which has been caused by the neglect and abandonment of Castro's government. I could have included photos of most other cities and towns of the island which are in similar conditions.

Since I came with my family to the United States, this great country has given us many opportunities and we feel extremely grateful. We have been allowed to work and to travel and we have enjoyed feeling free for the first time in our lives. We are considered by many as successful, hardworking people and part of the American dream and we are proud of it, but precisely, because it is the love and respect for freedom in this country that has allowed us to do this, we believe that we cannot forget that, just ninety miles away, where we were born, there is still a whole nation that deserves the same rights.

CHAPTER 1

‒‒‒

The reality of Cuba in 1959 and some misconceptions about Castro's revolution

Since the first significant appearance of Fidel Castro in Cuban politics, when he attacked with a group of followers the Moncada Barracks, in Santiago de Cuba, and especially after he started his fight at the Sierra Maestra in 1956, until our days, he has received wide media coverage. At the beginning, it came mainly from the Cuban media; later, it came also from the American media and gradually the world media gave as well a very extensive coverage of him. For reasons that are not easy to understand, this media coverage, in general, with very few exceptions, has presented an image that is extremely shallow and decorated. The fact is that Fidel Castro, who did not have very good references when he started his movement, soon became a media star, and he has remained the same way during all these past sixty years.

There were many other leaders and personalities in Cuban politics at that time who had more qualifications and definitively much better moral backgrounds than Castro, and the reasons why he managed to displace them to become the leader of the majority of the Cuban people are not easy to explain.

Castro was cataloged by many people at the University of Havana, where he initiated his political career, as a sort of a gangster. He was not a good student or a respected university leader, and there were some turbulent accounts about his participation in an obscure chapter related with the killing of another university leader who was considered his rival.

In my view, the reasons why Castro managed to succeed in such an almost incredible way seem to come from three conditions:

First, the general conditions established by General Batista and his corrupt and violent regime. While most of the other existing Cuban leaders at that time were trying to oppose Batista on moral grounds and using political means, Castro decided to fight Batista by using his same terms and conditions but bringing them to another level. The corruption and violence he generated since the beginning was much stronger than the ones Batista ever generated. He killed people right and left, ignoring the Constitution and all the other existing laws; he made deals with whoever he could use for his purposes, and he enrolled, to become the core of his movement, some of the worst people available.

Second, he took a totally different avenue compared with other Cuban politicians, in which he was practically the single runner. When he decided to break with all the traditional bodies of Cuban politics and start his armed movement, he had his way open because there was no real competition. When some time later, other organizations woke up and started their own similar efforts, it was too late, Castro had already the advantage.

Third, the world was experiencing a series of political changes and the well-introduced image of Castro and his people fighting against all sorts of social, economic, and political "demons," was very attractive for the most different spectrum of interests. The communist countries and specially the Soviet Union loved this image, but a good portion of the Western press and even some highlevel Western politicians and philosophers also did and it was very especially loved by the newly baptized underdeveloped or emerging world.

Practically nobody, other than the few people really very familiar with Cuban matters, really cared at that moment whether these "demons" I mentioned, were real in the case of Cuba or not.

It is a fact that very few people cared in many circles of the world at that time whether the conditions of Cuba were really as bad as they were being described by the propaganda and the press, or if the case of Cuba could be compared to other countries that were in a completely different stage of development. The fact was that Castro (and his movement) was quickly inserted into a worldwide perspective of underdeveloped countries in which he was able to avoid much competition as a leader once again, as had happened when he started his fight against Batista.

Most of the other leaders of the predominantly very poor countries of the world, including those countries in Africa, Asia, and Latin America, which were obtaining their independence precisely in those years or were fighting for it, could not match Castro's abilities and ambitions and especially his lack of scruples to deal with their political battles.

Castro's image as a leader of underdeveloped countries was promoted not only by his own incipient propaganda machinery, but mainly by some Western press and later by the Soviet Union, which became his main ally, in a way that made him accepted as one undisputed leader, even when Cuba had very little in common with those countries, and due to this, he soon became the adored and admired leader of millions of people in the world, something that was used by the Soviet Union in their own advantage for all their efforts to penetrate different regions of the world and enhance its influence in world affairs.

Most political leaders of the underdeveloped nations during that historical stage of the decade of the sixties and seventies could not match Castro's aggressiveness, and this allowed him to become not only respected but also feared.

Castro was allowed to do things that were unthinkable years before for a leader of any small nation: from international conspiracies to foreign invasions and wars, from blackmailing to killings of foreign political adversaries, from widespread sabotage of Western civilization standards to demonstrated drug and arm dealing in large scale, from imposition of political marionettes in some countries to support of guerrilla warfare, from well-established open espionage activities in developed and underdeveloped countries to recruiting and patronage of adepts within foreign governments and all sorts of international institutions.

Due to the above-described combination of factors, no matter what Castro and his regime did internally in Cuba, all this was practically minimized by many circles when Cuban matters were considered in the perspective of world politics, and the role allowed to Castro's movement within it, well if it was the destruction of the Cuban democracy and all political alternatives, or the killing of tens of thousands of his opponents and the incarceration in savage conditions of hundreds of thousands of people, or the destruction of the Cuban economy and the appropriation of billions of dollars of property owned by the private sectors, or the disruption of moral, educational, and familial values and the indoctrination of children, or the repression of the smallest sign of free thinking and all opposing political views, or the condemnation of the whole Cuban people to live in miserable conditions.

One cannot ignore the fact that, if certainly the Soviet Union and other countries within its sphere of influence patronized in large degree Castro's adventures for a long time in these past fifty years, there have been also many other accomplices of him all around the world, and the fact that the Soviet Union has not existed already for almost twenty years and Castro and his regime have continued existing and, even more important, keeping, with some logical adjustments, his same policy of sabotage of Western civilization and his oppression of Cuba, is a clear indication of this.

It is important to establish some very interesting facts: Cuba, in 1959, had the second highest standard of living in Latin America, comparable or better than the one that, at that time, nations like Italy, Norway, Spain, and many other European countries had. The world was less developed then and there were other standards, and even most of the countries, which currently belong to what is defined as the developed world, had much higher levels of poverty than what they currently have. Considering this, Cuba was not as such an underdeveloped country.

Many people do not presently understand that the figures frequently used by Castro for his propaganda and especially the images of Cuba in 1959, so frequently used by the defenders of his regime in many countries of the world, which present Cuba as a very poor country, with a predominantly illiterate population, an underdeveloped infrastructure, and a totally corrupted society, with very low economic, moral and social values, are very relative and may bring us to very inaccurate conclusions.

These mentioned images represent a partial vision and they can be compared with similar ones in many other countries, which later became developed nations, at that time, and they do not provide enough documented evidence to justify what has happened in Cuba during the past fifty years under Castro.

The justification of Castro can only be sustained by the ignorance on Cuban history or, in cases, by some dubious interest in supporting a wrong cause, ignoring the damage caused to Cuba by a dictatorship that has been there for the past fifty years. It is curious that most of the people who defend Castro in other countries are not ready to accept the same kind of regime established in their countries, which is an indication that their intentions are not always transparent.

There are all sorts of obvious and well-documented data of 1958 showing the following:

- Cuba already had had, for almost thirty years, social laws and a constitution, which were among the most advanced in the world, much more advanced than most of those existing nowadays in many developed countries.
- There was a very powerful and wide national industrial movement in full expansion.
- There was a fast-growing and modern transport and commercial infrastructure.
- There were excellent newspapers and press media.
- There were modern and fast-developing television networks and radio stations that reached the whole island.
- There was a huge tourism industry in full expansion, which one can estimate could have reached enormous figures of tourists by now, compared with the meager figures achieved by Castro.
- There were excellent, long-established, and prestigious universities, all in full expansion, and a large and growing network of public and private, elementary and middle schools.
- There was a fast-developing and well-established construction sector.
- There was a large mining industry including several large nickel plants.
- The Cuban agriculture had already, in those years, a much larger and diversified production output than any achieved by Castro in sixty years, and it was the source for a rapidly expanding export trade.
- There was a modern and well-established commercial sector, with modern stores not only in Havana, but also in all the main cities and excellent and diversified products of all kinds.
- Cuba could be proud of its cattle industry, which was very well developed and established and allowed Cubans to have the highest consumption rate of meat in the whole continent.
- There was no rationing of any product or food, and people were able to buy from a nationwide well-supplied network of food stores and the current limitations and rationing established by Castro for the past fifty years were unthinkable.

- The banking industry was at the same technical level than anyone in the developed countries and most of the main world banks were represented there.
- The Cuban peso kept a parity with the dollar, actually having a slightly higher value.
- The Cuban people were used to be ahead of most of the world in the introduction of all the main inventions and technological advancements.
- There were already assembling plants for new American cars established in Cuba and the figures of cars and trucks, as well as buses per capita, at that time, were several times higher than the ones existing there now.
- High-rise buildings and hotels were being built in the main cities and especially in Havana at an incredibly high rate.
- There were plans already being implemented for the protection of the coast of Havana and the remodeling of the city and the main roads as part of the development of a modern infrastructure and other cities of the island were also being transformed.
- There was a fast-growing telephone network established in the whole island.
- There was freedom to travel anywhere outside and inside the island.
- Housing programs were in process of development in the whole island and housing conditions were already, fifty years ago, much better than the current housing conditions under Castro, which can be defined as a huge disaster.
- There was freedom of expression and people were free to have any kind of ideology or religion, or to affiliate to the different political parties.
- There was a culture with moral and family values that was preserved by the educational system.
- There was a powerful cultural and artistic life.
- There was a very large network of theatres, cabarets, and night clubs and national recording and distribution centers.
- The already large national electrical industry was in process of rapid expansion to cover every corner of the island.

- Most of the main water distribution works and aqueducts had well-studied plans for their expansion, designed to satisfy the needs of the growing population.
- There was a very low penal population and most crimes were low-level offenses.
- There was a large national network of public and private hospitals and clinics, with very easy access to the population.
- There was a developing health control system to eradicate plagues and epidemics.
- The salary of Cuban workers were higher than in most countries and this was specially so in the case of a number of key sectors of the economy.
- Migration of foreigners to the island was higher than Cubans moving abroad, and many Americans and other foreigners liked to live there due to the mild weather and the island's low prices.[1]

I have described the above facts, which can be corroborated very easily by anyone with only studying the main statistics of the island before 1959, which can be found in practically any important library and were prepared by professional and impartial people, not like those created by Castro's institutions, which are full of irregularities, with figures intentionally manipulated.

After describing the above facts, one could question why, then, was there a revolution in Cuba and why Castro was initially accepted and supported by a vast majority of the Cuban people as if it represented their salvation, and even now, it is still accepted by many Cubans living there, if looking objectively at the present conditions of the island, this regime has evidently brought back in time Cuba, its economy and society for more than half a century?

Also, why so many people in Cuba, for so many years, have gone so far in supporting the wrong actions of this dictatorship, many of which include actions that anywhere else in this world could be cataloged as crimes? Why, for instance, all the hundreds of thousands of people who have serviced at the Ministry of Interior and in the different bodies of the army have devoted the best years of their lives to follow blindly whatever order they have received from their superiors that could go from repressing Cuba's own citizens to risk their lives fighting in Angola, a distant African country they didn't even know? Is this a case of collective craziness? Is there some kind of compulsory control of their minds by the impressive propaganda machinery of the regime? Is it that Castro has found ways to make idiots of them?

Is it possible that some kind of psychological pressure or the effect of a paramount repression had forced them to act in that irrational way? Why so many people and families that had never before in their lives been involved in any kind of politics, have accepted to put themselves in the hands of this regime for practically anything.

Even more complex, why so many people in other countries or in international organizations, many of whom have high levels of intellect and the capacity to corroborate these mentioned facts, or those who develop their activities in high government positions at them, have expressed their support in one way or another to Castro and his regime? Is it logical that people denounce their own family or friends to the government if they have opposing views about its policies, like it happens in Cuba every day? Why so many established artists and intellectuals, who do not need monetarily or professionally to do that, have been ready to defend this regime, avoiding to find out by themselves the reality Cuba is living by doing some basic research and ignoring the overwhelming evidence available? Are all those actions of so many foreign people an act of cruelty on those who have suffered the Cuban repression that allows them to satisfy who knows which internal aberration they may have?

Is it an act of arrogance or is just idiotic to underestimate the suffering of others? Why so many people, in democratic elected governments and nations, have accepted to spy and work for Cuba, against the interests of their own countries, an act of high treason? Obviously, the answers to the above questions are not simple. It takes some historical reading to find out how the same pattern was followed in other communist countries or in Nazi Germany. The crimes of Stalin were ignored by many for a very long time and his figure was exalted in numerous forums. The same happened for many years with Hitler, who copied a lot from the methods of Stalin.

It is my belief that, in 1959, most of the Cuban people wanted a democratic revolution in Cuba, because they believed that it was logical and important to introduce some necessary changes in Cuban politics oriented to guarantee the existence of a permanent democratic political system in the island, with regular elections every four years and with the enforcement of laws, to guarantee an honest and decent government, with transparent actions. They wanted more competent people in charge of their lives, and they wanted to eliminate the existence of those conditions that had allowed the continuing presence of corrupt politicians in one government after another and the periodic intrusion of authoritarian rulers who disrupted the democratic process.

The Cuban people was not able to compare what they had in regard to many other nations and give the proper credit and value to it, and they were incapable of recognizing their own virtues and achievements as a young nation or their enormous good luck in many aspects for having a prosperous country and a society that was achieving things that were unthinkable at that time in many other countries. This was a fault not only of the masses as such, but also of all the main intellectual and political forces the country had.

Castro utilized the above idealistic hopes that most of the Cuban people had and managed to convince a large portion of them that he represented those ideals. In reality, he was exactly the opposite of what they wanted, and once in power, he immediately showed his real intentions of transforming Cuba into a communist dictatorship, under his absolute control and with some of the worst people that Cuba has seen in all its history accompanying him in that process.

The perversity of Castro opened for many bad people the opportunity to realize themselves. Those are the people who have committed uncountable crimes in the name of the revolution, in Cuba and abroad, as well as those who have not vacillated in tainting their reputations by supporting consciously all sorts of wrong actions, while acting on behalf of this dictatorship.

It is a paradox that, sixty years later, after the whole disaster created by Castro has become obvious, each Cuban, dreams, in the silence of the night, in whatever other diffuse form of government that can exist, which could mean a liberation, and they pray, to the same God who one day they were brought to negate, for the same democratic changes they were dreaming then, sixty years ago. Cuba has become a land of broken dreams and a nation with no notion of time.

I am absolutely certain that Cuba was far from being a perfect place in 1959, and we do not pretend to justify Batista's regime, which I believe was responsible, as I explained before, for creating many of the conditions that came later. Cuba had advanced considerably in establishing its institutions as a relatively new free country and could show already extraordinary achievements in the development of its economy and political structure and this process should never have been broken. I consider that this was a very huge mistake, even considering the historical context of American politics at that time, when military coups were almost common.

It is also true that, if one looks in detail into each aspect of Cuban life in the decade of the fifties of the past century and even recognizing, as I did above, the numerous achievements Cuba already could show, that there were all sorts of problems that remained to be solved, from problems of administrative transparency to traffic of influences, from an unbalanced management of national resources to insufficient policies to resolve many pending development problems, including those in sectors like the education, housing, and health and in general in the infrastructure of the country. But it is only fair to say, that many of those problems existed at worldwide scale then and most of the world tackled them in a much more logical way, without getting into the kind of trouble we got.

The data that I mentioned before and any historical research shows that most of the developing world, at that time, could not even remotely dream about many of the economic and social achievements that Cuba already found normal and were well behind Cuba, and we should have had an advantage to achieve those development goals in regard to them if we had remained a democratic nation.

I consider, looking backward into many of the problems that Cuba had at that time, all of which were used demagogically by Castro to justify his assault to power, that a lesson may be learned from this kind of events, which can be useful for other countries that can find themselves now in situations similar to the one Cuba got into.

It is very easy sometimes for a demagogue politician, usually with well-fed and unlimited ambitions, to criticize the shortcomings that a country may have as a whole, ignoring the need for a more comprehensive analysis of what the relative weight of these problems represent, in comparison with the overall value of the positive achievements the country already has. To forget this very simple rule, or to allow one of these self-proclaimed messiah to manipulate these facts, may bring a whole people to very disgraceful times as happened to Cuba.

We have mentioned before in this chapter some of the many misconceptions that exist in regard to Castro's supposed achievements in the transformation of the different aspects of Cuban life and we will get into more specific details and comparisons on this later in this book, but it is the case that one also finds that his regime has also been presented and considered abroad, by many people and governments, as a great defender of causes like the liberation of peoples or the defender of rights against all sorts of inequalities, which is an aberration.

A closer look at this shows a very different set of conclusions. If one goes back in time a couple of decades, it was obvious how Castro, without any kind of scruples, sent his army, armed with Soviet equipment, to support the most criminal sort of dictators in Africa, people widely criticized as criminals and corrupt, like Mengistu Hayle Marian and Robert Mugabe and many others. Was he defending any ideal of freedom for those countries or just trying to increase a territorial area of influence by no other than the Soviet Union, an empire of corruption and crime? The historical answer is evident.

Castro has managed elected twice as president of the Non-Aligned Countries Organization. Has Castro being non-aligned ever? Does he represent any real hope or chance of improvement, with all his corrupt values, for any developing nation that hopes to be independent? I understand that this organization has many contradictions, like the world in which it has come into existence, but still, it is astonishing what Castro has been allowed to do, especially since many other democratic nations have never had this opportunity.

Castro's opportunism is anecdotic. Just few years ago, a representative of Cuba was in charge of the American chapter of the Commission for the Protection of the Environment of the United Nations. I found him, representing the president of that organization, in a symposium organized in Washington, D.C., to study the case of the area known as the Pantanal, in South America. He was in charge of delivering the speech to close the event! It was ironic that Castro, who has created a total disaster in every aspect of the Cuban environment, was representing the United Nations and America in this field. With what moral he could attempt to do so? It did not look serious. But this was just an example of the general misconception about Cuba and also the result of a very active policy of penetration of international organizations by Castro's secret services, which has occurred for many years without any apparent serious concern by many countries.

These are just some examples at random, but it is evident that we are in front of a very strange situation and sometimes it becomes almost incredible to see how this regime, which has violated every right of the Cuban people and the rules of world politics and diplomacy, has been able to convince so many people of accepting an image of it totally opposed to what it really represents.

If one analyses methodically what has happened in Cuba during these past fifty years, it becomes obvious that Castro's actions and ideas and the Cuban revolution as such, conform a huge gigantic disaster, which has nothing to do with this mentioned idyllic and respectable image.

It is incredible, when present and past comparisons are made and a logical perspective is found, to see how there is practically no aspect of the Cuban society, which has not suffered a huge damage due to the policies of Castro, his brother Raul and his cohort of followers after these sixty years but the same it is, to see how this regime has managed and has been allowed to perform a role of patron of the good causes of the world, when it represents in reality the worst model any country could have.

Due to the above, I have written this book and I will attempt in the coming chapters to describe some of the realities behind the fake facade of the Castro's regime.

CHAPTER II

≈

Power, privilege, and corruption:
The contradictions of the Cuban Revolution

Fidel Castro and the Cuban Revolution he has symbolized have been recognized and accepted by many people in this world as a paradigm of the fight for freedom, social and economic justice and equality and no matter how much has been said and published against this aberration by his opponents and critics, there is no doubt that the acceptance they have had in many regions and within numerous governments and organizations has been very large.

Even many people, who are normally associated with very respected circles and are considered part of a distinguished intellectual level, who most of the time are very careful with their image and paradoxically could be considered as political adversaries of Castro, due to their positions in regard to intellectual, religious, and political freedoms, have felt some attraction for this man or have accepted something from him, even if this was simply a little piece of his time.

Our generation grew up used to see Castro as the main acclaimed speaker in the United Nations or in some of the largest world conferences that this world has ever seen, or dealing with the main political, military, religious, social, literary, and academic leaders of our time, with famous artists and athletes, personalities of all kinds. In most of the cases, he has been the main center of attraction in those events, easily recognized by practically everybody. When, even educated people, have had difficulties to remember the name of most of the other world leaders, they all recognize easily Castro. One could say that Castro established his image at a different category, which makes him a widely recognizable figure.

We have seen also how many powerful men, who have represented the most influential economic and political forces of Earth, have shown some kind of satisfaction when they have visited him, sharing their time in discussions about the most varied subjects, after which they have expressed their respect for his power and influence, his reach and experience.

Leaders of the noblest causes in the world have dealt with Castro as an equal. There has not been any sign of repulse when he has dealt with the top ecumenical and ecclesiastic leaders, with presidents or queens. In cases, one could see in their faces some curiosity, for seeing closely this man, who has managed to survive all the other main figures of this world in the past half a century and is still in his elder years able to provoke interest and the most passionate arguments. Who remembers the names of all those, among the most selected personalities, who were at some, usually ephemeral, time, relevant figures during this past half century? Even some of the most high-profile politicians in developed countries are only remembered by their people and those who read about history. You can ask for Castro anywhere in this world and probably you will find people who have never read a book or watched television, who may not know where Cuba is, but they rather likely have heard of Fidel Castro and his revolution.

With the idyllic image of his revolutionary Cuba on his shoulders, Castro has traveled all over the world, even to the most distant countries, and he has received all sorts of honors and decorations. Likewise, he has received a hero's welcome in a little country in Africa, for few days in the news due to his visit, than he met in private with all the main Soviet leaders, at the top of their power, and was introduced by them to their people, as the leader of the Cuban revolution, during those gigantic marches in Red Square. He could speak for hours to the General Assembly of the United Nations, nobody having the courage to tell him that his time had finished, even if the whole program was altered due to this.

There is something very interesting in the way the image of Fidel Castro has been projected, which makes it rather singular and has produced the most incredible results. Since the beginning of the revolution, Castro, and other people around him, who evidently knew what they were doing, brought his followers to call him Fidel, creating what would seem an innocent and spontaneous familiarity around his name, and this established a repeated and repeated pattern that spread around the world, resulting in a very curious situation.

The projection of the image of Castro, then a young attractive leader with a university degree and extraordinary histrionic abilities, dressed in his military suit, his beard showing manhood and resolution became easily sold to the multitudes around the world and obviously, more than in any other place, in Cuba.

Soon, even his worst enemies started spontaneously calling him Fidel as well, and his brother became simply Raúl. The problem was that, after a very short time, Castro became a dictator and all sorts of other things, but people kept calling him simply Fidel. This way, he became the only dictator of the world, to whom the people refer in almost affecting and familiar way by his first name.

As a contrast, nobody in this world would have called the Chilean dictator General Augusto Pinochet simply Augusto, even when, despite many other violent actions and irregularities, it is a fact that he saved Chile of communism. Even Pinochet's style did not give the slightest room for such a familiarity. However, all the crimes, irregularities, and other serious accusations against Pinochet are just a pallid reflex compared with what Castro has been doing for fifty years.

Sometimes, one marvels how distinguished intellectuals refer to Castro and his brother with such a familiarity, after absorbing a drop of the poison of his well-sold image, and how they talk with such an easiness about them and the continuity of their regime as something that could result from simple calculations, leaving aside the moral factor in their interpretations.

There were other important elements added very early to the image of Castro, which, no doubt, contributed, to create a new kind of concept around him.

He was a leader able to mobilize enormous multitudes and the images of his speeches, surrounded by these huge crowds, in a state of catharsis, provided some sort of seal of legitimacy to whatever he was saying, and not many people really cared about the fact that this way of getting things approved could never replace the orderly and civilized process of discussion a democratic nation should have.

On the other hand, the projection of Castro's image, talking to the Cuban people and to the world from his tiny Caribbean island, was represented as an act of enormous courage, because he supposedly was defending the whole world, not only the Cuban people, against all sorts of monsters who exploited them and against all sorts of bad political and economic wrongdoings. It was difficult, indeed, to overcome the impact of this image and to find out what really has existed behind it during half a century.

It became part of the mentioned image that, when Castro delivered one of his long speeches, there were always people from around the world close by, who came to witness how the Cubans listened whatever he wished to say and applauded and cried his name, telling him they were willing to do whatever he ordered them, whether to approve the killing of his adversaries by a firing squad or to go anywhere in this world to fight and even die for whatever cause he told them required their sacrifice.

Castro became another kind of pope, a communist one, and he found followers from many other countries who became his fanatical apprentices and also helped to bring his image to unimaginable levels of recognition, ignoring in that way all that existed behind that facade of illusions and distorted concepts he was spreading in all directions.

One can say that, never in the history of this continent any political personality reached, even remotely, the peaks of power and influence, like this man has been able to do. Other politicians have had a huge level of power and influence for few years, during very crucial events, like the American presidents during the world wars, but they never were able to reach and communicate with so many different people, in so many ways, for such a huge long time, playing a continuing role in the most varied events of world politics in all corners of the earth. Castro did all this in his own terms and according mostly to his wishes. Bolivar, San Martin, Marti, Juarez, all our immense heroes, could never have the exposure Castro has had. Those were other times, when television and Internet did not exist, traveling was an adventure, there were no international organizations comparable to the present ones, and the possibility of doing the things he has been able to do during his life simply did not exist.

There are, however, some issues with this incredible trajectory that Fidel Castro has had. One can ask what has been the price the Cuban people has had to pay for having such an extraordinary famous maniac in charge of their government, their lives, and their destiny for fifty years? To answer this in a very simple way: very high. This vast publicity that has existed around Castro is the result of the uncontrolled power he has usurped and the unlimited privileges he has awarded to himself.

This incredibly expensive projection of the personality of Castro is perhaps the best example of privilege and perversion that could be given, and it was achieved by violating all the sound rules of democratic government. It is based on the most absolute and integral corruption and it has represented a total aberration.

This same Fidel Castro, from the small and beautiful island of Cuba, who was able to ensure for himself an important role in world events, was totally incapable of dealing with the most elemental aspects of the Cuban economy and brought Cuba to a whole economic disaster; he was totally unable to assimilate the moral values that the Cuban society intrinsically had and simply destroyed to an unimaginable level its scale of values, to make it unrecognizable. In his pursue of glory, he just forgot the most elemental human rights principles and killed so many people, who opposed his views, including many of his closest original followers, that no other figure in Cuban, and probably American, history, come close to him in his macabre record. In order to preserve his power, he decided to build horrible and barbaric prisons in every corner of Cuba and fill them with hundreds of thousands of people, destroying their lives and those of their families. Castro's absurd policies, and the general misery in which he immersed most of the population, created a climate of frustration and persecution, and more than a million Cubans had to emigrate from their country, many of which were so desperate as to willingly risk their lives trying to escape in primitive rafts built furtively. Nobody exactly knows how many of them were never seen again by their families. Cubans died by the thousands, fighting for all sorts of causes, following his orders. The conditions of living of what he inherited as a prosperous country were brought to the level of some of the most backward countries of the world, the same ones that he tried to represent in his philosophical diatribes, the difference with them being that the Cuban people had a much higher level of culture and education. The assistance that he managed to receive from some of his strange allies, mostly to pay for his "revolutionary" services, was dilapidated in his overseas adventures and his multiple irrational projects, which did not bring any improvement to Cuba. His need for having a totally faithful and unconditional machinery, to administer his plans and every aspect of the society, left aside all the best talents of Cuban society and instead, brought to the most important positions some of the worst and less competent and opportunistic people, creating a total chaos in every aspect of it, causing an immense disaster.

In order to make possible that there was no dissent in the interpretation of his will, Castro confiscated and destroyed all the newspapers, television and radio stations; he advised to the artists and writers what they could say or not and prosecuted any dissident; he prohibited all the political parties, social organizations, and independent cultural centers, destroying all their valuable inheritance. He fired all the judges, the magistrates, the clerks and brought people that he could trust to create a new kind of pseudo justice. After all, he had finished his studies of law at the university somehow, without going to classes, because he was busy in other "revolutionary activities," and he managed to get his law degree, which he never professionally used, but that he felt was enough to give him enough knowledge to change all the laws of the country, eliminate the constitution, which was one of the most advanced of the world and establish new laws, the first one establishing the death penalty for anyone who opposed him or pretended to conspire against his new order.

Since he needed all the economic power he could get to develop his ambitious plans and ideas, Castro confiscated for his revolution all the private industries, the most productive lands, the farms, the sugar mills, the banks, the transportation companies, the railways, the airlines, the commercial stores, the mines, the hospitals and clinics, the houses of all those who were forced to emigrate, the private schools, and everything he found that could help in his mission to become the undisputable leader of Cuba, in his way to become one of the best known leaders of the whole world.

Castro had never had the slightest previous experience of work of any kind, nor had he managed any business of any size, nor he had been involved in any cultural or academic enterprise; nor he had any record of political or administrative achievement of any kind, thus, the only thing he could do was to improvise a number of primitive laws and decrees to handle all of the above and as a result, this brought to the most incredible and absolute destruction most of the accumulated richness of Cuba.

Obviously, in order to be able to control Cuba after such a radical change of system he needed to have his own armed forces, which had to be unconditional to his authority; therefore, he dissolved the regular constitutional army, as well as the national police, which he said were totally corrupted, sent their members home or to prison, and created new ones under his own command as commander in chief, with some of his bearded followers in charge of the main units.

He sent a large number of his most unconditional supporters, many of whom had a very low level of education, to the Soviet Union, to be trained in the operation of planes, tanks, missiles, torpedo boats, and all sorts of arms while some of those he considered the most loyal received special training to command military units.

Incredible as this may seem, few years later, these same people were already instructors of people from all over the world, in training camps built in the island, while there were also several Cuban armies, equipped by the Soviet Union, fighting in Africa against all sorts of enemies, according to Castro to "liberate" that continent, and of course, there was even a cemetery in Angola just for Cuban soldiers!

Since the traditional structure of the army could not give him enough control on the people and he needed to be totally in charge, he decided very early to create the Ministry of Interior, with some of the people who had been with him at the Sierra Maestra and had proved to be the cruelest and with less scruples.

His new secret services quickly became a terror machinery and made him capable of materializing some of his boldest ideas in regard to achieving an absolute control of Cuba, but also, thanks to them and to the new "advisors" he was getting from his Soviet and German friends, he could start thinking as well in other more complicated objectives abroad.

Castro realized that he was already in a position in which he could do whatever he wanted in Cuba, but this was not enough for his ambitions, and soon he expanded his activities to many other countries. Cuban agents started showing up in every corner of the world. As soon as in 1963, four years after he had taken power, there were already rumors of Cuban involvement in the death of President Kennedy, and there were hundreds of infiltrated agents working for his secret services within most governments in Latin America and thousands of people were coming to Cuba to "study," from every continent, many of whom had obviously been recruited to work with the Cuban secret services.

Astonishingly, few years later, some of these same people were already established in all sorts of important positions in their countries, and in some cases, they even became presidents or prime ministries while many others occupied other high positions not only in their governments but also in armed forces and in every organization Castro found important, even within the most important churches. Some people in the world started to realize that they were dealing with a new kind of secret service machinery never seen before in any small developing country like Cuba was.

Castro justified the development of such an organization and its actions by considering that it was essential to protect his revolution. He never worried that this large military and intelligence machinery was out of proportion in comparison to the capacity of the Cuban economy and the size of Cuba as a nation and obviously, the cost of this was astronomical, not only in terms of money and resources, but also in terms of human and organizational energy, and obviously not all this cost and effort was necessarily assumed directly by the Soviet Union.

At the top of Castro's involvement with the Soviet Union and some of the main countries that were in its communist bloc, specially East Germany, Cuba was receiving incredible subsidies, mainly from the Soviet Union, but a large portion of those resources were never used to develop its economy or to improve the conditions of living of the Cuban people, because they were absorbed by these other mentioned activities, which could certainly serve Castro's interests, but did not produce any other real improvement to Cuban society.

All of the above represents the most absurd abuse of power Cuba has seen. Castro has established a new level of privilege for the world we have lived in by using a whole country as his own property, introducing the most absolute corruption in the process.

When the Soviet Union dissolved and all the other satellite countries were free again, Castro found himself in possession of this huge military and secret service machineries, but with no more funding to operate it while Cuba became a country in bankruptcy, with a state of total disaster existing in every aspect of its economy and society.

For the past twenty years, Castro has seen how most of the military equipment inherited from the years of the alliance with the Soviet bloc becomes more and more obsolete at the same time that his huge army of hundreds of thousands of people has become unemployed and there is no much he can do with it. This has become a symbol of the enormous waste of effort and resources occurred under Castro.

The Cuban economy, which is totally stagnant, obviously has not been in the capacity to generate any way to find employment or use for this large number of men and women.

Not surprisingly, the conditions of living in the island have been in free fall all these past years, and no matter the subsidies he manages to get, here or there, from some newly found allies, like Venezuela's Hugo Chavez, who actually is one good example of the above-mentioned recruitment system established by the Cuban intelligence, these subsidies are not enough to sustain any kind of serious development in Cuba.

Castro, however, was able to use the remains of his formerly powerful military machinery and specially his secret services to keep intimidating his own people, who are defenseless against them, while his propaganda machinery helps to maximize the image of his decaying forces, trying to preserve his image as a powerful dictator.

He also used a large portion of the resources he got from Cuba's foreign trade and tourism to keep his intelligence service in operation in the world and to maintain his reign of terror on the Cuban people. Many of the old factories Cuba received from its former allies may be closed or totally depreciated, but his regime has been careful to keep operating all the infrastructure of his secret services and the enormous network of prisons developed in those days when he was the favorite ally of the soviets.

An analysis of all this shows a strange duplicity, because, while Castro was being able to keep a very high profile for many years in the world arena and was practically in total control of the Cuban people, thanks to his huge terror machinery, he has brought Cuba to a whole disaster in practically every aspect of its society and economy.

Theoretically, the ideals of Castro's revolution consisted in the establishment of a system in which people should see equality and achieve economic progress and a basically acceptable level of living, including the possibility of individual realization. The problem with this is that the Cuban revolution has denied all this to the Cuban people, who has seen how, while Castro, his brother and his closest group of followers have used all the resources of the country to satisfy their unbelievable egos, living a privileged life with all sorts of resources, traveling all over the world, spending huge amounts of money and resources in propaganda designed to promote Castro's image at incredible levels, enjoying with their families all the pleasures and using as their servants as many people as they wish, all this paid by the state, the Cuban people, in general, have become poorer and poorer, living in extremely difficult conditions, with all their rights limited, with no chance to achieve any improvement and a policy of terror on top of them at all times, with hundreds of thousands of their own in prison, millions others in exile, with thousands young Cuban lives lost in the waters of the Florida Strait while trying to flee from this catastrophe in rustic rafts, with no way to have even a modest home or a car of their own and even worse, a terrible forecast for their immediate future waiting for them when they wake up every day.

Cubans are forced to accept the diatribes of Castro and many other functionaries of all levels, who on top of being totally incompetent like their leader, pretend, with total lack of scruples, to put on their shoulders the responsibility of every disastrous result, requesting from them more and more sacrifices, never accepting their own responsibility for the situation in which they have brought the people to live.

A recent report by Kenneth Rijock, a very well-informed international authority on financial crimes at Complinet, in London, describes in detail the fortunes of Castro, his brother Raúl, Vice President Ramiro Valdes, and a long list of people who have been within the top circles of Castro's government during these decades. It describes how these fortunes were accumulated with total impunity, by deviating funds from the sale of Cuban assets, arms, trade makes, factories, lands, oil, money laundry schemes, drugs, kickbacks, and other sources.

The mentioned report shows that Castro accumulated a billionaire fortune, something ratified by *Forbes* magazine and other sources, which includes properties in Cuba and in many countries, a network of bank accounts in foreign banks, investments in foreign companies and all sorts of assets, managed under an intricate system of facade companies, in some cases registered under the name of other members of his family or people who work for them.

As mentioned before, this report refers in detail to the also large multimillionaire fortunes of a good number of people who have been around Castro, including prominently his brother Raúl, who has an estimated fortune of more than three hundred million dollars.

The mentioned report establishes by size different categories of illicit fortunes and gives the names of the people who own them, describing sophisticated bank schemes used by these people, and it establishes the complicity of foreign banks and people, who have been used to mask these fortunes in countries like Panama, Brazil, Mexico, Canada, Britain, and Spain among others.

Evidently, in a country like Cuba in which the control over numerous transactions has been almost nonexisting, this made so on purpose, there is very little chance of tracking any financial irregularities. Obviously, all this has been organized and allowed under Castro's administration. There is no doubt that many of the people in high positions have seen the doors open to appropriate as much money and other resources as they can, which after all, is only a way to imitate their main leader, trying to ensure a possible good future for them and their families when the system disappears, this, obviously, if the next government does not go after them in international courts, which would be an interesting "after chapter" of the Cuban revolution.

I have tried to put things into perspective in this chapter, to illustrate the situation existing in Cuba, where, in one side, one finds a number of very corrupted people with Castro at the top, living at full speed and surrounded with incredible illicit richness, while in the other side, there is the whole Cuban people, who are suffering all sorts of abuses, disgraces, and limitations.

To make the things worse, in Cuba there is no chance to make a choice of new people to replace the existing corrupt leaders or to try to change things under a system of free elections, because all people elected in the so-called parliamentary yearly elections, must come from a pool of acquaintances of Castro. Even when the propaganda and terror of the regime may force the Cuban people to live with this, the fact is that Fidel Castro and his revolution have become a disgrace for them.

As time passes, more and more secrets, for a long time well kept, have emerged. They corroborate how Castro and his family have accumulated these mentioned huge fortunes in foreign banks and how they have bought numerous properties in many countries of the world, hidden behind other names. People have learned in detail how all these people have been traveling everywhere they have wished and how they live with full access to all what they have been denied for decades.

Most Cubans by now know how the members of Castro's family have been enjoying all sorts of privileges and how other people around them have also been able to keep their own large fortunes in foreign countries and they see how all of them enjoy all sorts of incredible privileges, properties, and means in Cuba while they have nothing.

The participation of Castro and other of his people, who have had high positions within his regime, in drug traffic activities, including their connections with some high-profile leaders of the drug cartels like Pablo Escobar, has been described in enough detail to leave no doubt, by people who were close to him and have escaped from Cuba. The same has been the case with their role in arm traffic and all kinds of obscure international criminal activities during the past half a century, which have been described in all detail by former participants who have escaped from Cuba.

Sometimes, the schemes created by Castro and implemented by his intelligence services are so elaborated that they become astonishing, but in many other instances they are just elemental schemes, carried on with total impunity and disregard for any international rule or laws, with the complicity of foreign authorities, banks, and individuals.

Apart from the long list of crimes of all kind Castro committed in Cuba during the time he has been in power, he was involved, among other things, in conspiracies associated with the killing of foreign leaders, in state coups, in political conspiracies in large and small countries, in elaborated fraud schemes, in espionage, in bank frauds, in drug traffic, in the creation and development of schemes for the distribution of drugs in the Unites States and Europe, in military expeditions to overcome governments, in blackmailing schemes, in all kind of dealings with the worst kind of people and somehow, this has been mostly ignored by the international community, who has become indirectly accomplice of these actions.

Even the most innocent or idiotic people, those who have come to believe blindly in Castro and his revolution, at some time, must ask themselves how is it possible that he has come to live with so many privileges all his life.

In total contradiction with the above, many people who have been enrolled in the armed forces, or the security services, all these years and have undergone what they consider numerous sacrifices, following Castro's orders, wonder what is going to be of their lives because they have devoted to Castro's system all their lives and they have received very little reward out of it, and what is even worse, they do not foresee any improvement in their elder years.

They can see time passing, their lives flowing without clear direction and no progress whatsoever. They also realize that, for many who have brought their support for Castro and his system to fanatical levels, the future may be very confuse, if eventually there is a change in Cuba.

There are many people in the government, who have not been involved directly in crimes, or in any activities of repression and have not been involved either in the mentioned corruption activities, who no doubt wonder what their situation will be after Castro. Like anybody in this world, they also wish a better life for their families and many of them realize how complicated their situation is.

They feel that, in any event, they should be able to work and live like any citizen in any other country and even develop and run their own businesses and enterprises, something for which they feel to be competent, without the need to have an omnipresent corrupt government controlling them and even more, without the need to pledge their support for any political figure if they wish to do so, with no risk of having any problem.

Many observers have noted that the case of corruption in Cuba has expanded through the ranks, following the reality of what people realize is happening at the top of the existing system and has become generalized and this obviously is true. In Cuba, practically anybody nowadays considers normal to simply take what they can and bring it home, to help to sustain their families. This practice has become so extended that, after several generations practicing it, it has become almost normal. This is a reaction to the system and does not mean that the people are necessarily corrupted, and it will take some time and education and the introduction of new rules of discipline, under a radically different set of circumstances, but these practices will gradually be eliminated, once Castro becomes part of our history.

There are also many people, the worst of the worst of each generation, who Castro has used once and again as part of his schemes and also there are those who always have been ready to brutally repress any presence of dissent in the name of his revolution. It may well be that, at some point, social frustration reaches a boiling point that the regime cannot manage and this people will find themselves in serious trouble.

Castro, like Stalin, Hitler, Mussolini, and other dictators, has also had his troop of unconditional people at every level. He created the Committees for the Defense of the Revolution to spy on the lives of all the neighbors in each bloc, but as time has passed, many of these people have learned that things are not what they are told, and many of them try to deal with their neighbors, avoiding more trouble because they also realize that they need to survive.

Castro also created the Brigades of Quick Response to deal with cases of more direct confrontation to his authority, formed by people who are willing to go to any place they are sent by the government, wearing civilian clothes, armed with batons, pieces of rebars wrapped in cloth and all sorts of brutal instruments, to repress any act of dissent, crying slogans of support to Castro and the revolution.

The people of those brigades have been filmed once and again by the foreign press and many of them have become notorious for their abuses and offenses.

But there are worse people than these. Castro has always had a number of faithful followers, who are always ready for any repressive action. Those are the guys who have kept him in power through all his political life and he was extremely successful in using them every time he has needed to do so. They have been his special weapon to sustain his corrupted machinery.

They are the opportunistic people, in charge of intimidating any of his adversaries, the ones with the lowest instincts, those who lack all sorts of scruples and find pleasure in the worst actions, his unconditional men and women. Sometimes, it becomes difficult to identify them, dressed as commanders of the revolution, generals, attorney generals, or members of the Communist Party Politburo or the Central Committee. In reality, behind their fake identities, they are just thugs!

It is necessary to follow the itinerary of each of them within the revolution to discover who they really are. They have ascended the hierarchy based on their crimes, their total servitude to the worst causes, their lack of principles and scruples, their opportunism and the fact that all their long list of atrocities, in each case, has been done in the name of their undisputed boss, Fidel Castro, the one who have brought them along during all these years, allowing them to share his pleasures and corrupt power.

From time to time, one of these guys has some bad step and is removed from his position, most likely provisionally, something that, after all, also serves the purpose of remaining to the others that they mean nothing without Castro, but most of the times, they are called back, because in the deepest of his mind, Castro knows how valuable they have been and still are for him. There may be rivalries between some of these people, but they have learned to behave orderly, controlling their ambitions, and not to provoke the ire of their boss.

In this past half century, the Cuban revolution has been able to create a kind of breed of terrible people, who, on top of what they are by nature, are trained to be extremely bad and lack most of the moral values that a standard person would have. They have been found and selected by Castro and his system through the years and the long time he has been in power has allowed him to keep his own renovated reserve of them, in case he needs to replace one at any level. He has based his power on them.

I have observed some of this people in action and I must say that they can be incredibly bad. They reach a level of insanity in their pleasure to be bad. The Cuban revolution has sold to its followers the idea that it was creating a new man. That kind of people is its new man!

CHAPTER III

⟞

The failure of communism in the island

I am sure that there are people, among those who still stubbornly feel sympathy for Castro, despite the evidences that have accumulated on his corruption and crimes, who consider that the term failure may be too drastic to be applied to the case of Castro's revolution, however, numerous historical and economic facts show that this is not the case. There are all sorts of evidences and comparisons, which allow one to reach that conclusion.

Castro's regime has experienced numerous changes in its political and administrative machineries during the past half century, which have been mainly directed to try to accommodate it to the changing conditions of the world, as well as to make possible the permanence of it, however, these changes have not been able to avoid the existence of a permanent chaotic state in almost every aspect of life in the island.

In my view, this large complex of organizations, ministries, and all sorts of entities, always under the overall guidance of Castro, well through his Communist Party or some of the organizations he created during the early stages of his regime, has never been designed to govern Cuba properly, but mainly to ensure the total control of Castro on the Cuban people. This may explain in part the overall disaster the Cuban revolution has brought.

The main failure of Castro's revolution has to do with the people, who are the ones suffering the consequences of his regime. Even many of those who have been deeply involved with it are far from being an exception.

One finds that the different main organizations created by Castro have had many different people involved in the management and operation of each aspect and level of them along different stages, but very few of these people have had a permanent presence. Most were people selected and promoted by Castro to carry on some function, were used by him for some time, until one day they disappeared of the public radar. They became an object thrown in the trash. Even those who participated in the most important roles and positions of the party and the government at some time, who one should expect could receive a different treatment, have not been exempt of this treatment.

It is equally impressive to observe the case of so many people who have sacrificed their lives in the name of the revolution in the most different functions and are almost unknown for anybody outside their families. Among them is also the case of a good number of people who have died in mysterious circumstances, who also have never been mentioned again.

There are very few selected figures, who have been immortalized in idyllic terms by Castro's propaganda, their memories becoming valuable for different reasons to him, despite the fact that their deaths had numerous obscure aspects, like the well-known cases of Camilo Cienfuegos and Che Guevara.

Cienfuegos was a popular and charismatic commander who disappear in obscure circumstances in what Castro said was a plane accident in 1959, few months after Castro took power. His remains and the plane were never recovered nor has any trace of them been found. He participated actively in the fight against Batista, as commander of one of the columns that came from the Sierra Maestra, the other being commanded by Guevara. Camilo, as the people called him, accepted the initial measures of terror applied by Castro after he took power, but there are indications that he was not happy with the communist path Castro was following and there have always been many speculations about this since his disappearing.

Castro has used one side of Camilo's image to show to the people the loyalty he expects from them, which obviously is a decorated image. Castro has established that people go to the sea coasts one day per year to through flowers in his memory. Evidently, Castro hides something in this case, like also is the case with Guevara.

In the case of Che, who survived eight years the triumph of the revolution, Castro has used the irrational ideas of Guevara with many different purposes. He has tried to convince the Cuban people about the possibilities that they can get, thanks to his revolution, a system of social justice and individual achievement based on moral grounds. He has presented Guevara as the symbol of austerity and honest values and total devotion to a cause, which he implies was Castro's cause. There is nothing more separated from reality than this.

Guevara was a criminal mastermind, with unlimited ambitions of power and total disregard for the life of others and his ideas do not represent any improvement for human mankind. His personal life reflects a very discouraging example considering that he irresponsibly abandoned his wife and children in his ambitious and crazy pursuit of power and recognition, which brought him to try to copy, in a wider scale, Castro's model of guerrilla warfare.

All records indicate that, when he was captured in Bolivia years later, he only thought of himself and his ego and how to save his life, when he said to the officers who had apprehended him that he was Che and he was more valuable alive than dead.

Guevara was captured by the Bolivian army in 1968, when he was trying to develop a new guerrilla war in that country, after being in Congo as a military advisor before. His diary and other recollections, by different participating witnesses, indicate that there were differences between him and Castro and it is clear that his chances of success in this operation were very small and Castro evidently knew it. Many people considered that Castro facilitated that he left Cuba to get rid of him.

Guevara was not a competent manager or a knowledgeable authority in practically any field. His image has been projected and used by many for the most varied interests, including commercial ones. The fact is that he was a reputed accomplice of Castro in some of his worst actions and in fact, he performed some of the cruelest actions during the early years of the regime when he executed the death penalty of numerous prisoners.

The own lifestyle of Castro, his family, and his cohort of followers have shown how false are those slogans and symbols, manipulated through the image of a false Guevara. Castro has been a despotic and corrupt dictator of the worst species and he has tried to use the image of the dead Guevara as a way to make others believe that he promotes austerity and honesty, which would be a joke if we were not discussing serious matters.

Castro has used the case of Camilo and Guevara to make others, including all the Cuban children, believe in the rationality of following blindly his orders, to do whatever he has wished they stupidly do, even if they have to lose their lives in the name of his supposed cause, which in reality is no other than his unlimited ambitions of power and corruption.

In reality, Guevara has come to represent the failure of the human side of Castro's revolution and the destruction of all the main family values and the basic principles of education as well as the free entrepreneurial will of modern societies. He epitomized the total lack of respect for the life and ideas of others and the independence of human beings in the name of some dubious and corrupt ambitions, which are defined wrongly as revolutionary, in order to give to them some validity and prestige.

He symbolizes a total lack of recognition for the accumulated achievements and efforts of society, under the pretention that everything done before these sorts of pseudo leaders take power was wrong and lacked merit.

Castro pretended that the Cuban revolution, at the end, became the history of one man, Fidel Castro, and perhaps few others among those close to him, well at some stage or in the long run, whom he cannot erase completely from his version of history.

If certainly, one can observe numerous changes, as mentioned, in the case of the organizations and people representing the regime at different stages, the case of the ideology of it is relatively different. One can say that Castro's ideology has remained being the same during all these years, so much so, that his regime has become at some point a dinosaur of world politics, even when one can identify a marked intention of Castro in doing so on purpose perhaps considering that his system, no matter how disastrous, has kept him in power, after all his main goal.

Castro and his regime have been through so many difficult situations that compared with these years, the rest of the history of Cuba in the twentieth century may look boring, despite the fact that it was full of achievements and continuing progress.

Before 1959, Cuba had a political structure with many similarities to the United States. It included a legislative branch, with the Chamber of Representatives and the Senate; an executive branch formed by the president and the Council of Ministries, that managed the main branches of the government and the judiciary branch, which included the supreme court and the lower courts. The Cuban Constitution of 1940 was a very advanced document that had been periodically improved through Cuban history.

Each of the six provinces existing then had a governor, and each city or town had also its elected officers, mayors and commissioners, to deal with its administrative matters.

There were many political parties representing all ideological trends. It was established that Cuba had elections every four years, even when Fulgencio Batista altered this, with his military coup, in 1952. Unfortunately, Batista's own attempt to bring back in track this system was not successful, because the elections lacked transparency and mainly because Castro's revolution took power before the newly elected president could assume his functions.

The economy of Cuba was based on a system of free enterprise and there were all sorts of businesses in every aspect of the economy, including important foreign and national firms.

When Fidel Castro and the people who had been fighting against Batista, well under the Twenty-sixth of July Movement created by Castro or under other organizations, took power in 1959, they found some vacuum of leadership, created by the sudden fall of the government of Batista, but the machinery of public administration was intact and there were many competent people at all levels of Cuban society, on top of all those who were in charge of the private sectors. Even when practically all the main figures of Batista's government abandoned the island in a rush, the revolutionaries inherited a well-established administration, plus a country with enormous human and material resources.

The first government of the revolution was mainly formed by educated people, selected among those who had been involved in Castro's movement or in some of the other organizations, who came from many different backgrounds, many of them with considerable political knowledge and experience and very high education.

Even when Castro included a number of his closest associates in positions within that government, most of them without any managerial capacity, keeping for himself the total control of the new army formed by his *barbudos*, it was very clear that some of the personalities designated for a number of important key positions were democratic, competent leaders, who had been fighting to establish a representative democracy in Cuba and wanted social improvements, freedom, and honesty for their country.

Even within the Castro's army, there were educated people who were independent and had been given high ranks by Castro within his Twenty-sixth of July as a way to improve the presence and relevance of his movement with their political prestige and the moral value they represented.

In a matter of days, however, the above situation started to change since it became obvious that Castro evidently had different ideas in comparison with those of the most relevant personalities and leaders around him. As a result, Castro first forced the resignation of its prime minister, Jose Miro Cardona, a respected personality, taking those functions for himself and then he provoked an unjustified conflict with the new president Manuel Urrutia, who was forced as well to resign and was replaced by an obscure man, never mentioned before within the leaders of the revolution, Osvaldo Dorticos, who came from the old Socialist Party (Communist Party), an organization considered a relatively minor participant in the revolution before 1959, this converting the position of Castro, as prime minister, in the main authority within the government. Meanwhile, Castro followed having problems with most of the newly appointed independent leaders who had assumed other positions within that first government and one after the other, they had to leave their positions.

In the middle of all this mentioned quick process, there were some strange incidents, in which people who had important positions in the government or in the new revolutionary army, died under obscure circumstances, this being the prelude of something obscure that has been present all these years and has become an element of the way Castro has operated.

Once of the first steps that Castro took, immediately after he arrived with his forces at Havana, was to establish revolutionary courts, all presided by officers selected from within his army, people without any legal competence or educational background, in order to judge those officers of Batista's army, as well as some people related to the former government, who were accused of crimes during the insurrection against Batista and parallel to this, he established the death penalty, not existing until then in Cuba, to punish a number of newly defined categories of crime.

The public trials of the former officers of Batista's army and others of his followers became a bad show mounted by Castro. These trials were arranged in different locations of the island and usually they ended with the sentencing to the death penalty of most of those men, who were executed by fire squads then, after a quick process of appeal, all this again being covered profusely by the national and international media.

The cry of *paredon* (the wall where people were shot by the fire squads) became a sudden hit among the populace following Castro and with it the Cuban revolution evidently lost any remain of innocence it could have had. Many people in Cuba and outside it realized at that point that Castro was not what the media had been presenting to them.

At the beginning, the death sentences were applied against some of the middle-ranking officers of Batista's army, who had remained in Cuba when Batista left and had been accused of committing crimes against the population, even when, in many cases, this was not clear, because they had fought under a constitutional army and had obeyed orders.

When many of the other democratic leaders who had fought against Batista started realizing Castro's intentions, their discrepancies with him immediately grew and many of them started to conspire once again, this time against him, and the same did practically all the main democratic political parties and organizations, which had also fought against Batista. Castro decided then to use those same revolutionary tribunals against all these other opponents and practically anybody who tried to conspire against him in one way or another.

The consequences of all the above decisions were tragic for Cuba and its people and the way these revolutionary trials were organized violated all the rules of law until then existing in Cuba and created a circus atmosphere, establishing a precedence of terrible consequences, creating a climate of violence and hatred within the Cuban society, which closed the door to any possible movement toward democracy and progress in Cuba.

Within few months of the existence of the new government, some of the best people within the main organizations that had fought against Batista decided that Castro was moving in a direction they did not like, and they started to try actively to oppose him and soon the first ones of them, who were discovered by Castro and his recently established Ministry of Interior, were brought as well in front of these mentioned revolutionary tribunals, which became a new violent symbol of Castro's revolution and established a disparate terror in the whole island, something that no Cuban generation had never before seen. The number of people who lost their lives in front of these firing squads during the years of Castro's rule or were killed fighting against him or while in prison can be counted in the tens of thousands and one can say that Castro killed many of the best men that Cuba had.

The above was complemented with the creation by Castro of a vast network of prisons and centers of torture and interrogation, located in different provinces of the island, where those who were not killed by firing squads were sent, the same if they were men or women, with incredibly high and disproportionate sentences, not supported by any legal principle.

The conditions of those new prisons ranked them almost immediately among the worst in the world, and hundreds of thousands of Cubans, at one time or another, have been sent to them, where they have suffered all sorts of humiliations, tortures, and abuses, many even losing their lives. Incredibly as it may be, after fifty years, these prisons are still in full functioning, and Castro continues incarcerating his opponents under the same terrible conditions, with total disregard for any international denounces and despite the condemnation of all the human rights organizations.

The Constitution of 1940 and the existing law system that Cuba had in place before 1959 were a democratic set of principles and practices and could not serve the purposes of Castro; therefore, he replaced them by introducing new primitive decrees, which were replaced by new spurious laws and a new pseudo constitution years later and were not supported by any kind of legal concepts but anyway were used by him to apply his terror on practically anybody that opposed him.

Due to the terror established by Castro, the rest of those people who had fought against Batista and had democratic ideals very different to Castro's ideas soon started to leave Cuba, trying to save their families and their lives, most of them migrating to the United States. This process gradually grew more and more, becoming an exodus of more than a million and a half people, which has continued for the past fifty years, something never even imagined in Cuba before, considering that more foreigners used to go to live at the island before 1959 than nationals emigrated from it.

Obviously, in order to be able to take such violent actions, Castro had to be supported not only by some close followers, but also by, at least, a large portion of the Cuban people, and with this in mind, Castro created a huge propaganda machinery by confiscating all the independent newspapers, television, and radio stations, which were then, in many cases, reopened under new revolutionary management and Castro's political orientation and supervision.

At this stage, Castro's government prohibited any kind of opposition including all the political parties and he started a campaign against the private industry and commercial sectors.

The above process created a state of panic in the Cuban society and affected all aspects of life, destroying numerous families, which started to suffer the separation, in one way or another, of their members.

At the same time, due to other aspects of his policies, the main values and traditions of the Cuban people started to be destroyed and replaced by a new set of slogans and unscrupulous practices.

It becomes evident that the magnitude and impact of Castro have been such that they have affected every aspect of life, creating a climate of emotional instability within the Cuban society, in which it became impossible any peaceful and equilibrated development.

As time has passed, most of the Cuban people have become disenchanted of Castro's demagogic promises and there is practically nothing he and his followers can do that could convince them that they will get any improvement under his regime. This is why they simply do not work and have become cynic about the political system and do not care about anything around them.

To establish their new order, Castro and his followers not only could not allow any kind of independent thinking, but they also required substantial economic power, and as I explained before, in order to achieve this he decided to nationalize practically all the economy of the island, this including every existing industry, all the banks, the commercial establishments, most of the land and the cattle industry, all the transport infrastructure, this is, all sorts of businesses and undertakings.

As part of the above, Castro created a new law of agrarian reform, but it was so badly managed and conceived that it destroyed the productivity of the agriculture of the island, failing in achieving any improvement of the conditions of living of the population. After a few years, most of the best crops of the island were destroyed, including the sugar industry and large portions of the territory became desert lands, because of the wrong exploitation, the wrong systems used in their cultivation and the out of control pollution and erosion.

The result of all the above-mentioned process in a country with a predominantly agricultural economy, has been the worst catastrophe the Cuban economy has lived during all its history.

Since Castro obviously saw the lack of result of the people's work under his regime and he did not trust most of the qualified people still living in the island, he started the practice of using some people who come from the highest ranks of his revolutionary army, whom he appointed to manage important sectors of the government, usually with the rank of ministers or in other high positions. However, these men, called "commanders" based on the ranks they had when they lowered with him from the Sierra Maestra (their range changed later to "generals" when some categories of the army were changed) could offer him some loyalty but other than that, they were not made of any special material, and through the years, they have become due to their limitations and weaknesses, a symbol of the real disaster of Castro's effort to manage the different branches of government.

They were sent to those positions by Castro, without having, in most of the cases, any previous knowledge of them or any organizational or managerial skills, and due to this, they have become notorious for their disparate initiatives.

One can say that the overall process of the so-called Cuban revolution has destroyed the total administrative infrastructure of the island, which has been replaced by all sorts of incompetent mechanisms and a wild class of pseudo administrators promoted by Castro's government from his own supporters. Castro practically not only has eliminated most of the accumulated richness and the patrimony of Cuba, but he also has managed to vanish the immense amount of resources he has stolen and received for many years, including the richness he confiscated to previous former owners and also all the money and resources given to him by the Soviet Union and other countries of the communist bloc and also from other Western countries to which Castro owes enormous amounts of money.

The amount of money that Cuba received during only the first thirty years of Castro's rule was already several times more than all the money that had entered in Cuba through all its history, according to the statistics of trade.

To illustrate some incredible aspects of this disaster in more details, it is important to explain that, after he took power, Castro appointed Ernesto "Che" Guevara as president of the national bank and later as minister of industry, during the initial years of his government, with a wide range of influence on economic matters. As a remembrance of those days, one can still find Cuban monetary notes with the signature "Che" as president of the national bank and nothing else. The case was that Guevara was a physician, not an economist, and he totally lacked any managerial or entrepreneurial experience when he was appointed to those important positions by Castro. The physician Guevara, after doing some basic readings of political economy and Marxism, arrived at the conclusion that the law of value, a basic element of economics, was in contradiction with the new system Castro wanted to establish and due to this it had to be eliminated. He decided then to promote the idea of using the system of barter to replace it, this becoming for some time the basis for all the interchange of products between the many different nationalized industries, enterprises, and ministries in Cuba.

Guevara's concept was accepted by Castro, who similarly had the most total lack of knowledge of economics, being a lawyer who had never worked in his life. Apparently, due the terror already implemented at that time by the regime, there was no substantial opposition to implement this concept nationwide, apart from the frustrations and incredulity of all the qualified economists that still lived in Cuba at that time. The result was that Castro's government, in a short period of time, lost all notion of the value of all the products that existed in the island.

Since the above happened simultaneously with the suppression and destruction of all aspects of the accounting system of the country, which was declared unnecessary by Castro and Guevara, suddenly there was no basis anymore to measure the value of each product. To make things even worse, Castro ordered that all the monetary transactions between government entities were eliminated. Incredible as this may seem now, Castro considered this a huge success in his fight against bureaucracy, an obsession he had at that time.

To explain this better, if the director of an enterprise needed a product produced by another enterprise, he simply called the director of the other enterprise or sent a slip with an order for it and a truck to pick it up and that was it! From one day to another, all the economic controls were eliminated and there was no notion of the financial conditions of any branch of the economy. Castro's propaganda simply explained to the Cuban people at that time that they had achieved a new level, never reached by any other country, in the management of the economy.

To make the disaster worse, Castro closed all the schools of economics of the country at different levels, from the university to the base, because he considered that those people studying economics, accountancy, or even to become secretaries, were no longer needed, because they were a bad seed of capitalism and no matter in which year of their careers they were, they simply were sent home to start all over their studies again, or to start working in whatever other field they could find employment.

No need to say that this mentioned incredible set of events placed Cuba in a situation so primitive that even the Castro's friends from the Soviet bloc found difficult to deal with it. The Soviets had already realized the disastrous consequences of similar policies in their own country and were trying to correct them and had discrepancies with this side of Castro's policies.

It is necessary to remember that all this came on top of the previous total rupture of Cuba with the United States and other countries with which Cuba had most of its economic links, which had been the main historical source for its international commerce.

We must note that in order to be able to find the support he needed to stay in power, without any support or income from the United States, which was Cuba's traditional partner, Castro procured the establishment of new links with the Soviet Union and other communist countries and started projecting himself as a leader of the developing world.

The establishment of those links with the Soviet Union had other effects on Castro's actions, because the Cuban communists, who were grouped under a so-called Socialist Party, became more visible within the ranks of Castro's government, and based on that, Castro found it necessary to reorganize his movement, adding them, together with people from other movements that had fought against Batista and had remained at his side, to his own forces.

In 1961, he created what he called the Integrated Revolutionary Organizations, merging his own Twenty-sixth of July Movement with the Socialist Party (communist party), presided by Blas Roca and the remains of the Thirteenth of March Revolutionary Directory, an organization which had played a role in the fight against Batista and had influences among the students of the University of Havana, of which Faure Chomon was the main remaining leader.

The above event illustrated the degree of isolation that Castro had reached from the point of view of the traditional Cuban political organizations and parties, none of which were anymore at his side, but at the same time, it gives a clear idea about the degree in which Castro was already achieving his goal of concentrating absolute powers in Cuba. A closer look shows that even the participation of those few leaders of the only two political organizations that remained beside Castro was rather limited and controlled and mostly symbolic.

Many years later, the main leader of the Socialist Party, Blas Roca, became the president of the National Assembly of the Popular Power while another communist, Lazaro Peña, served as the secretary of the Workers Federation. Faure Chomon was sent to Moscow as ambassador of Cuba there. Incidentally, when Blas Roca died, years later, Castro ordered that he was buried beside Antonio Maceo, one of the main national heroes of the war of independence against Spain, at the Cacahual Mausoleum in Havana.

The mentioned process of concentration of powers continued at full speed, and by 1962, Castro was able to create what was called the United Party of the Cuban Socialist Revolution. The inclusion of the word *socialist* was a clear illustration of his purpose to convert Cuba in another communist regime, something that would allow him, based on the use of the communist doctrine, to preserve and develop his absolute powers. This was the same Castro that had proclaimed in 1959, only three years before, that his revolution was not communist.

Finally, in 1965, this is six years after he took power, he changed the name of that mentioned party to Communist Party of Cuba, and paradoxically, with this name, which showed his alignment with the communist bloc, he managed to be accepted as an undisputed leader of the non-aligned nations!

While Castro was conforming the mentioned new political establishment designed to keep him in power with unlimited powers for as much as he wished, there were many other changes occurring in every aspect of society as well as the economy, caused by the radical departure from previous institutions introduced by his regime.

Under Castro's rule, there has been a total restructuring of the traditional government Cuba had before him, not only in the form but mainly in the content of functions and organizations and especially in the fact that they have become dependent of the Communist party, which is the main ruling body.

Castro's government has ministries to handle the administration of each of the main sectors of the economy and society and these ministries have had different branches to handle the main aspects under their field, including representations in different regions and abroad, one would think that as in most countries, but the differences with them appear, however, when one analyses the contain of their functions.

All these ministries and other institutes and government entities must operate according to Castro's orientations and must follow his rules and those emitted through the channels of the Communist Party, which keeps a vigilant eye on all what they do. They must respond to the policies of Castro and their first obligation is to fulfill the duties assigned to them to such effect. It is this sort of first commandment what has made most of them very difficult or almost impossible to manage successfully.

The Cubans have seen regularly how a note published in the *Granma Diary*, Castro's newspaper engender, created to replace all the best newspapers and magazines of the island that existed before 1959, in which it is informed to the population that a certain minister has been demoted and assigned to other usually unclear functions, because of his bad work or whatever irregularities were discovered in his ministry. In cases, these irregularities have brought them to long terms of isolation, what the Cubans jocosely call pajama plans or just to disappear from Cuban politics, and this kind of notices serves to remind everybody that, in Cuba, only Castro and his family, or those very closed to him, can have mistakes or be corrupted.

The functionaries are also alerted that they can try to get some privileges because of their functions, but if this is uncovered one day, it may bring them disgrace. The fact is, however, that most of these people, who are appointed to carry on functions at different levels of the government, learn that their status is most likely provisional, until Castro disposes of them, and they usually try to get the most they can from their stay in those positions. I have known of ministers with twenty-six cars in their garage and a private train to visit their children when they were sent to work to the fields with their schools!

As I mentioned before, corruption at all levels of Castro's government and party has been rampant, so much that it has extended to all levels of society—and, since people live in the middle of the most absolute poverty levels and there is scarcity of practically everything, they have got used to steal whatever they find, to satisfy at least a little portion of their needs.

Castro established a network of prisons for common crimes, in order to brutally punish anybody caught doing this and hundreds of thousands of people have been through those prisons, but Cubans are so desperate that they keep stealing from the government everywhere and whatever they can. The fact that, in their subconscious, all the Cubans know, even when they may be afraid of mentioning it, that Castro, his family, and his main followers have all sorts of privileges and assets, make them feel that they are also entitled to a little portion of it and this, together with the fact that most of the people have lost all interest in the protection of government assets, has created a state of abandonment for all aspects of Cuban society. The image of Cuban cities in many aspects is similar to the one of those cities that were bombed during the Second World War.

Supposedly, the main organizations that should take care of the administration in Cuba are the mentioned ministries, but there are as well as the local representatives of each community, who have seats in the so-called National Assembly of the People's Power, but since there is a total lack of supplies and the machinery of the government does not work and the top levels of the Communist Party are totally incompetent and do not care about these problems, nobody can do anything to solve any situation.

It is obvious, when one looks at the pictures of present Cuba published abroad, that we are in front of a total disgrace of enormous proportions. There is no way to hide this.

Curiously, it has become more frequent in recent years to find qualified people in charge of ministries or in other important positions of them than to find them in the Communist Party, but they cannot do much to solve any problem and their presence in those positions usually does not last much, because as soon as they start being recognized as successful leaders, no matter what little good thing or improvement they achieve, they become in some degree popular and this is something Castro does not like—and they are soon removed..

In those few cases in which charismatic personalities have had the audacity to be more independent, introducing some modern elements of management, or only of expressing some criteria different to Castro's, they usually end clashing with him and his convincement that he is the only one that can have the power of acceptance by the people and the power and capacity to decide what is right or wrong.

As I mentioned before, the Cuban people are already used to the sudden demotions and disappearance from the public eye of ministers that have been considered successful at one time or another in different branches. They have all found out that they had been appointed by Castro to basically follow his orientations and guidance, not to become generators of change or successful personalities and also they have learned that they, like many others, are just disposable pawns.

Cuba has also had, since 1976, this is seventeen years after Castro took power, the mentioned National Assembly of the People's Power. This body came into existence at the same time than the new pseudo constitution introduced by the regime; the real Constitution of Cuba, a document that was not possible to manipulate like Castro wished, was abolished in 1959, no matter that it was one of the most advanced of the world at that time.

The National Assembly meets regularly twice a year and the people elected to it come from the pool selected and approved behind curtain by the regime. Even when it is a larger body, with more than six hundred members, there is no space within it for any serious dissent. It has some legislative and constituent capacity and takes care of national plans.

Every year, its members listen to a report from the national government and of some branch of it. Since there are many branches of the government, the chances that the issues been discussed are seen again is very small and the process of tracking the solutions for any issue is very ineffective. This so-called National Assembly has been a puppet inefficient institution and it has been presided for a long time by one of the most servile followers of Castro, Ricardo Alarcon, a repulsive opportunistic character.

Due to some wording introduced in a paragraph of Castro's constitution, the National Assembly should be able to allow the creation of new political parties, in the event that somebody decided to present an application for this, with ten thousands signatures, but as my own experience shows, if one tries to do this, not only they are not going to accept it, but one can end in prison like I did, because, like all what Castro does, the letter or his words may mean something, but the reality says that it is not true.

Since practically all the industry leaders, who represented most of the energizing and administrative forces of Cuba, had to leave their country and as I explained, Castro closed all the schools of economics and accountancy, which he considered were teaching wrong capitalist theories, Cuba has lived in a state of permanent administrative and entrepreneurial disaster.

At some moment, when he could no longer ignore the economic disaster that had been created, Castro decided to reopen a number of those schools that had been closed, in which he started teaching socialist concepts to manage the economy, mainly brought from the Soviet schools.

However, the fact that the economic system established in all the communist countries was also a total failure and the newly introduced theories, which were always complemented by Castro's paranoid ideas, were totally divorced from the Cuban reality, meant that, for all these years, Cuba has lived in a growing state of economic disaster, no matter how much the level of subsidies, for years enormous, it received from the Soviet Union and other countries.

To make things worse, when the Soviet Union was dissolved, Cuba remained in a sort of limbo, because Castro decided to keep attached to the same absurd communist concepts and they are still being used as the guidance for the management of every aspect of the society. The magnitude of Castro's disaster continues growing and it will be in that way, up to the infinite, unless the present regime is changed.

It is interesting to explain that, in the case of Cuba, Castro has managed the country according more to his wishes than to the traditional communist political and economic theories. An analysis of his rule during the past fifty years shows that, no matter the existence of the Communist Party of Cuba, Castro has done whatever his wishes have been, the party only being something decorative that he can use to satisfy his almost unlimited ambitions of power and keep under control his opponents. It has happened that at times, for very long periods of years, there have been almost no meetings of the central committee or any other relevant activity of it other than sporadic meetings of the politburo to discuss particular issues.

Proof of the above is also that there has not being regular calls to congresses of the party, as it is established in its rules; for instance, the last congress took place in 1997 and we are in 2009, this is a period of twelve years without congress, which is in violation of the own rules of it.

We must explain that, even when Castro has assumed personally the main government and party decisions, this does not mean that things were going to be very different if the politburo or the central committee were the ones taking the decisions. There are so many incompetent, corrupted, and opportunist people appointed to the highest levels of the party and the government, that it would be very difficult that there was much difference.

Theoretically, cadres of the party should be selected based on merits and capabilities and they should be promoted based on their studies and intelligence and their achievements. The number of members of the party and the communist youth organizations represents the existence of a very large political organization and they should have been able to fulfill a more successful role during all these years. The fact, however, is that the appointment of cadres for the different positions and levels of this structure and also for the positions of the government has been totally capricious, based mainly on their unconditional and opportunistic support to Castro. Whenever this key requirement is challenged, even slightly, Castro and his machinery are always ready to repress the challenger and destroy him or, at least, limit his ascension to higher levels.

An analysis of the composition of the main group of people in charge of the key aspects of the party shows that the most influential of them are very old and have been around since the times of the Sierra Maestra or before, and in general, they are people who lack a proper level of education and competence, even when their representation sometimes almost hide that fact.

They are also people with serious moral problems in their background, and in many cases, they have been accomplices of the worst actions of the regime in these past fifty years.

It should not be strange then, based on the above, that the capacity of this huge political machinery to orientate and provide guidance at the different levels for the proper management of the society and the economy has been nil and has resulted in a total failure.

The presence of so many contradictions makes impossible any attempt to justify the absolute power of Castro and the privileges of him and his family and in a group of close followers. In order to be able to perform any role of leadership within the structure of the party at any level, its members must renounce in fact to any individual freedom of dissent and this has created a whole spectrum of incompetent and opportunistic cadres.

No matter how much the party rules pretend to give some limited and carefully measured opportunities to its members to discuss their ideas, the result is a total fiasco, in which the slightest dissent is forbidden. The only valid rule is that people are there to preserve Castro's rule. If they get some kind of privilege, well small or big, because of their position, they must know that it will last until they stop giving total and unconditional support to Castro, avoiding any challenge to it. The fact is that Castro, his party, and all the political infrastructure they represent are a political, social, and economic aberration.

Not only the Cuban revolution has failed in achieving any level of development for Cuba, but has dramatically brought backward the economy of the island to levels of poverty and lack of progress only comparable to some of the poorest countries on Earth.

The continuing propaganda of Castro has managed to make many people around the world believe that Cuba has achieved important educational, medical, and social results under its rule. It has represented the image of Castro as a benefactor of the Cuban people, a progressive mind. For decades, it was even elegant to support the Cuban revolution among some intellectual circles of the world. The crude facts show a very different picture.

The Cuban population has been living in precarious conditions and most aspects of the society and economy are totally stagnant or going backward, and this has been so for many years. This situation has come to a point in which many sectors of the population have arrived at a level of frustration and desperation and they do not see any chance of fulfillment of the empty promises and slogans the government of Castro has been repeating for half a century.

It is important to note that the Cuban government presents regularly to international organizations all sorts of statistics and data, which show important achievements in many branches of Cuban life. It is likely that honest people, in many countries of the world or in those international organizations, tend to believe that information. The fact is that most of this information is manipulated and altered by Cuban authorities with a total lack of scruples. This is easily corroborated when people travel to Cuba and move out of the arranged itineraries they usually are offered by the people operating the tourism industry there.

During the time in which Cuba received huge subsidies from the Soviet Union, there were some aspects of Cuban life that showed a certain degree of improvement in comparison with the early years of the revolution, but they were ephemeral and they never represented what they could have been, if things had been different and another kind of democratic system had been operating in Cuba. It is most likely that Cuba was by now a sort of Singapore of the Caribbean, if one considers the speed at which many developments were being introduced in practically all aspects of its economy and society before Castro took power.

After the disaster caused by the initial years of Castro, he obviously has had a very long time to develop a new government infrastructure and new people to run it, but this has also become a huge failure. Cuba is nowadays a very backward country, with a very low level of industrialization, horrible housing, and living conditions, a totally unproductive agriculture, incredible limitations, or even a total lack of products, to satisfy all the basic needs, an obsolete infrastructure, and worse than all this, Cuba is not a free democratic country. There is no way to justify the existence of a dictatorship of fifty years in Cuba. No philosophical doctrine, or political creed, can justify so many years of rule by the same group of people. The terror used against the Cuban people to maintain this situation cannot be ignored and must be denounced. The chaos engendered within Cuban society by Castro's rule has made impossible any achievement or sign of progress or the functioning of an effective administration.

Cuba currently has a deficit of almost three million housing units; the water supply infrastructure is totally inadequate and underdeveloped; the hygienic conditions cannot be worse; the transport infrastructure is basically obsolete; the educational system is in shambles; the health system and hospitals are a disaster, lacking the most elemental supplies; the environmental conditions in which people live, especially in the cities, are comparable to the ones in some of the most underdeveloped countries; there is a total lack of freedom for any kind of expression; no free newspapers, Internet, television, radio, nothing.

There is practically not a single new modern industry oriented to satisfy the needs of the population, much less a national industrial program; the foreign commerce is by far insufficient and the Cuban government has not been able in fifty years to organize the production to establish a balanced trade and to satisfy national needs.

Cuba is perhaps the country of the world with the largest debt per capita and there is no chance that the Castro's regime, used to violate all the rules, will be able to improve this.

All the incipient industries that were in process of development in 1959, which included practically all sectors, have gradually disappeared or have become relics after all these years; the tourism industry, which in the past decade has become the main source of income for Castro, is not even the shade of the one Cuba would have by now, if things had been different, as the growth rate of the statistics of tourism in 1958 show and it is also a source of discrimination against the Cuban people, who lacks the economic power to share its services.

The use of Cuban doctors as a source of income, by sending them, with miserable salaries, to other countries, to be used as Castro's propaganda, while the Cuban people are lacking medical services, is a criminal act. The use of the educational system as a machinery of indoctrination of Castro's ideas in Cuba and abroad is also a criminal act.

The discrimination of the Cuban people by prohibiting their right to free traveling while Castro, his family, and his followers go anywhere is a crime; the virtual condemnation of most of the population to live in the worst conditions with no hope of improvement is also a crime.

We have mentioned before in this book some of the many myths included in Castro's propaganda, in regard to the supposed achievements and transformations of the different aspects of Cuban life by his regime. Sometimes many people abroad do not realize how far these myths have gone.

The failure of all this complex of organizations in charge of the political and administrative aspects of Castro, including the Communist Party, the government, the National Assembly, and many others not discussed here, is overwhelming and has impacted and damaged the life of several generations of Cubans in every aspect.

The effect of this disaster in every branch of the economy and the society has been enormous, but it is the human side of it the one that is more terrible. Many people in this world have been able to see the documentary images brought from Cuba by tourists and visitors, which show the degree of destruction of the cities, the sadness and poverty of the people, their mental confusions and lack of hope for a better future. It is easy to see how they feel afraid of expressing freely because of the terror established within the Cuban society.

This destruction of the human condition is the worst result of Castro and his regime. The families that have seen their best members killed by firing squads or in horrible jails for decades; those who have lost their sons and daughters in the Strait of Florida trying to abandon the island looking for a better future; those expelled from their schools or working centers due to their dissent; the ones that have seen their families divided; those who have expend their whole lives there and do not see any progress. They represent the crudest aspect of the failure of the Cuban revolution.

CHAPTER IV

The living conditions in present Cuba

One would assume, in simple terms, that a revolution is a historical process, essentially motivated by the needs of the majority of the people of some country, to remove a certain established type of government or regime, which is being bad for them and their society, in order to replace it by another one, which they hope will be better and will eliminate a number of contradictions, which do not allow them to progress as they would like.

Like it was also the case in many other countries, Cuba had, indeed, many problems in 1959 and the majority of the Cuban people wanted to solve them. Some of these problems required an urgent solution and affected considerably different sectors of the Cuban society.

Even when Cuba had advanced enormously, since it had finally got its independence at the beginning of the twentieth century, there were still many development problems, and there were important sectors of the Cuban society who lived under conditions of poverty, with low levels of education and without access to many important services and possibilities. There were also large differences between the standard of living of the rich and poor people.

Cuba had been struggling during most of the twentieth century, trying to establish on permanent basis a democratic system, with regular elections every four years and freedom and transparency. The conversion of some of its main leaders from generals of the war of independence against Spain to politicians of a democratic new nation had in most cases not been simple. Conflicts between some leaders developed within the national army and the other civilian ones, who were in different political parties, were frequent.

Corruption had been rampant in most of the governments Cuba had had and the one of General Batista, which resulted from a military coup, was far from being an exception. The traffic of influences had become normal and the distribution of wealth was unbalanced and unfair.

There were powerful foreign interests, especially American, which had found very favorable conditions to flourish, in cases due to corruption schemes, dominating many of the most important sectors of the economy and they had a large influence in Cuban politics.

Most of these foreign interests and firms had started coming to Cuba during the American intervention that followed at the end of the war of independence Cuba had fought against Spain. After the Spanish-American War finished in 1898, the United States stayed in Cuba for few years, until 1902, time in which they developed some good and necessary works and helped to arrange the transition to the new independent state, but also many American interests used this time to procure access to develop numerous businesses, which in many cases presented administrative irregularities.

The ownership of the land was basically unfair. Some Cubans, as well as foreign interests, had managed to acquire in dubious ways enormous extensions of land and a large proportion of the lands remained underutilized, or were exploited under abusive terms while a large portion of the rural population did not have any land to work. There were sectors of the population, which received very low salaries and had to work under bad conditions.

The agriculture still was the main source of income and specially the sugarcane industry and the state of Cuba's economy was still linked to the price of sugar in the world markets, even when the United States had established a system of preferential quotas, with special prices for Cuban sugar, which represented an enormous help for the development of the country.

Having mentioned the above facts, it is necessary to consider that, as we mentioned early in this book, the world of those times was different to the one in which we live now. Cuba was not the only country with those problems and even many nations that are considered within the developed world now, had many of those problems as well then.

A detailed analysis shows that Cuba was already experiencing serious progress in the diversification of its economy and the development of a number of other industries, which satisfied a growing percentage of the national market and also were becoming the source of new exports while tourism was growing very fast and all elements indicated that it was going to become shortly the main engine for the national economy.

There were important and effective efforts taking place to improve and extend the education of people at all levels and new schools were being built; the universities were exceptionally good and were autonomous institutions.

The construction industry was growing very fast and Cuba was building new roads and highways to communicate to the most remote areas and all sorts of new works while new industries were being built for practically all products consumed by the national market and new housing developments were taking place, public and private including new high rise buildings, similar to those existing in the United States. There were also new water systems in progress and the whole infrastructure of the country was being transformed.

The commercial network had all sorts of supplies and was expanding and developing and the transport industry was developing at the same rate than in any developed country.

There was a whole new industry of telecommunications and new channels of television were developing at a much faster rate than in any other country of Latin America and there were also excellent newspapers, magazines, and radio stations.

The agriculture, which was the main Cuban economic sector, was producing new products that were increasingly sold in the American market and the population had available all sorts of food products.

In general one can say that there was a sense of progress among the Cuban people and they were used to the quick introduction of all the new inventions and to pursue their improvement in every aspect of life.

Cuba had very progressive and advanced labor laws and the labor unions were an important institution oriented to the protection of the rights of workers and the also advanced Cuban Constitution established important rights for every citizen. People were free to travel and everybody could participate freely in all sorts of political or social institutions.

In other words, as I explained before and in the previous chapter, Cuba had problems, but not even remotely comparable with the ones it has now, after fifty years of Castro's rule. Also, one must consider that it was perfectly possible that Cuba had found the way to stabilize its democracy, like many other countries did, without the need to go through a process like the one Castro established.

The obvious facts show that the problems Cuba had in 1959, no matter how important, were in comparison much smaller than those existing in Cuba now, and one has to reach the conclusion that the portion of the Cuban people who believed in Castro and followed his political aberrations and personal ambitions suffered the worst kind of historical mistake any nation could experience.

How are the Cubans living now, after fifty years of communism and Castro's government, and how does this compare with the rest of the world? We will try to describe that in detail in the next paragraphs of this chapter.

Cuba currently has a housing deficit of approximately two and a half to three million units, which come from the fact that the construction of new houses has been practically nil for several decades as the relatively few that have been built by the government or by private owners have not been enough to replace those that have destroyed due to their very old age and poor conditions or due to natural disasters. Those houses that were destroyed by hurricanes were in general never rebuilt or replaced and there have been people living in provisional facilities for decades.

At the beginning of Castro's government, he promised to build hundreds of thousands of new housing units and he created an institute to deal with these matters. Soon, this institute started the construction of new buildings in a new neighborhood at the east of Havana and the same happened in some other important cities like Santiago de Cuba. At that time, Cuba still had many resources from those construction enterprises that existed before Castro that he had confiscated; therefore, the mentioned institute had some power to build while the quality of those buildings was relatively good.

Unfortunately, once the mentioned institute finished those neighborhoods, they stopped building anymore due to the lack of interest of Castro's government, until many years later, when the pressure for new housing became too much and Castro announced a new crazy plan, which consisted in allowing people, who need desperately a place to live, to abandon their regular work, whichever it was, to go to what he called micro-brigades, which basically were inexperienced construction brigades, that started working in many locations.

The result of this new plan was a huge failure, not only because there was a lack of all sorts of materials but also because the people working at them had a very low productivity and they lacked the knowledge to achieve the quality required, The resulting quality of the buildings they finally managed to build was atrocious.

To complicate more things, in many cases, the new buildings did not have any site work done around them and many still remain there, after many years, without proper streets, landscaping, and other common facilities around them, just isolated in the middle of big lots.

At the same time that Castro made his promises of building new houses in 1959, he introduced a new law to reform the structure of property of Cuban homes. By this law, the government nationalized all rental properties existing in Cuba, to become the only centralized owner to collect rent in Cuba. He made available, to those people that were renting until then, the possibility of buying those properties in a number of years, paying to the government for these properties that he had confiscated. In other cases, the government simple kept collecting the rent of the properties that had been nationalized. He ordered the reduction in half of the rents, to make many people feel happy in the short term and try to get their support, even when this, of course, was done with the money and properties of others.

In some cases, Castro's government established a value for those properties that had been nationalized and paid them accordingly to the former owners, in fixed monthly amounts established for a period of years.

One big problem with the mentioned law, however, was that, as it became common in Castro's plans, there was nobody really competent and with enough resources and knowledge to manage and maintain all those properties and soon they started depreciating and deteriorating. Since the population had the same limitations or even more and there were no materials available, most of the inventory of Cuban homes started to decay and destroy and this ended in the current housing crisis Cuba currently has.

The Cuban population almost doubled in the past fifty years, growing from six million to eleven million six hundred thousand approximately, and there are close to two million people of Cuban origin living abroad. This means that, if there has not been practically any construction of new housing units, because we do not consider the first houses built a significant result in terms of percentage and the micro-brigades can be considered of such a bad quality that they should better be replaced and also considering that many of the homes existing originally in 1959, have since then collapsed and disappeared due to the effect of time, natural disasters, and other causes, each existing house must have now as an average more than twice the number of people than before Castro took power.

If we consider that most of the existing houses in the different cities, as well as those in the rural areas, must be, at least, more than sixty years old (in reality they are much older) and there hasn't been any distribution of materials to repair, enlarge, or improve them during most of this time, one has to conclude that the existing inventory of houses has to be in extremely bad conditions, something that is coherent with the images filmed by tourists and Cubans visiting their relatives, which are frequently shown in TV programs in Miami.

It is also well-known that, as we mentioned before, most of the large number of people that have lost their houses due to hurricanes, failure of their structures, floods, and other causes during these past fifty years have been moved to collective provisional facilities called *albergues*, where they usually have remained for many years until our days.

It is also obvious that in a country like Cuba, where there is a whole long season of rain every year, it is necessary to paint and repair every existing building periodically. It may seem incredible, but this basic maintenance principle has not existed in Cuba for fifty years because the government, even at the times when Castro was getting huge subsidies from the Soviet Union, never has engaged in any serious attempt to solve this situation.

Even worse, those people that become desperate and try to buy materials outside of the government distribution network may end in jail if they are caught, something very easy, since the Committees of Defense of the Revolution and everybody else are seeing when a neighbor repairs or paints his home, because this makes his house look very different to all the others around. Based in elemental calculations, one has to arrive at the conclusion that it seems logical the deficit of three million housing units for the population of Cuba, according to the parameters that a civilized country should have.

The question that comes to everybody's mind after the previous paragraphs is: how do so many people live in those conditions? The answer is that, obviously, they live in terrible conditions. They do not have any kind of privacy, with all the implications of this and the hygienic conditions are very precarious, especially considering that on top of the housing problem, the water systems of every city or small town are also in a state of abandonment and water is each day more scarce there.

The few very old pieces of furniture they may have, if they have a house for themselves or their family, usually come from their grandparents, because there has not been any stores in all these years to sell new furniture or factories to fabricate them, and most of the many very good ones that existed before 1959 have long ago disappeared and there has not been any significant production of new mattresses either or new factories opened and the old ones closed due to lack of supplies and people have to use the same mattresses of fifty years ago, with all sorts of patches and broken springs.

The electrical home appliances they usually may have in a whole house are old Russian TVs or perhaps a better even when cheap one, if they receive dollars from relatives in the United States, an old Chinese refrigerator or maybe an even older American one with an improvised engine from other equipment, an old radio and maybe an old fan. Most families usually have a very old kerosene or electrical kitchen. In general, Cubans cannot have any of all the other types of appliances existing now in most countries.

Most of the old Cuban houses, which have resisted this long time almost without maintenance, are usually very small, and many people, especially in Havana, have tried to increase their space by building small illegal mezzanines at them, which are called *barbacoas*. Most of these are built without any proper construction code and usually they represent an additional risk to the overall structure of those houses. It is frequent to learn of old houses that collapse, especially after heavy rains. When a person walks along the main streets of Havana, he can see everywhere the empty spaces where these collapsed houses or old commercial buildings were.

There are also many old houses that were built larger and they are now crowded, because the families that owned them have had to split them to house the several generations of their families who were born during these fifty years.

Cuban architects have elaborated many plans to develop and improve Cuban cities, but Castro's government has failed to devote the economic resources to materialize them, saying that there has been a lack of means to finance their development.

The infrastructures of all the Cuban cities are destroyed and in an advanced degree of abandonment. There are primitive living facilities erected everywhere. They remain visitors of the famous favelas of Brazil and Venezuela, but much poorer. Currently, they can be seen even at the center of some neighborhoods of Havana.

Most Cuban towns usually lack paved roads and their residents must improvise unsafe connections to steal the services of electricity and water from the regular lines.

Cuban houses and apartments, specially their bathrooms and kitchens, usually are full of accumulated dirt because there are no cleaning products of any kind available in the stores and the government never bothered to build factories for this.

The walls and roofs of most buildings and houses are damaged, this creating dangerous conditions and there are patches of humidity everywhere.

There are also mosquitoes everywhere and all sorts of insects, mice, and vectors because there are no fumigation products available.

The windows and doors are generally cracked and damaged because there has not been any painting product available for decades and most houses have their walls in very bad conditions.

The supply of electricity is very irregular and people cannot be sure when they are going to have it or not.

And all this, of course, refers to those lucky ones that have a house. All the others living in collective units or in the most unbelievable places one could imagine, live in much worse conditions.

Could anybody believe that Cuba has fewer houses now than fifty years ago, when Castro took over? Is that possible? Unfortunately, yes, it is possible. People can believe it or not and I know that, especially Castro's followers, may have a problem to believe this. I respect that, but according to the stubborn facts, this is the incredible case. Does this give a clear idea of the disaster Castro has created? I sincerely hope so.

In general, Cuban people currently have very few clothes because the stores are regularly almost empty, and they do not have the capacity to buy them, unless they receive presents from their relatives abroad or they can get dollars in the black market or through some work in the area so-called dollar of tourism, which would allow them to buy in some special stores established by the government, which sell only in dollars or in a certain hybrid monetary unit introduced by Castro to collect the dollars.

Since there is very little space where they live and sleep to keep properly their clothes and other belongings, this may become a very serious problem, especially considering that thieving has become a standard practice.

Cubans have tried to keep their old tradition of dressing well and people do the most astonishing things to procure clothes to look better, no matter how poor their living conditions are. In the past, they were well-known for their pride in regard to the way they dressed, but now visitors can see everywhere men without shirts and with very poor clothes and women dressed in very elemental clothes.

There is a shortage of shoes because the old well-known Cuban shoe factories, which existed before Castro and had a well-established reputation of quality, have not been replaced by any new factories, and even those few old ones that are kept precariously operating have become technological antiques. They also have problems with their supplies and since the livestock industry of Cuba is also in a very bad situation, it cannot satisfy their demand for leather; therefore, they cannot fulfill even remotely Cuban needs.

Food has become a big issue in Cuba all these past fifty years. The small and limited rationing quotas established by the government have kept reducing as time has passed and every day the range of products has become shorter and their quantities smaller and obviously they are by far not enough to satisfy even remotely the demand.

All the people, and especially women, have to dedicate a huge amount of time to look for whatever they can find to feed their families. Anything outside their quotas is very expensive, and since salaries in Cuba have the level of the poorest African countries, they have to do marvelous things to find food. Pilferage of food and any product is everywhere, especially in working places.

Most of the traditional plates of Cuban cuisine are very difficult to prepare now, because the ingredients are scarce or nonexisting, except for Castro, his family, and close followers, who have an abundance of everything.

The supply of fruits, vegetables, yucca, sweet potato, and potatoes is very limited and traditional Cuban fruits like mangoes, mamey, bananas, and others have almost disappeared because their plantations were destroyed by Castro's brigades of earth movement many years ago, when he was planning the restructuring of land use.

Meat, ham, and fish and their derivates are almost impossible to find in government stores and people have to pay astronomical amounts for them in the so-called dollar or "shopping" stores or in the continually persecuted black market. This in a country that had the highest rate of meat consumption in Latin America in 1958.

Cuban agriculture, traditionally the main source of food for the Cuban people, has contracted to very low levels of production of most products under Castro's management, and Cuban farmers are not willing to work for the government in government farms because of the meager salaries and bad treatments.

The regime has not been able either to supply properly those private farmers and cooperatives still existing in Cuba. As a result, the agricultural production does not satisfy by far the demand of products of the population.

To complicate even more the situation, since some of the main export products Cuba had, especially sugar, have decreased their production to levels only seen during early colonial times, Castro needs to sell every product he finds available, in order to be able to get some hard currency, leaving the people without practically any food to satisfy their needs.

In the past, Cuba was able to produce enough agricultural products to satisfy almost all the national demand and also to export growing quantities of them. Under Castro, this has not been possible. One can say that the development of Cuban agriculture is in a dead point.

It became an obsession of Castro and his government to dedicate to the export market every product available that has a relatively good quality, leaving the Cuban people the worst of them for their consumption. However, despite this, Cuba has an enormous unbalance of foreign trade and the commercial balance has been in the red for almost all the time these past fifty years.

The result of all of the above is that Cubans do not have access to any kind of possibilities and they are forced to live in the worst conditions. Obviously, this does not apply to Castro and the other people around him, who have almost unlimited access to all sorts of articles and luxuries.

A good example of the above are lobster and shrimp products, as well as the best fishing species, which are captured for the export market or for the table of the party and the army leaders, but the people cannot buy them because, if caught with one of them, they can go to jail.

Oysters, a traditional plate in every corner of Havana before 1959, have disappeared, like all the kiosks that were so familiar in Cuban urban landscape and engaged in selling all sorts of delicacies.

The scarcity of products have been so widespread in Cuba during these years and it is so complicated to satisfy a basic demand for it in each home, which many people consider is a premeditated policy oriented by Castro, to keep the people busy and unbalanced all the time and avoid that they can have time to think about their situation and start looking for a way out of their nightmare.

If one considers the high fertility of Cuban lands before Castro took power, this mentioned reasoning acquires some logic.

It seems almost incredible that Cubans do not have food, considering how productive the land and the seas around the island were.

Since urban and rural transport is very scarce, and usually because of the lack of proper maintenance, even new buses lasts very short time in good shape; it is not easy to travel inside Cuba and between its cities. A trip to one of the provinces from Havana or wherever people live may become a real adventure. As a result, people try to work close to their homes or wherever they live, even if the jobs they find are more elemental and do not require the knowledge they may have.

The transport crisis, especially in rural areas and provinces, is such that many people have built primitive horse carts to use them for their transportation and for rent, like during the colonial times.

Work is also scarce because most of the few remaining old factories are closed, well for lack of supplies or for bad conditions, and the construction industry, a traditionally important source of employment, is very limited, and most urban services are in a state of total abandonment. To make things worse, most people who live in urban areas are not willing to go to work in the agriculture. Since most working activities are paid very little, according to the government's abusive scale of salaries, many people prefer to find their living by doing all sorts of irregular activities, something that they call in slang "inventing."

There is a large portion of the population without any permanent job. Many men in working age are seen regularly expending a lot of time playing domino with their friends in any corner of their neighborhoods, usually accompanied by some beers, obviously if they manage to get them, or drinking a bottle of one of the very bad liquors produced for national consumption, because the good ones are again for export. Not surprisingly, there is an extended problem of alcoholism in Cuba.

Those people who work regularly in a government entity have to dedicate a lot of time to take their buses, or whatever more rustic way of transport they can get, to go to work and come back, and they must look later for their supply of food at the abandoned and run-down stores that still exist and most people, especially the elder, look very tired and thin. It is noticed that even young people look older than their age and women have very limited beauty products available and creams and other skin products are almost inexistent.

Private cars, like good houses, are the top luxury, only available for people in good positions within the government or for very few professionals and also for those who manage to keep operational one of the old American or Russian cars still existing, which may have parts from who knows what other make or source. Since fuel is rationed, many of the people who own cars have to keep them parked most of the time and go out to work by bus or truck or whatever other means they find. This has made bicycles very popular.

Buses are usually extremely crowded and scarce and there are all sorts of things that can happen at them. Desperate people can try to take your jewelry and run away.

As I said, the use of bicycles has become popular during the past two decades, given the transportation problems, but it has some inconveniencies, among them is that if it rains, like so frequently happens in Cuba, they get wet, and also, if somebody tries to steal your bicycle, it is not easy to find new bicycles.

The main recreation is to watch TV, but the programming is very boring and of very poor quality and lacks variety. This is when it is not full of Castro's indoctrination. People have felt relieved, noticing that his brother Raúl prefers to give his "orientations" in other ways and they are less frequent, after Castro gave more powers to him, after his illness. There are no foreign TV channels allowed, and if somebody is caught with a clandestine improvised antenna, he may get a big fine or even go to jail.

Considering that Cuba was one of the pioneering countries to introduce television, in black and white and in color, immediately after the United States and much before all of Latin America and most of the European countries, the contrast is obvious. The same happens, in general, with many other inventions. There were already several channels in 1959 and a very varied programming and there were plans in process of implementation to expand them considerably.

Cubans were the first to see the World Series directly from the American television. There were also many national and local radio stations with excellent programming.

When Castro nationalized the media sector, he decided to use all these TV and radio stations for his propaganda. Many of the best artists had to leave Cuba and obviously again, what came later was another big disaster.

The current television and radio network that Cuba operates is very backward and its technology is rather old and this does not allow it to achieve a good level of quality, but the programs elaborated in Cuba are also very limited and show very low quality and there is a lack of all sorts of modern means and technologies to create sceneries comparable to the ones made in other countries that were well behind Cuba in this field in 1959. To make the programming even worse, Castro only imports very few foreign programs, which makes the programming miserable, and this is even more considering the constant shortage of electricity, which makes the watching of TV unreliable.

The existence of freedom is an essential requirement to facilitate the development of any branch of art to its full potential, and since it does not exist in Cuba, the radio and television networks have become another Castro's disaster.

Castro has used the radio and television networks for his own personal propaganda, to project his image once and again to the Cuban people, and he has not been interested in any other role for them, among other things, because he does not like the idea of allowing the projection of any other personalities and figures. Castro is obsessed with this as part of his paranoiac personality. As a result, Cuba, a country used to produce excellent artists, singers, and musicians in the past, has only allowed very few of them to reach a level of international recognition during these past fifty years, and even in these few cases, this was allowed only after they have shown a total compromise with his regime and once they have been willing to represent Castro's interests and be used for his propaganda purposes.

In the past, there were many cinemas in each neighborhood in Havana and in all Cuban cities and towns, and Cubans liked to go to them to see films, especially if they were American or European, but there are only a handful of them that are still in operation because the government never gave any maintenance to those buildings and most of them have collapsed or being demolished due to their dangerous conditions. In other cases, their very old equipment broke and replacement parts never came.

As I have mentioned before, Cuba had many internationally famous night clubs, cabarets, bars, casinos, and all sorts of entertainment centers before 1959, but most of them have gradually disappeared because Castro did not find them good for his plans of oppressing the Cuban people. Most of their buildings were abandoned after they were closed by Castro and their structures collapsed years later. Few of the best known places, like Tropicana, are still open but for tourists mainly and they are not even a remote shade of what they were before, when famous people from all over the world, Hollywood actors, and famous singers were frequent visitors of Havana and the city had its lights on day and night and tourists were everywhere. A comparison of the projections of the tourism industry that Cuba had in 1959 indicates that Cuba would have by now one of the largest number of tourists per capita in the world and its tourism industry was among the most profitable because it came mainly from the United States. It is easy to visualize how this tourism had impacted the Cuban economy, considering the effect of tourism in the development of other countries, most of which started much later to develop their tourism industries, like Spain, Greece, and other Caribbean islands. Even now, most of these countries cannot compare their natural attractions and the level of their installations with the incredible network of entertainment and beautiful places Cuba was already offering fifty years ago.

Open access to Internet is not available to the population at their homes as there is no network available for them and the only services available in the country are controlled by the government and its secret services. Only the lucky ones who have dollars or convertible currency can use the government-controlled system available and they must go to some hotel for tourists or to one of the few centers opened for this in order to be able to use the service. Some people also try cautiously to connect to the Internet from their place of work, when the service is available at them. Nobody, except obviously the people at the top, can use without limitations that service.

To have a personal computer is an almost unthinkable luxury for a regular citizen and most of them have not seen them except in films or television or in selected working places. This in a country used to be totally updated of all sorts of new inventions in the past!

In 1959, Cuba had excellent newspapers and magazines and the best of them, like *Diario de la Marina*, *Informacion*, *Prensa Libre*, and *Bohemia* magazine, were comparable to any good newspaper existing at that time in the world. They were all closed by Castro, as we have explained before, and their printing machineries and building facilities were then used by him to publish a newspaper called *Revolucion*, a name he later changed for *Granma*, in honor of the yacht that brought him from Mexico to the Sierra Maestra to start his guerrilla war against Batista. Two other newspapers called *Juventud Rebelde* and *Trabajadores* are also published, both with very limited editions, terrible quality, and both devoted to publish Castro's interpretations of events and ideas and to give a very extracted briefing of national and international events. It is so ridiculous that the current level of the Cuban press is not respectful to pretend any comparison with what Cuba had before Castro. The fact that the Cuban people are all the time looking for copies of *Granma* to use them as toilet paper, another basic product almost nonexistent in Cuban stores, gives a clear idea of the best use one could find for this newspaper and the two others.

It is illustrative to try to put oneself in the case of regular Cubans in front of some possible situations anybody in the island can experience.

If, for instance, by any chance, somebody has a medical emergency being at his, or her, home and needs urgently to go to a hospital, this may become a very serious challenge because most likely there won't be ambulances to call and it is not easy to find a neighbor that may have some sort of transportation and even less that has enough fuel to bring the patient to the hospital. It may take a long time to solve this, but on top, if the patient is finally able to get to the hospital or a clinic, there is no guarantee that the doctors will be available because there is an increasing shortage of doctors, especially in small clinics, due to the fact that Castro has converted medical services in an export and propaganda commodity, and there are so many doctors being sent, with miserable salaries, to other countries around the world, that there are many locations in which they are scarce. If the above was not enough, it most likely will happen that the medical facility where they go does not have the medicines needed, because the shortage of medical supplies is also serious problem and if the patient needs to stay at the facility, almost surely there won't be clean sheets or pillows available and people have learned that they must bring with them their sheets from home in cases like this. The mattresses of most hospitals regularly are in terrible shape and the general hygiene of them is rather poor because there is a total lack of disinfectants and cleaning products in the island.

The look of the facility may also be rather deplorable because of the lack of paint and maintenance, but since everybody has got used to this, they will consider this "normal" and the same will happen with the clothes of the doctor and nurses, which may be stained because there are no washing products available either. Finally, if there is a need for some medical equipment, like for instance an x-ray machine, it is possible that there is no electricity, or that the hospital has its electric plant broken due to a maintenance problem. This is obviously if the equipment is not broken due to a lack of spare parts and even it may happen that the technician, or even the doctor, may have had some problems with his transportation and may be late or have not come.

However, if everything luckily goes on well and the patient manages to get to the medical facility in time and be treated by the doctor, the medical equipment works well and the medicines are available and he does not need to stay there overnight, the problem may be, then, to find some transport to go back to his home, unless they had found a good neighbor with transport, who stays there waiting all the time.

Of course, if the patient happens to be one important figure, *dirigentes* they are called, then everything is easier because he surely has a car and fuel is not a problem and he can also go to a special facility, restricted to other people. If the patient was a tourist and can pay in dollars the medical bill he won't have much problems either because almost surely the facility to which he is brought will be better equipped and supplied and even cleaner than the regular ones and the doctor will be immediately available. There will be clean sheets, pillows, and a TV in his room if he needs to stay.

To make love may be, for many people in Cuba, apart from the pleasure that one can expect, is a real adventure. If the couple is married or living together, something frequent, because social customs have changed according to the new reality and most couples do not marry, they must find a private moment in their home and obviously, considering the conditions of living explained before, this may not be easy, especially considering that there are many people of different generations living together in the same limited space. They must find the time to try to see if the others are sleeping or are not there. They must also have some planning, depending of the conditions in which they live, to keep some stored water because to have running water is a luxury in Cuba now due to the obsolete water supply systems. They also need to take some protections, and condoms may be scarce. Some people, given the complexity of the problem, may decide not to go to work that day, no matter what and they must see that their children, if they have children, go to school and their parents or other relatives that live with them as well also go out, well, to work or to look for their food quotas, which is another problem, because nobody knows exactly when they arrive at the store. In many cases, people get so frustrated that they do not care anymore and their love making becomes a sex show, and everybody, even their neighbors, become used to this.

There is no need to say that the rate of divorce is very high in Cuba and the frequency with which people change partners is even higher. It is not easy to live happily on these mentioned conditions. But things can be more difficult.

If the couple does not live together, they must find a place to have their intimacy and this may be very complicated. Unless one of them can bring the other to his or her home, and this may not be possible because there may be some reasons why they do not live together, they must look for some other place. In Havana, and in most cities, there were many motels (called *posadas* in Cuba) before Castro took power, but his government nationalized, almost fifty years ago, them. From that moment on, these motels never received any kind of maintenance and gradually, they, like it happened with the cinemas, disappeared, after being in a state of total abandonment for many years.

It may also become a real challenge for many people who do not have a place to do it to find a dark corner or a hidden spot, to make their furtive love, or they may better decide to discretely pay somebody they know who owns a house and rents a room, to get some additional money or even dollars. Again, they must decide how they manage to find the time and how this matches within their other activities and their families, especially if they have children, who may live with one of them and they need to keep attended. In Cuba, there are many hundreds of thousands of children who live with only one of their parents due to different reasons, the extreme housing shortage being one of them. This obviously leaves many prints in their young lives.

If the couple is just friends and may be starting a relationship, it may become a complicated matter to arrange for these things, and most frequently, this becomes somehow frustrating. This is one of the reasons why there are so many problems between Cuban couples and many of them do not to marry. People want to have something to enjoy and to feel free and happy but they find that there are so many obstacles in their lives that make this difficult to achieve that they do not care anymore about the appearance of things.

When a woman gets pregnant in Cuba, she and her partner will have to deal, in the first place, with their housing problem. Since usually every Cuban home is crowded and there is no chance at all of moving to a larger one, the couple usually needs to convince the rest of the family to somehow open more space for the new child. Most of the times, this is not feasible and this is one of the reasons why the rate of abortions in Cuba is astronomical.

Another issue is that the level of salaries in Cuba is very low and many young couples find they cannot afford to have children. On top of this, they find that their living conditions are so difficult, in every aspect of life, that they don't think they can deal with them with a baby.

The level of salaries in Cuba can only be compared to those of the most underdeveloped countries. In Cuba a professional receives approximately the equivalent of $ 20 per month in Cuban pesos, which are practically useless, while an average worker receives approximately $ 12 only. Those who do not have access one way or another to dollars are condemned to live in the most absolute poverty. Castro argues that Cubans receive a number of services like education and health free, but not only this was also so in the past, when salaries were comparatively much higher, but the fact is that whatever these services represent, the total current income of the average Cubans is so low that this has brought them to live under conditions of misery. Compared with people in other countries, Castro has converted the Cuban people in beggars.

Practically nobody in Cuba can visualize a better future under the present system, even if they try to be as optimistic as they can be. It has been half a century of empty promises and slogans and unlimited appeals for sacrifice and continuing hopes for some kind of improvement that has never come. The people have come to realize that they have dedicated the best years of their lives to something that basically has become a big lie and an empty myth.

Theoretically, a Marxist regime is supposed to be the government of the workers. In the case of Cuba, this interpretation seems more like a joke, because the Cuban workers have been exploited, humiliated, deprived of most of their rights and brought to live in miserable conditions and their presence in the upper ranks of the regime is minimal,while all the fat cats, followers of Castro, who are allergic to work, are occupying those positions.

The Cuban population is practically not growing nowadays and it is easy to understand that. Under the present conditions created by Castro, having children has becomes a very complicated matter.

There are other problems apart from those mentioned before, which make very difficult, especially for women, the decision of having children in Cuba.

The values of Cuban society have become different under Castro, and most of the traditional moral and family values, which had passed from generation to generation within the Cuban society, are gradually being eroded by the cynicism of the communist system. There are hundreds of thousands of children without father in Cuba because they are virtually abandoned by their fathers, who are young people with a level of irresponsibility and lack of scruples very high. These are the people who have grown up under that engender of a system and have a totally distorted sense of moral and family values. At the same time, they lack any working discipline and capability that could make them good workers and citizens. This is just one result of the huge failure of Castro's revolution.

If one considers that religion always had played an important role in Cuban society, which had per se enormous reserves of moral and family values, and that now, after fifty years of chaotic materialistic indoctrination, several generations of Cubans have grown up without any notion of any of these moral and religious values and principles, it is obvious that it will take many years and lots of efforts to bring back on track the Cuban society once the Castro disappears.

The situation with the above-mentioned problems, which widely exists in the Cuban society now, deserves some other considerations.

Some people in the world may say that these problems are not only present in Cuba, considering that, indeed, there are other countries that are experiencing somewhat similar situations, but the case is, that Cuba, fifty years ago, was in a much more developed stage than most of those countries and the only reason why this situation is so extended in Cuba now is that Castro has brought back the level of civilization and social and economic development that existed in Cuba, which is now at a very primitive level.

The poor conditions of living created by Castro have another, even more terrible aspect, which is the possibility that Cuba is impacted in the coming years well by a strong category 5 hurricane, or another natural disaster, especially if the hurricane affects Havana or some of the main cities. The degree of abandonment of all the housing and industrial infrastructure of the island and the lack of maintenance that comes with it could result in a human catastrophe of gigantic proportions. Only Castro and his regime would be responsible if this happened.

Unfortunately, the statistical records of hurricanes that have affected the island through its history show that the time that has passed since the last category five hurricane that impacted Cuba, in 1944, is several times longer than the historical average of time between large hurricanes. This is, according to the historical trend, there is a huge possibility that a very large hurricane impacts Cuba, and if this disgrace happens, the Cuban people will suffer the result of all the wrong policies of Castro in a much worse way.

The above is perhaps the most dramatic example of why Cuba needs a new, more responsible government, which is able to change course to the disgraced situation created by the current system and can start rebuilding the whole infrastructure of the island immediately, including the development and implementation of new plans to repair and transform the housing facilities of the whole country in a short time, something that Castro's government has not been able to do in fifty years.

I believe that Cuba may be able to develop its economy and infrastructure very fast once Castro and his system are gone, even when I believe that it will take many more years to revert other damage done by them to the Cuban people.

It will take a lot of educational efforts to cure the many wounds left by them and to develop a new system of values within the Cuban society, which includes moral principles that are almost extinguished there now.

CHAPTER V

≈

The educational system

Castro's propaganda has sold the image of Cuba as a world power and success story in the field of education, of course, thanks to his policies. They have repeated this so many times, in all kinds of forums and events and they have expressed this concept in so many publications in all languages that many people around the world has come to believe that this is true.

Castro's propaganda has been designed to convince all those that come across it at one moment or another, who are relatively ignorant of Cuban history, that Cuba was a very underdeveloped country in 1959, full of illiterate people, without a proper educational system, and that all Cuban governments before Castro had had a total disregard for the improvement of those conditions. It presents Castro as the savior of Cuban education and the benefactor of Cuban children and youth.

I must start by explaining that, when Castro took power, sixty years ago, Cuba had an educational system that covered most of its territory and all the large and small cities and towns.

There were rural teachers that went to work in the most isolated parts of Cuba, including the mountains and all teachers had to be graduated from pedagogic institutes and many thousands came from the School of Pedagogy at the universities. They had to win their positions by exams and teaching was a respected profession.

There were excellent books, which not only facilitated learning the whole spectrum of knowledge, cultural and scientific, but also served the purpose of creating better citizens, by introducing moral and civic principles and the best family values. Those books were reverent with the heroes of our nation, those who had fought in our wars of independence of the nineteen century, and Cuban children grew up learning of their courage and sacrifices as well as their patriotic values. The textbooks did not include political indoctrination or any kind of veneration to any living political figure.

Good manners were taught in every school and children learned to respect their parents and elders. There was freedom of religion and race was not an issue to go to those schools. The idea was introduced in their minds that if they made a good effort, they were able to be successful in life.

As we have explained before, Cuba still had many development problems in 1959, including problems of education. Illiteracy still existed in many areas, especially in rural areas, but Cuba already had at that time a whole and growing network of centers to gradually reduce that problem and advanced scientific methods to teach illiterate people. Practically all the schools nationwide operated night centers for adults, in which every citizen had free access.

Cuba had excellent public and private elementary schools and the teaching of other languages, specially English, was very extended. There were also excellent private schools in every Cuban city, some of them managed by the church. These schools worked under the same educational guidelines established by the Ministry of Education.

There was a whole network of institutes of midlevel education in the island and they had very competent and professional educators, many of which were authors of excellent books in their fields. These institutes were established in all the main cities of each province. All the students could buy at very reasonable prices their books and even those who came from very humble families had access to them. All these institutes had well-dotted laboratories and educational facilities, including gymnasiums.

Cuban universities had a long tradition of excellence. There were public and private universities. The University of Havana, the main one in the island, had two hundred years of existence and all the members of its roster of professors and lecturers had to win their chairs by opposition. They were usually well known for the textbooks they wrote in their fields, something that was a tradition. The Universities of Cuba were autonomous and the government could not influence on them. Students were free to believe in any ideal or to follow any political doctrine; the police could not come into their buildings.

The students who graduated from Cuban universities could find work practically anywhere because their programs had equivalencies with the best universities of the world in the most advanced programs. There were careers like medicine, engineering, pedagogy, and law, which had a well-established prestige, due to their long traditions and there were many Cubans that excelled on them.

The Cuban society was literally full of distinguished and prestigious scholars and Cuba was up to date in all branches of science, literature, arts, and technology. Cuban scholars carried on research in every aspect of our culture and their books were considered valuable pieces of the national patrimony and were considered obligatory pieces of lecture by any cultivated Cuban. They were open minds, without any kind of vestige of discrimination and their influence on Cuban thinking and education was enormous.

Cuba had a vast and expanding network of libraries, some with the most advanced reference systems, in which every Cuban, poor or rich, white or black, had free access. Anybody could borrow books from these libraries because all of them had their loan systems, available for everybody who wanted to read a book.

Cuban archives were carefully preserved by knowledgeable and specialized personnel and they kept the most valuable information about every stage of our History. They were the most valuable source for every researcher.

It must be said that education was not only a matter of the National School System and the Ministry of Education. It was something in general spontaneous in most families because there were some values that were established too deep in the Cuban society, no matter is people were rich or poor.

Maybe some people reading this book can think that I am exaggerating and that I am trying to decorate the image of what already existed in Cuba in 1959 and I understand their feelings after all the propaganda that has existed giving a different view. Since I can be mistaken, I invite them to consider carefully just few things that to me reflect these facts:

- How is possible that in the Cuba of 1959 there was such a small number of people in prison? The number of prisons existing in all the Cuban territory at that time was incredibly small, and apparently, the system existing in Cuba had to produce some kind of result to keep people acting in an orderly way. If Cuba had so many problems, one should expect a larger prison population. Instead, Castro has multiplied the number of prisoners by hundreds of thousands, and this is my imagination, even when he has told the whole world he has achieved a large success in educating the Cuban people.

- How is possible that all the most important and advanced inventions of the first part of the twentieth century were almost immediately and extensively introduced in Cuba? Cuba necessarily had to have a very progressive economy and society, with many educated and competent people, in order to be able to achieve that. Under Castro, Cubans have not known about even some of the most elementary new products existing in the developed world, not to mention more advanced ones.

- How is it possible that, fifty years ago, Cuba had more or less the same number of houses the country currently has, but obviously in better shape; and how could Cuba feed without any kind of rationing all its people and have all its stores well supplied of all sorts of products; how Cuba could have, year after year, a positive balance of trade, all this never ever achieved by Castro? There must have been some qualified and educated civilization in Cuba before Castro, in order to be able to achieve all that.

In reality, it becomes obvious that Cuba was a very progressive country, which was achieving important economic and social advances in all branches and its educational system, even when not perfect, was good enough to be the key element in those achievements. That other image of Cuba as a poor country, with a very underdeveloped and backward educational system, which has been sold to the world by Castro's propaganda and has found echo in many places and media is not real.

By the contrary, we can say that it is the educational system created by Castro, despite all his propaganda, the one that has proved to be a total failure, because it has being part of a chaotic political and administrative infrastructure, which has created the worst situation Cuba has ever had in all its history.

In 1959, Castro promised to build thousands of schools, because he considered that the speed in which new schools were being built in Cuba by former governments was not enough. He did not explain, however, that he was going to replace most of the educational programs existing in all Cuban schools by a new one, designed to ensure the indoctrination of students according to his political ambitions. He did not say either that he was going to build many of those schools in remote locations, not to satisfy the needs of those areas, but in order to separate the students, arbitrarily brought from the cities, from their parents, with the same indoctrination purposes and to use those students as cheap labor for his absurd agricultural plans. Much less he explained that he was going to use all this for his propaganda.

When one starts analyzing how the educational system of Castro has worked, one finds that all Cuban schools have all their programs mixed with political indoctrination and the political propaganda of the regime is part of their agenda; children are forced to become pioneers of the communist system since they are in the first grade of the elementary school and they must use a red necktie as part of their uniform and they must repeat every day a pledge: "Seremos como el Che" (We will be like Che Guevara), as if Guevara could be a role model for them!

Castro and his followers have used the Cuban educational system to reinforce their control on the Cuban people. It is not true that Castro introduced improvements in Cuban education, but on the contrary, he destroyed many of the most important achievements Cuba already had in this field when he took power and has poisoned, with premeditation, the minds of several generations of children.

Cuban children may be more or less intelligent and get good or bad results, like any other children in any other country. Some may excel in their studies, like always happens anywhere. But the problem is not there. The problem is that Castro's educational system has been designed to introduce into the minds of all those children, a whole set of wrong political and moral values, which work like viruses in a computer; this demoniac purpose has been achieved with all perversity, with the assistance of many of his most corrupted followers and one can foresee that it is going to take probably several generations to remove them, once this regime is gone.

Anybody visiting Cuba can see that most Cuban schools are in deplorable conditions due to their lack of maintenance by the government and that, after fifty years, there is a scarcity of qualified and professional teachers and school managers at all levels of the educational system. Many of the most competent Cuban teachers have decided to abandon their profession because they have become tired of the ideological pressures of Castro's government and the bad conditions existing within the educational system, as well as the low salaries and lack of incentives.

Most observers do not realize the main problem of present Cuban education because they are not allowed to go into the full details of it. They do not realize that, not only the teaching of moral and patriotic values has been removed from all the programs, but emphasis is now done on Castro's slogans and communist principles and theories and this is only the tip of the iceberg of what Castro has done in this field, with a total lack of scruples.

Based on the above facts, it is easy to understand why so many teachers, who may have had any kind of dissent with government policies, have been removed from their classes, in a country with a large shortage of teachers. I have known personally many of those teachers, who explain that they were retired early or were force to leave their profession because of the pressures applied on them. Many of these teachers were forced to migrate. Those teachers were the main remaining barrier between Castro and his goals of controlling the minds of Cuban children.

Castro nationalized all the private schools existing in Cuba and all these valuable educational facilities have suffered the same abandonment of the rest of Cuban schools. Most of the teachers and the main personnel of them had to migrate. Obviously, Castro knew what he wanted and had planned how he had to proceed to achieve it.

The loss caused by the incredible destruction of Cuba's educational system by Castro's government cannot be calculated.

Practically every action taken for the past fifty years by Castro and his regime in regard to the Cuban school system deserves to be carefully reevaluated in order to discover Castro's real motifs and what exists behind decorated images his propaganda has presented. When doing this, it becomes obvious that all Castro's actions in this field have been taken based on his political ambitions and not with the intention of educating better any Cuban children or students in general.

I can illustrate many examples of this. For instance, during the initial years of his government, Castro brought from the Sierra Maestra mountains to Havana, with grand fanfare, several thousands of children. He said that those children were going to have much better conditions if they lived and studied in Havana and he presented this as one big achievement of his revolution.

Many of those children were brought to live, in fact, at houses of Miramar, one of the best neighborhoods of Havana, which had just been left behind by the first waves of Cubans who were forced to immigrate to the United States due to the policies of Castro. Those houses belonged to the families of the Cuban upper society, formed by professionals, business owners, lawyers, and bankers, among others.

The intentions of Castro were not precisely altruistic, however. Not only he was trying to destroy the economic power of the people who were his political opponents, but in reality, these children were separated from their parents to be intensively indoctrinated on communist doctrines since the first school levels and not to be properly educated. I could witness many times how they were forced to repeat hours after hours the same communist slogans, in order to convert them into blind followers of Castro's government. This is the reason why they were brought to Havana from where their families lived, instead of leaving them there, to be educated by their rural teachers.

But things did not end there. The purpose of Castro was not only this. He really also wanted to separate those children from their parents because he knew that many of the people who lived in those mountains were very independent and it was going to be very difficult to convince them to accept his communist ideas and his new rules and they could become a very serious problem for him. Having control on their children facilitated to have much more control on them. In fact, after few years, Castro was able to enroll most of these indoctrinated youth in some of his military and semi-military organizations and use them at his will.

At the same time that he achieved the mentioned purposes, Castro used this in his propaganda, in order to justify the confiscation of all those homes, the same he already had done with other productive properties of those Cubans and foreigner investors in the island, whom he forced to migrate with his policies. This had never happened before in Cuban history because the private property was protected by the Constitution.

After a short time, Castro removed all those mentioned children and youth from those houses and brought them to collective military units or to other centers where they followed their training and indoctrination. Then, he ordered the repair of most of the best of these houses, which had been practically destroyed by the children, who obviously were not used to live in this kind of environment, and he gave them to his closest followers and their relatives, including his own family, while some were also rented in dollars to the people of the main embassies represented in Havana.

It is interesting to mention that most of the valuable pieces of furniture of these houses, as well as the collections of art they usually had, were taken out when they were confiscated. Many pieces ended in the houses of some of the new leaders of Castro's government while others were sold in international markets, as a way to collect hard currency; there were also many that were brought to the warehouses of the former Havana Docks Co., at the Port of Havana, where they stayed deteriorating for years, stored in big piles, until someone in Castro's government found that they could be repaired and sold as antiques in foreign markets.

Many of these homes had valuable libraries and it became frequent to see the big piles of books thrown in the middle of the abandoned gardens, under the rain, or people putting them on fire to get rid of them.

All of the above represents the real "educational" values behind Castro's actions. Castro and his followers have destroyed the Cuban patrimony. Most of the accumulated wealth of Cuba has disappeared and by this I do not mean simply the loss of richness, which becomes obvious only by seeing the deplorable state of abandonment of all the houses, lands and cities of the island, but also the patrimony represented by Cuban traditional values, including moral and civic virtues and the patriotic education as well as all those principles of decency, honesty, respect to the others, good manners and educated behavior, which were part of Cuban culture.

One of the reasons, almost always used by Castro in his speeches to justify the radical changes he was introducing in every aspect of Cuban society at the beginning of his regime was the corruption of Batista and other members of his government. Soon, he extended similar accusations to all successful elements of Cuban society and identified practically any personal or business achievement with corruption and the exploitation of people by the rich class. This concept was introduced by Castro very early and it is included in all the millions of new books ordered by his government to replace the existing school texts, which were distributed in all Cuban schools and used as well as in all sorts of crash courses created for every participant in the activities of the revolution.

Private property was demonized in all those books and the ones that have followed during the past half century and identified with all sorts of problems of Cuban society and this principle has been taught to every Cuban, enforcing it in all educational programs.

The above was the main element of the so-called Castro's revolution in the Cuban education. From there on, education and indoctrination were the same.

For Castro, a real parasite who had never worked in his own life, there was no merit in the effort of anybody to create and develop any kind of private economic enterprise or richness and there was no reason why the society had to respect the accumulated work invested by a person in this. He considered that a society that respected private property was a corrupt society, and many generations of Cubans have grown up and lived under that premise.

However, the above concept was soon in contradiction with the actions of Castro himself and most of his main followers because, once installed in their positions of power, they started to procure for themselves, according to the level they were, all what they could; a kind of philosophy spontaneously developed to justify this way of acting and it was that they deserved those things, because of their revolutionary merits and sacrifices. Castro got for himself an immense well-dotted and fortified house in each of the newly created fourteen provinces, a whole fleet of specially prepared cars, planes, a huge personal security force, military compounds for them and their training, all sorts of equipments, missiles and the most unbelievable machinery of propaganda, by using all the newspapers, TV stations, radio stations, and printing factories for his personal needs.

Under Castro, every functionary of the top of the party and the government, as well as the people who command his armed forces, started the practice of stealing whatever they have found, which they understand corresponds to them due to their merits.

The Cuban Ministry of Education is no exception to the above. On the contrary, since it is such a key ideological element within Castro's infrastructure of power, it has moved vast resources and has always been in the middle of this absolute system of corruption, which is huge.

The system of corruption established in Cuba is so vast that there are difficulties to compare it with other cases of corruption in the world, and within this, the corruption existing within Castro's educational system has been atrocious, especially at its top level, where people like Armando Hart and Jose R. Fernandez, among others, who have been ministers at different times for many years have committed all sorts of barbarities.

These mentioned figures belong to the core of Castro's circle and have been among the most abject of his close followers and their corruption, in every sense, has been total. They have enjoyed doing everything, like faithful dogs, in order to satisfy their boss and convert the Cuban educational system in an instrument of oppression and discrimination and a new kind of gigantic psychological prison.

The real facts show that, after fifty years of absolute dictatorship, the real Cuban education, which is diametrically different than the false image internationally represented by Castro, is a colossal lie, one of the biggest myths of Castro's so-called revolution.

The truth is that, in 1959, Cuba already had a good educational system, especially if compared with other countries, and it is only logical that by now, after fifty years, it should have been not only much better, but it had been established on principles of freedom and democracy, and these principles by themselves would have represented something radically different for the Cuban people.

Those mentioned principles are most valuable as well when one analyses the situation of Cuban universities after all these years of Castro's rule.

Castro frequently repeated that Cuban universities have seen a large increase of students in all these years; however, this is not an achievement of Castro's government necessarily. An analysis of the universities of the world during this same stage shows that, beginning at the end of the decade of the sixties of the past century and from there on, there has been an explosion in the number of students at most of the universities all over the world, even in countries that were in a much backward stage of development than Cuba at that time. It was a worldwide phenomenon and Cuba for sure was going to be part of it. The increase in the number of students is not an achievement of Castro nor is it a result of his policies. On the contrary, considering the number of young people who were at the university in Cuba, plus those who were about to enter at them at the end of the decade of the fifties and the large percentage of them that had to leave Cuba because of Castro's policies, it is almost sure that Cuba had had more students at the universities by now than the numbers of university students under Castro.

As I explained before, Cuba had excellent universities since many years before Castro came to power and some of them, like the University of Havana, were among the oldest and best in America.

A detailed analysis about present Cuban universities shows some very serious issues that must be mentioned. These are as follows:

- All the present Cuban universities have a serious shortage of qualified personnel and they lack the quality of teaching and the prestige that was a tradition of Cuban universities before Castro.
- Many people selected by Castro's people to teach at the universities do not have the required knowledge and culture to do so, and they have been selected due to political reasons and ideological confidence.
- The individual personality and character of the people teaching at Cuban universities under Castro has been systematically crunched by the policies of the Communist Party.
- Most of the programs of the different careers being taught at Cuban universities have not been updated according to present standards due to the lack of free contacts with other similar centers and people in developed countries and the almost total absence of modern literature on the different subjects, as well as the inefficiency and incompetence of their administrations.
- The continually and meticulously applied censorship by the government of any reference to new ideas and any new developments in the different fields of knowledge makes impossible any real progress of Cuban universities.
- There are numerous research fields, authors working on them, and key technological and scientific achievements that have been censored and are not mentioned in Cuba and, as a result, have been eliminated from the curriculum of most careers being taught at Cuban universities.
- There has been a very repressive policy toward all those students and lecturers who show some kind of dissent with Castro's policies, and they are frequently expelled from the universities and not allowed to continue their studies or their work.
- Castro eliminated the autonomy of the universities, something that is a crude violation of the traditional rights established in Cuba for many decades. This has converted Cuban universities in mere appendixes of the Cuban regime, which are used according to the political interests of Castro.
- Under Castro's government, all the main authorities of the different universities are not appointed anymore by their prestige or achievements in their careers, but mainly by political reasons and the degree of confidence the political establishment have of them.

- There is a growing feeling among Cuban students that their educational effort will become sterile because of the shortage of possibilities and the small salaries they will receive when they finish their careers. These salaries, as well as the positions they may be assigned, are in close relation with the political evaluation and decision of people within the government and the Communist Party and have very little relation with their competence and capabilities.

- Castro eliminated the system of opposition exams to award the main positions at the universities, a well-established and respected tradition, and replaced it with a system of selection based on political influences and guidelines.

- There is a scarcity or, in cases, total lack of modern educational means to teach at the universities, including modern textbooks, magazines, electronic audio-visual equipment, computers, and documentation, which makes almost impossible to achieve the same educational standards of other countries.

- Access to the Internet is prohibited by the government at most levels of society and it is even persecuted, when the services detect any kind of free expression, which is critical of the system.

- The secret police is constantly observing the behavior of both students and lecturers, and any manifestation of dissent is immediately punished.

- Students and lecturers are not allowed to travel freely to other countries or to participate in any free and independent seminars, conferences, or symposiums abroad.

- The only contacts allowed between Cuban universities and other universities and research centers abroad are those of members of their staff that are considered politically accepted due to their political orientation in regard to the system.

- No independent publication of any kind is allowed, and any new piece of research or article requires a long and complicated process of censorship and approval before it is allowed to be published, most times in limited editions.

- In general, the publication of new works on ideological, economic, or technical matters, which may be critical of the current system are totally forbidden.

- Research work is limited and based on political and ideological appreciations and there is a very limited participation allowed in any of the very few programs of post-graduate studies.
- Masters and PhD programs are based on political considerations and people are only allowed to participate in them after detailed ideological screening.
- If a piece of research or a subject in any course result in any kind of critics on the current system or any aspect of its policies, this may be punished severely and the author can be expelled, or at least stranded, from the university and isolated from any further participation in his field.
- In general, the physical conditions of most university installations in the whole island are deplorable, some being really in state of ruin and they all suffer a total lack of maintenance.
- There is an absence of modern facilities, except in few specialized centers, which are mostly used by the government for some privileged tourism or political purposes.
- Private universities were dismantled in Cuba many years ago and have been prohibited since then, despite the fact of their very old existence and achievements, among them some prestigious institutions run by the Catholic Church, like the University of Belen.
- Curiously, none of these above-mentioned issues, which are only few among the many others we could mention that would make this a much more extended chapter, were present in the Cuban universities before Castro took over.

It must be said, based on my own personal experience, that it is very frustrating for any Cuban student, lecturer, or professor who loves his country and wishes logically to develop something new, to contribute to the development of his field or simply to improve some aspect of Cuban society or economy, to realize that he is not allowed to do so by the government and that he is victimized, due to his independence of mind and also as a result of the envy for his achievements that comes from the establishment.

The existence of a censorship, which has been established with the well-defined purpose of crushing any sign, no matter how small, of freedom and progress, in order to satisfy the sickest ambitions of absolute power, is a barrier in most cases insurmountable for most of the people.

CHAPTER VI

⁓

The dangerous conditions of the environment

Even when many people, especially those who have suffered deeply the consequences and crimes of Castro's tyranny, may argue this, I must express my view that the environment is most likely the aspect in which Cuba has suffered the most severe and permanent damage during these past decades, and I understand that this is a lot to say considering the magnitude of the disaster Castro has caused.

I will attempt to describe, within the limits of this chapter, at least some main aspects of the enormous damage caused by Castro's policies in this field, but I must explain that this mentioned damage is so widespread and diverse that it is very difficult to quantify and even describe it accurately and, even less, to find exact answers about how future Cuban generations will have to deal with this side of the disaster they will inherit from the current system.

Going back in time, one finds that, in Cuba, like in other islands of the Caribbean, large portions of our territory were devoted to plantations of sugarcane during colonial time, when Cuba became the main producer of that product in the world, and there were also large extensions of land used for cattle raising, all this causing the destruction of most of the original forests that existed in the island when the first colonial settlers arrived.

The above pattern of land use was basically maintained during the first part of the twentieth century.

A review of the conditions of the environment at the time when Castro took power shows that most of the Cuban lands, which were well known for their high fertility were, in general, environmentally clean. The air of all the main cities did not have any problem either, and Cuban rivers were also generally clean and the same happened with the seas around Cuba and the waters of most Cuban bays, where people were used to regularly develop commercial fishing.

Most Cuban cities were modernizing their water distribution systems to adjust to the main trends of growth of the Cuban population and the same was the case with their sewage processing plants.

There was a trend to enforce by law all the main existing industries fulfilled a number of regulations that were being introduced by applying similar standards to those being applied in the United States for the protection of the environment and the same was required from the many new ones that were being developed, which usually came with the new environmental technologies already incorporated.

Obviously, considering the stage of development of the world at that time, the above does not mean that there were no problems in this field in Cuba before Castro.

Among the main environmental problems existing at that time were those created by the erosion of land by some mining enterprises, the largest of them in Moa and Nicaro, at Oriente Province, where the digging for nickel and cobalt, even when it had not been continuing, was leaving considerable damage in the surrounding areas. Other mines of manganese and tungsten also presented problems, as well as those areas that were dig to produce construction materials for highways and buildings.

The use of inadequate septic systems in most homes in rural areas was a problem because of the pollution they created, which affected the underground waters and the wells used by the rural population around them.

There were also serious problems in regard to the exploitation of the water reserves in some of the regions with larger population.

There were also other industries, in different locations of the island, which created environmental problems as well, like the tanning plants in Havana and many plants processing construction materials in different provinces. In most of the cases, this was the result of the operation of industrial plants that still lacked the filters and dust and smoke collector systems that were being introduced widely in the industries of developed countries at that time.

In general, and especially if compared with what came later under Castro's government, one can say that Cuba did not have a situation of crisis of the environment, even when certainly there were already some serious problems in regard to this. I believe that, in most cases, it was comparatively simpler to design solutions for the problems that existed at that time than for the much more extended and serious that exists nowadays. There is no doubt that the situation of the environment became dramatically serious after Castro took control of Cuban government.

Castro's totally ignorant policies in this field have caused some catastrophic effects, one of them being the destruction of enormous extensions of the best Cuban soils and lands.

A report prepared in 1997 by Castro's own Ministry of Science and Technology, with the assistance of Dutch authorities, mentioned as the main environmental problem of the country the degradation of soils due to the erosion, bad drainage, salinity, acidity, and compaction, among other factors. This report considers that around 26.44 millions of acres of the Cuban territories have the soils affected. This representing 60 percent of the national territory and it describes an advanced process of desertification and deforestation. In other words, a large portion of Cuba is becoming a desert.

The above gigantic environmental disaster was caused by a number of wrong actions taken by Castro personally and other people of his government, who followed his instructions blindly. The case is that, even when he did not have in his background any kind of knowledge of agriculture or any managerial experience in this field, he started acting as if, on top of his political functions, he was the top Cuban scientific agricultural authority, ignoring all the many alert calls expressed by a number of competent authorities that Cuba had in this field, as well as those of other foreign experts, who visited Cuba and expressed their views on what they saw.

Soon, the Cuban people could see how Castro assumed direct management of all the sugar industry and agriculture, personally developing and introducing a number of ideas, which he tried to implement at the scale of the whole country. These actions and ideas reached a level of craziness and the overall cost of these stupidities may never be calculated.

One day Castro could become one of the fastest cane cutters of the country and his "productions achievements" were widely covered by the newspapers and all the media while another day he was embarrassing some of the best scientists in the field of agriculture in the world by refusing their theories and accusing them of not understanding the situation of Cuba.

All this, obviously, created a huge disaster in the agriculture of the island, but in the middle of all this craziness, it was the environmental damage created by his actions the one that represented the worst part of it.

Following Castro's pseudo-agricultural policies, which were followed by all levels of the Communist Party and Cuban government, the mostly incompetent people he appointed to manage the agriculture in all the main agricultural areas tried to cultivate many extensive areas of land, without any kind of sense about the rotation of crops and using the wrong kind of equipments, inadequate cultivation and irrigation methods, as well as wrong amounts of fertilizers and pesticides and all this caused deep and extensive damage, which may be irreversible, to those lands, which gradually diminished their productivity more and more, while they became eroded by the weather elements, until they became useless for agriculture.

When it became evident that those mentioned lands were not producing any more, Castro and his people moved their agricultural operations to higher lands, including the hills and smaller mountains, and started doing the same at them. The result was that many of those other large extensions of higher lands started as well experiencing a growing process of deterioration and erosion, also becoming unproductive and part of a process of desertification.

To make things even worse, Castro oriented an intensive and indiscriminate exploitation of the underground water reserves existing in many agricultural areas, ordering the installation of batteries of heavy pumps in most of them, without any concern for the capacity that those natural water basins could have. The result was that, when most of the potable water, which was floating in the upper level of those basins was pumped, this allowed the penetration of the salt waters that were under them. Thus, most basins were contaminated by salt.

Since most of Castro's people had no idea about any irrigation techniques because they had not studied any of this, they followed strictly Castro's instructions, and when they exhausted the existences of usable water in some dry seasons, they kept pumping the saltwater under it because they thought they were irrigating their lands and had no idea about what they were doing, and as a result, instead of irrigating the crops, what they did was destroying enormous extensions of the best Cuban lands, which became salty, also polluting with salt all the walls of the large underground basins. It will take many decades for this salt to be eliminated by nature in those soils and basins and any other process to try to do so will be enormously expensive. Obviously, Castro does not want to talk about this anymore.

On top of the above, the rains, which are rather heavy in Cuba, picked some of the mentioned salt on these lands and brought it to rivers and creeks, this also causing a large ecological damage at them, which caused the disappearance of numerous species.

The intensive and indiscriminate use of pesticides and fertilizers, which were used to try to overcome the increasingly low productivity of the damaged lands and eliminate some plagues, also contributed to make this mentioned ecological disaster a worse one, because the rains also carried these products to the rivers and creeks, also affecting the already contaminated underground basins.

Cuba built, with assistance from the Soviets, some large fertilizer plants, which not only represented a serious challenge to the environment by themselves due to the pollution they caused due to their old technology, but also allowed Castro to intensify the indiscriminate use of these products in the Cuban agriculture, which became a new source of contamination of the environment and at the end did not produce any improvement of the productivity of the soils, which continue decreasing due to the wrong exploitation of the lands.

Another factor that affected large extensions of land was the compaction of soils due to the construction of many miles of rural and military roads in many zones of Cuba, as well as numerous military bases, with total disregard for the damage caused to the agriculture due to the reduction of available cultivable lands.

It is impressive to see how Castro and his people selected the best agricultural lands to develop some large industrial plants that he built with Soviet assistance, leaving without use those areas that were unproductive. At the end, most of these industrial plants became a total failure, but the damage caused by their large buildings and yards, which remain in existence, has been very large.

Perhaps the best example of this was the nuclear plant that Castro tried to build in the province of Cienfuegos, which took all the construction materials of several provinces for almost a decade a never could be finished. The enormous buildings with huge thick walls of concrete and steel and all the large space of land used remain there idle as a monument to Castro's incompetence.

The case of the mining of nickel and cobalt in the province of Holguin has become another gigantic environmental disaster, and the whole area around these plants has been polluted to unimaginable levels, this producing the appearance of a number terrible illnesses, which are affecting the workers of those plants and the people living in this large region, which have been directly associated to the toxics detected in the environment.

All the vegetation of the area has disappeared and the people living there give detailed accounts of the strange conditions of the environment in which they live, explaining how every metal of any item they may have become corroded in a very short time and how there are a number of strange occurrences regarding health problems.

While all this has been happening for decades, the Cuban government and those occasional partners Castro has found to develop these plants have done nothing to study the problems and protect the inhabitants of the region.

It is evident that the cost of restauring the zone around those gigantic mines and plants, after the brutal exploitation it has suffered, will require several times more money than the one Cuba has received for the exploitation of these resources.

The mentioned Cuban-Dutch report has obvious limitations of scope and did not include many of these facts, but despite this, I consider that it is an exceptional report, considering that most of the other reports published by the Cuban government usually include all sorts of manipulated data.

The Dutch report referred in very categorical terms to the deterioration of all the urban infrastructures and services. I have mentioned some aspects of this in previous chapters, but I believe that some more details must be explained on this.

Practically all the main Cuban aqueducts are the same ones that existed in 1959, and some of them, like the famous Albear Aqueduct, which was an extraordinary project, come from the nineteen century. After fifty years of Castro's government, absolutely all Cuban cities and towns have their aqueducts in advanced levels of deterioration and abandonment.

The fact is that they have been exploited all these years without much concern for the capacity of their underground basins and applying higher pressures to their pipes than the ones they were designed for, this causing all sorts of damage to their distribution lines.

The distribution of water in Cuba, in general, is totally unreliable and irregular and this is valid for practically the whole country and the lack of potable water has become a serious headache for a large percentage of the urban population, no matter where they live and in some extend for the rural population as well.

The losses, caused by this state of abandonment of the water distribution networks, have been estimated in more than 60 percent of the water pumped. This evidently makes the whole system a physical as well as economic mess.

Approximately 90 percent of the water distributed in Cuba comes from underground basins, which exist all along the island, while 10 percent comes from rivers and dams. There are different regional water systems, which operate separately in the island because most of them have not been interconnected, except in Havana and other large cities, where the exploitation of some of the main basins have been interconnected.

The operation of the different water distribution and treatment systems existing in the island is based on the supply of electricity, but since the electrical system also has numerous problems, this affects the operation of all the different parts of them. The treatment process for most of these waters is not adequate because of the lack of development and obsolete technologies of the existing plants.

The main underground basins existing in Cuba for human consumption are of good quality and they are a very valuable natural resource, however, this has been endangered by the excessive exploitation of them, their bad administration, the pollution of the lands and the underground and the salinity, as well as by the obsolescence of the different systems used to exploit them.

Most aqueducts existing in the island have their pipes and valves in very bad condition and they have numerous leakages. Since the distribution of water is not regular, they have become a source of contamination for the water that people consume. As a result of the extent of this contamination, some types of parasites, which are present in the pipes and, therefore, in the water, have become endemic within the Cuban population and represent a danger for foreign visitors.

Many materials used in the construction of these old aqueducts, as well as in some extensions of them built under Castro, are no longer used in modern systems, as is the case of the fiber-cement pipes, which have cancer genes and are forbidden in other countries.

These pipes should have been replaced long ago, but the almost absolute lack of maintenance and the lack of capacity for the introduction of new developments in this field, for the past five decades, have not allowed this. The types and thickness of most pipes are not adequate for the elevated pressure they have been operating during all these past decades and this has caused the partial destruction of important portions of these systems.

Practically all the existing treatment plants, in charge of producing the potable water consumed by the population, are old ones and they lack modern filtering systems and chemical products. Castro's government has ignored the need to introduce new modern equipments and proper repair and development programs in this field and they have all been severely affected by this.

Due to their advanced state of decay and millions of leaks, all the mentioned infrastructures of water lines of the country are no longer able to keep a proper pressure of operation anymore and this makes impossible to bring the water to many buildings and other elevated locations, forcing the people that live at them to go to places where there are still old fire hydrants, usually many blocks from where they live, to try to get few pales, or other recipients, of water, after waiting for hours in very long lines.

The distribution of water in provinces like Pinar del Rio, Granma, Cienfuegos, Sancti Spiritus, Las Tunas, Holguin, Villa Clara, and Guantanamo, as well as in Habana and Santiago de Cuba, is precarious. In reality, one can say that a very large portion of the population do not have access to potable water in their homes anymore.

If one considers all the other limitations Cubans have to deal with on regular daily basis, the problem created by the lack of water for their most basic needs has become a real nightmare.

As we have explained, most of the old aqueducts existing in Cuba have all sorts of problems because they have very old equipments and usually they experience a total lack of proper maintenance and they do not have spare parts, or adequate chemical products, to operate efficiently. The same situation exists in regard to the sewage systems of most urban centers, as well as in regard to the different existing industries and the tourism industry.

The sanitary systems existing in Cuba are based on the collecting networks of pipes existing in the different cities, which are separated from the ones that collect the pluvial water. There are also numerous areas where there is no sewage and the population use septic tanks and artificial oxidation lagoons. Only 45 percent of the population of Havana currently has sewage service and this indicator goes down to 6 percent in some areas of Cuba, with a national average of 30 percent.

The use of septic tanks and oxidation lagoons, which usually are not well maintained, is another source of pollution and they are one of the main sources of parasitism existing in Cuba.

For many years, the Cuban government has been building oxidation lagoons to process the sewage of industrial plants and all sorts of schools and urban facilities, and usually, they are an important source of contamination because of their poor conditions and the lack of maintenance.

The existence of proper treatment plants has become very limited, and in most places, they are almost inexistent. Since Castro stopped the construction and development of new sewage plants for almost five decades and the maintenance of the existing ones has been totally absent during his government, most sewage waters have been thrown at the rivers, beaches, and different areas of the coasts, and this represents another huge source of contamination and a dangerous situation. People who go to the beach there have no idea of the dangers to which they may be exposing themselves.

Some years ago, Castro's government finally started the development of a new large treatment plant in Havana, with assistance from Japan. Apparently, the situation of pollution in Havana Harbor had become so grave that it was practically impossible to continue allowing people to live around it and also operating the port. There were so many denounces of this situation in front of important conferences and events that, apparently, Castro was forced to do something in this direction. These mentioned works and others are trying to clean, at least partially, the harbor, which had become one of the most polluted in the world.

The existing systems for the collection of pluvial or rain waters are also in state of total of abandonment as they have not received proper maintenance for the past five decade either and only a small portion of the few new housing zones developed under Castro has these services. Since the cleaning of the drainages and pipes of these systems is very irregular, it is usual to see them clogged and surrounded by stagnant putrid waters in most neighborhoods.

During the hurricane season, citizens are ordered to clean these drainages doing voluntary work, but due to the lack of proper equipment, it is usual that whole areas of all the main cities are flooded in periods of heavy rains.

Castro's government was without any kind of control of the sands that existed at the sea in front of some areas of Cuban coasts, like it is the case of Havana City. Many years ago, Castro bought a whole fleet of used dredges in Britain for this purpose and these large amounts of sand has been used for construction purposes, without proper washing systems and with disastrous results.

One of the effects of this indiscriminate exploitation of the old existing sand embankments is that it has destroyed the natural protection of those coasts, and now, when there is even a small storm or a north wind, the sea penetrates almost a mile in very long portions of Havana.

When Castro took power, there was a project ready for execution oriented to protect the Havana coasts, where many new buildings were being built and even the molds for the concrete pieces (called tetrapods) that were going to be installed all along the coasts were ready, but like everything he has done, his government ignored this and simply abandoned and never pursue the project.

The fact is that Castro's government has been unable to assign the proper resources to maintain and develop practically all the main aspects of the whole Cuban infrastructure because of its incredibly inefficient administration. It would seem that Castro's mind was fully busy, with all those strange aberrations of fame and power in his head, and his only real concern was to stay in power while the people around him seem to have been busy trying to keep afloat in that sea of disaster that has been called the Cuban revolution.

While Castro immersed in those mentioned aberrations, to have a simple bath has become a real luxury in most Cuban cities and towns. If one adds to the lack of water, the irregular supply, or even total lack, of electricity, which, most of the time, affects most Cubans, one can imagine the conditions in which they live. This in a country which sixty years ago already had an existing and extensive infrastructure of services and was developing rather fast, with the introduction of the most advanced systems of every kind existing in the world.

Castro has allowed and at times provoked the conversion of many rivers and small creeks into open sewage canals, where all the sewage, from practically every city and town, hospital, factory, school, prison, and all sorts of installations, go. These gigantic sewage canals represent a large source of pollution for extensive urban and rural areas before reaching those locations at Cuban coasts or within Cuban bays where they bring all their sewage. No need to say that all the areas of the sea, or the bays surrounding them, have become also deeply polluted, and they represent a high risk for the population, also affecting the ecological systems. This reflects the degree of barbarism Castro has brought to Cuba.

One has to understand that Castro's government has failed to address this situation by simply ignoring every aspect of it for half a century. The only thing one can deduct is that this man is a monumental idiot in regard to every aspect of administration of the country, but also, with his insistence in remaining in power, ignoring the damage he has caused, he shows that he is a very sick mind and perhaps even more are those who support him.

The factories that existed in Cuba before 1959 were regularly required to have installations to process their waste. These facilities were simply abandoned by Castro and his people, and nobody bothered to repair or maintain them when they started to deteriorate, until finally they became inoperable.

In 1990, there was a World Conference on the Environment in Brazil and Castro went there, trying, like he usually does, to project himself as the main leader in this field in the underdeveloped world. However, this time, a group of us, who were part of the Cuban Environmental Association (known as AMAC), went also there and we were able to denounce in detail, by distributing our well-documented studies, the conditions existing in Cuba in this field and all this was transmitted to Cuba by Radio Marti and the Voice of Americas, having a serious impact in the island, where people identified our denounces with what they live every day.

After this, Castro took a number of actions, but curiously, these actions were not really oriented to correct or solve any of these enormous environmental problems he has created, but mainly to allow him to produce some propaganda on this, in order to show to the world a false image of the situation Cuba has in this field. In other words, since he was found defenseless when confronted by the crude facts, Castro appealed to his same repeated tricks and demagogic arguments.

He moved fast to create a department under the Cuban Academy of Science, which supposedly was devoted to these matters, and he managed to place, almost immediately, some of his people in important positions within several organizations of the United Nations, which have to deal with these aspects. One easily can imagine all the meetings and coordination of his secret services to arrange all of this smoke curtain. The problem is that, as the old saying says, it is not possible to cover the sun with a finger.

A short time after that mentioned conference took place, Castro managed to get some funds from United Nations, precisely to study the ways to clean the Havana Bay, which, as I said before, is one of the most polluted in the world. He also got some cooperation from the Dutch government to study some aspects of the Cuban situation, which produced the report that I have mentioned before, and one can only express gratitude to the Dutch government for having allowed, with their studies, to corroborate our denounces.

Almost thirty years later, Cuba keeps using the United Nations for its propaganda and to get some funds, the people of the Academy of Science are still there, and Castro's people are in important positions within the main ecological bodies of United Nations, but Cuban environmental problems have only aggravated. This is a good example of Castro's "achievements."

The problems Cuba has, in regard to the environment, are integral, that is, they include every aspect of it. We have given some illustrations about some of the problems affecting Cuban lands and waters, but the air of many areas of Cuba has also been seriously affected by the development of new plants of different types, many of which have obsolete technologies. This is the case of many electric plants, the main cement industries, fertilizer plants, and all those industries producing derivates of sugarcane and also many others.

Castro built numerous underground facilities to hide the equipments of his army, his navy, and his air forces, and for this purpose, he has used some of the largest systems of caves existing in Cuba, this causing the destruction of the habitat of these caves.

He also built numerous military and prison facilities everywhere in the island, and many of them were located in those valleys that had the best agricultural lands, which from there on were abandoned for their agricultural use.

It is no surprise that, under Castro, Cuba has not had enough agricultural production to satisfy its needs during all these past years.

The conditions of living in all Cuban cities and towns have been in constant decay along the past half century and a good example of this is the collection of garbage services, which has become comparable to the almost nonexisting ones of the most underdeveloped countries.

In cities like Havana, it takes several weeks sometimes to see some truck, or one of those primitive house carts I mentioned before, collecting the garbage bags that the people leave in front of their homes or the piles of them located in one corner or those hanging from nails in the trees.

To complicate more this situation, those sites used as dumpsters to which all the trash of the cities and towns is brought are basically large lots of land, without even the most elemental facilities to process the trash and with total lack of proper hygienic control. Since they are frequently located very closed to, or even within, the urban areas, they represent a real danger for the health of people.

The conditions at most Cuban hospitals and clinics are also worrying, because these facilities usually lack the means to process their residuals and they also lack all sorts of cleaning and disinfectant products, something we have mentioned before.

All the services to maintain the installations and parks of the cities and towns have almost disappeared in the island and the few places that still have them are mainly tourist facilities or institutions run by foreign or religious organizations. The same happens with the services to take care of the landscaping of parks and public areas in the main cities and towns.

It is important to note that, in Castro's Cuba, it is necessary to distinguish between the stubborn reality and the idyllic facts presented by the authorities, which usually are manipulated for their propaganda.

Cuba has created or introduced during the past two decades a number of rules, laws, institutions, and other mechanisms, which have to do with environmental matters, but these have not represented any improvement for the Cuban people. On the contrary, as it happens in every other aspect of Cuban society, the failure of Castro and his communist system to properly manage and develop Cuba in these matters has been absolute. One can use this as an example to explain that the communist system represents a backward step of mankind, all the contrary of what its apologists like to say.

The impact of this environmental situation on the Cuban standard of living is enormous, and it seems incredible how this could happen in a country that in the past was so receptive to all the advances of civilization.

During the decade of the sixties and seventies, Castro got obsessed with disrupting beyond any possible recognition the structure of ownership of the land in Cuba, and to this end, he created a huge equipment brigade, with large bulldozers, converted war tanks, and all sorts of heavy equipments, which he baptized Che Guevara, and he oriented it to go west to east, from Oriente Province to Pinar del Rio Province, at the other corner of the island, breaking huge extensions of unproductive lands, demolishing fences, and destroying all marks of previous ownership of those lands.

In reality, on top of all those "heroic" actions, which cost a fortune, the mentioned brigades also demolish as well all sorts of existing plantations, which were in the middle of their way, and this not only caused the crazy new distribution of land that Castro had in mind, including new limits for all sorts of state-controlled farms, but also it resulted in the destruction of all sorts of very old and established plantations in the whole island, destroying one of the main aspects of the Cuban agriculture.

Apparently, the changes he had caused, with the agrarian reform he had introduced at the beginning of his revolution, were not enough for him and he defined new goals for this. The case was that this brigade started its move along the island in the eastern provinces and did not stop until it reached the western ones. By the time it reached its goal of reaching Pinar del Rio Province, there was no significant productive achievement that could be identified, but instead, the destruction it caused was legendary.

Many important plantations of all kinds of Cuban fruits and all sorts of valuable trees were demolished because Castro wanted to change the kind of products that were cultivated on those lands. The result was the almost disappearance of many traditional products and specially fruits, which the Cuban people were used to regularly consume, as well as the destruction of huge extensions of old forest areas of precious woods, many of which were irreplaceable.

I must explain that when Castro nationalized all the largest land properties of the island and subdivided them in all sorts of ways, at the same time he confiscated as well all those smaller agricultural properties and livestock farms, which belonged to the many Cubans who opposed his government, including those who had to emigrate from Cuba. All this caused a very large decrease of the agricultural production of the island.

Incredible as this may look, to this day, several decades later, Castro's government has not been able to achieve the recovery of agricultural production to a level that allows it to satisfy the needs of the Cuban people.

Among the main reasons for the above are not only the bad management of agriculture by Castro and the lack of stimulus for the Cuban people to work the land, but also the destruction of the environment in most agricultural zones of Cuba, which has reached incredible levels.

I feel that the attenuation of the problems created by Castro's government in this field, if possible, will require the establishment of very strong policies and regulations in the management of all aspects of the Cuban society and economy, once Cuba returns to a democratic path.

To try to reverse the damage caused by such a long time of wrong administration and the most indiscriminate political actions will necessarily require the investment of important resources. This will make this field once again an important element within the context of the Cuban society.

The role of education in achieving some improvements in it will be critical. Even when a new consciousness is achieved, it will take many decades to reverse most of the damage.

It is interesting to note that, in the middle of all this disaster caused by Castro and his policies, we have observed how, several times during the past two decades, precisely when Castro needed some help in his propaganda on these environmental issues, he allowed some reporters from the best magazines in this field to visit Cuba, and somehow, he managed to achieve that they published long articles, in which they describe the "wonderful and pristine conditions" they have found in Cuba in regard to the fauna, with all sorts of references to the wonders of the locations they visited, including colorful pictures of some half-destroyed and decayed towns, which, in the context of the articles, look funny.

These articles have presented the views of these authors, and most likely of Castro, about how some species live and reproduce fantastically well in some areas of the island and how they consider that Cuba is passing for a great moment in this field.

How these people, who one could consider very competent, have failed so incredibly to ignore the conditions in which Cubans live and the enormous impact of all the disparate policies introduced by this communist system on all sorts of species and all aspects of the environment in the island, is something beyond my comprehension.

I have seen many similar cases, in which people who go there are attended like kings and are allowed to enjoy all sorts of privileges, which are negated to the average Cubans or have been favored by Castro in one way or another. At times, they somehow became fascinated with the Cuban communism and ignore its disaster.

It may also be that they were brought by Cuban authorities to some planned areas in order to facilitate that they could publish their experiences and ignore the rest of the Cuban reality, but the fact is that they were used by Castro for his propaganda.

I believe that it had been more honest from them to have made some deeper research, trying to illustrate the real impact that Castro's policies have had in all aspects of Cuban ecology, presenting all those existing and available facts about the many species that have been damaged by them everywhere in the island, starting with the human beings.

Surely, if they had done that, they would have found out how most Cuban rivers, bays, and surrounding seas have been polluted and most of the marine life of them has been destroyed. They would have found how many bird species have become almost inexistent, how different mammal species have been decimated. They would have also found the impressive deterioration of the Cuban conditions of living during these past fifty years. Probably this had been more valuable for the Cuban people, even when, obviously, this had not favored Castro's tourism plans.

Tourism became an important element of Cuban economy after the disappearing of the Soviet Union and the end of its subsidies to Castro's government. At that moment, Castro gradually started to accept that foreign hotel firms, mainly from Europe, which until then had not been allowed to operate in the island, could develop new hotels in different regions of Cuba, including some of the best known cays around the island. It was extremely important for Castro that a wonderful image of different Cuban attractions was presented to the world and these ideal images of some surviving aspects of Cuban ecology presented by those reporters were excellent for his purposes.

Unfortunately, the mentioned articles did not cover that. It had been very interesting that they had been able to describe the destruction caused in many of those cays, until then practically virgin, when Castro decided to build long roads to link the coasts of the island with them, not leaving any space for the transversal passage of the tidal currents of sea water, which caused a huge increase of salinity levels in those waters due to evaporation and the death of many species. Or perhaps, they could have described how the Cuban frontier guards detached on those cays shoot the exotic species on them to practice their aim, practically annihilating them.

It is really sad for somebody who loves Cuba to see how contradictory is the presence of tourists in many of these semi-isolated hotels, which have been built in many Cuban locations while most Cubans do not have the most elementary conditions to live properly. If certainly, I understand that most of these tourists do not have a clear idea of what is happening in Cuba outside those facilities and just want to expend their vacations as well as they can, I still hope that this book helps to understand better the Cuban reality and this awakens their interest for the real Cuba.

CHAPTER VII

The health system

Castro managed to present his government as a leader in the field of medicine and health services among underdeveloped countries and even people from developed countries, or from important international organizations, tend to look at Cuba with admiration for what they believe are Castro's achievements in this field.

He successfully convinced them that the improvements described in his propaganda and the elaborated figures included in Cuba's reports were absolutely true, and they consider his achievements the result of his almost magic leadership and management skills. Nothing, however, can be more misguiding.

It is a well-known fact, for instance, that Castro and his brother have sent a large number of Cuban doctors to many countries, under agreements of cooperation with them, and they also have brought to Cuba a large number of students from many different countries, to study their careers in medicine in Cuban universities.

He has been doing this for six decades and it is something that, obviously, has impressed many people in the world because practically no other government has been able to do so, even less in such a scale and especially considering that Cuba is a small country.

Nobody really has cared if these mentioned doctors are exploited by Castro, who pays to them miserable salaries and keeps their families in Cuba as hostages to avoid that they defect, and even less, that Castro uses them as propaganda or as secret agents, to facilitate the penetration of these societies for other political ambitions.

Some people want to see only the medical side of their function and do not consider other relevant aspects. They underestimate how communist mechanisms operate and how far the penetration of their societies by Castro go, as well as all what Castro's intelligence achieve through this apparently humanitarian assistance.

The Cuban people have a natural disposition to help others and this side of our cultural and moral character has been exploited by Castro in his advantage. The same way that he sends medicine professionals to other countries, other Cuban medical professionals in Florida have brought their medical services to different countries, obviously with much more limited resources because they have not had the whole power of a government behind them. In the case of these other Cuban exiled doctors, they have performed their assistance to those countries without establishing other ties and their work has been purely humanitarian and, in most cases, paid by themselves.

I feel that any humanitarian mission the Cuban professionals develop is positive and must be applauded and encouraged, however, I cannot accept that a criminal regime uses the sacrifices of these doctors to clean its image and get credits for something that it does not deserve.

It is also known that many people from around the world, from heads of state and high-ranking foreign officials to common citizens of different countries, have gone to Havana to receive free treatments for their illnesses or to have operations at Cuban medical facilities.

Castro also sent to other countries some of the best Cuban specialists to treat presidents and prime ministers and some of their top leaders. These personalities look first to their personal interests, but at the end, many of them, were ready to help Castro in other ways and many have served later as collaborators of Castro's intelligence once they left their positions.

The number of foreign students of medicine in Cuban universities has increased considerably during this past century and Castro and his regime have used this as an important element of his political propaganda. What most people don't know is how many of those students are recruited by Cuba's intelligence during the time they expend in Cuba and the important missions they are assigned once they go back to their countries. To underestimate the role of them within the schemes of Castro's regime penetration of the political infrastructures of those countries can be a serious mistake.

There is almost no international organization related to the field of medicine that have not had Castro's representatives appointed to all sorts of important positions within them and the propaganda brochures and books published by the Cuban government, oriented to describe what Castro presents as his achievements in this field are widely distributed at them.

Most of the main functionaries of these organizations have been invited to visit Cuba and have established links with Castro's government. Most people cannot imagine how many of them have been objectives of the Cuban intelligence. They cannot believe either how far Castro has gone in the penetration of all those institutions and the goals he has when doing this.

These propaganda books and brochures that I mentioned before, usually give a very romantic image about how Castro found his country with a very underdeveloped medical system and very few doctors, who were mainly located at the main cities.

According to them, a large portion of the population did not have access to medical services or medicines, and Cuban children were exposed to a number of illnesses typical of underdeveloped countries.

Usually, these books published by Cuba have impressive photos, showing the contrast between the past, represented by some photos of little children with rag clothes and without shoes, in the middle of very poor living conditions and those happy and well-dressed pioneers who live under Castro's revolution.

The same simple and direct pattern is used to represent Castro's assumed success in other areas and all this is usually backed up with some well-elaborated figures and statistics, which carefully avoid getting into deeper analysis.

None of the above actions of Castro's government is based on a noble cause. They are all part of an elaborate political and intelligence machinery.

Cuba can be a very poor country, with an economy in state of permanent failure and with its people living in very bad conditions, but Castro's ambitions are above all that. He does not care how Cubans live or what they suffer. His main goal is to project his image at whatever cost and the use of fields like education, health, and sports play well within this maniac intentions.

Obviously, his government does not have many resources and is not able to satisfy even the most elemental needs of the Cuban people, but even under the worst circumstances, he deviates from his limited funds what it takes, in order to promote his image and to keep his intelligence machinery very active. After all, it is this intelligence service the main mechanism he and his followers have used to stay in power for so long and to influence numerous events during his life.

The fact is that this carefully elaborated propaganda scheme has achieved its goal, and many people around the world, who may be innocent or accomplice, has come to accept as true most of what Castro has wanted them to accept.

Even in many of the world's most-renowned centers and organizations dealing with medicine and education, one will always find some well-known authority who is ready to defend Castro's views and achievements and it becomes a difficult task to convince them that what Castro says is not true.

Castro's government statistics, which usually are the main source of reference, for people looking for information on Cuba, ignore a number of facts and are very misleading and this is even more so when dealing with the situation of Cuba before 1959. It is very important then to present some information on the situation Cuba had before Castro took power and put it in perspective in comparison with other countries:

- In 1958, Cuba had a number of doctors per capita comparable to those of developed countries.
- The number of hospital beds per capita in Cuba was also at the same level of the existing in developed countries.
- Cuban mortality rate was lower than the one in the United States.
- The number of hospitals in Cuba had double in the two decades before the revolution and the technological level of those new hospitals could be compared with any other center in the world.
- Cuba had a national network of well-dotted hospitals, clinics, emergency hospitals, and mutual medical institutions. There were public and private services.
- The schools of medicine of the main Cuban universities were prestigious institutions and had been functioning for a very long time. In the case, for instance, of the University of Havana, this school was created in colonial times.
- Those schools were at the same scientific and academic level than the best schools of developed countries and they had

well-established links with other similar institutions of the United States and Europe.

- All the new methods, concepts, and technologies in medicine were immediately applied in Cuba.
- One can say that the distribution of hospitals and medical institutions existing in Cuba in 1958 was not even, and some rural areas had more limitations than urban centers, but this situation was gradually improving. Cuba was not alone in that problem. Many developed countries had the same situation fifty years ago.
- Cuba had a large and growing network of emergency clinics and hospitals, financed and managed by the government, which were free for all Cuban citizens.
- There were national, provincial, and municipal hospitals and there were specialized hospitals of very high scientific level in different areas of the country.
- Cuba had private hospitals, many of which were managed as mutual institutions and the cost of having excellent medical services at them was extremely low.
- Doctors of those centers had some important service traditions including visiting their patients at home when this was necessary.

Castro's propaganda specializes in manipulating the time factor in their analysis and people sometimes forget that Castro has been fifty years in power. One needs to consider what Cuba had been able to achieve in this same long period of time if consecutive democratic governments had existed like in many other countries.

There is a fact always ignored by Castro's figures on these matters, which is that most of the main hospitals existing nowadays in Havana and other provinces were built before 1959. One can easily imagine the kind of institutions they must necessarily have been at that time, when one considers that most of them have been operated by Castro's government for fifty years, without practically any kind of maintenance and they are still in service, even when most of them are in a state of total abandonment and run-down.

Obviously, if one compares anything, mostly anywhere in this world, with something that existed fifty years ago, one has to establish some basis or criteria of comparison because the world has changed.

Castro's propaganda, however, ignores this basic rule, comparing things of the past with the present without any qualification, which obviously makes the comparison absurd. Curiously, one can find that there are many people in the world, who seem to accept the views expressed by Castro, perhaps because they are repeated and repeated, or because they are ignorant or mostly, because they come within the political package Castro's propaganda presents, which for one reason or another they may sympathize with.

There is no doubt that many people, who sympathize with Castro's ideas and with the communist doctrine in general, want to accept and recognize what Castro says and they are not interested in digging for more data to get a more objective information.

A typical case are those people who, incredible as this may seem, want to establish in their countries a system like Castro's.

In his documentary *Sicko* made in 2007, Director Michael Moore gives credit to Castro's health services and uses a comparison between them and the situation of health care in the United States.

Evidently, Moore used this comparison as a way to irritate a good portion of the public and attract attention to his film. I doubt that, despite his obvious political preferences, he can honestly believe that this comparison is valid and the conditions of Castro's system are as he showed in his film. The case is that his documentary planted a doubt in many people, who do not know all the real facts on Cuba and this has helped Castro.

Castro has created a very large administrative machinery to deal with the government-controlled medical and health services. The cost of operating that gigantic institution is enormous and its efficiency is rather low. It represents a bureaucratic burden for the Cuban economy and it has been the source of all sorts of privileges and corruption within the Cuban society.

Any measures or actions taken by Castro in this field, like it also happens in others, have been designed by his political ambitions, without any concern for the proper use of Cuban limited resources. The results, considered under the light of the resources employed and the extent of human mobilization, have been disastrous. It is virtually impossible that any country properly administered can use as a model the wasteful and inefficient system that exists in Cuba as it is that people at them can accept in general the conditions of living imposed by the Cuban system.

Among the many institutions, traditions, and practices that Castro destroyed in the field of health services and medicine was the private practice of medicine, which had been traditional in Cuba for centuries, also eliminating all mutual institutions existing in the island for many years. He intervened with the universities, including the schools of medicine and this caused that many of the best Cuban doctors were forced to migrate.

The long list of excellent hospitals and clinics confiscated by Castro, which were placed under his Ministry of Health, were well-supplied and equipped institutions, run and administered by competent professionals. All of this successful sector was placed under the incompetent management of Castro's officials.

The result of all of the above was a huge loss for the Cuban national patrimony. As time passed, those facilities became more and more deteriorated due to the lack of maintenance caused by an administration that lacked proper expertise to run them. Castro's government has not been able to keep, much less update, any of these facilities at a level comparable with their past success.

Cuban hospitals and clinics are mostly in a state of abandonment due to the absence of proper maintenance services, including the lack of construction materials to repair their facilities and of spare parts for their equipment.

Since many of the medical facilities developed by Castro's government in the past fifty years are old and were built without proper quality control, they have all sorts of problems.

The lack of all sorts of modern products, among those available nowadays everywhere in the world, to provide the hygienic conditions needed at medical facilities and hospitals creates a very unfavorable environment and there have been numerous cases of operation rooms of the main hospitals that have become contaminated by bacteria and staphylococcus.

Many Cuban hospitals and clinics, as well as local medical offices established in many neighborhoods, do not have enough doctors and nurses, because, among other factors, as I mentioned previously, Castro has sent thousands of Cuban doctors to other countries, to use them as an export commodity, at the same time that they are used for his propaganda and to penetrate their societies for his political designs. But even when they have the medical personnel available, their services are very limited due to the lack of medicines and all sorts of supplies, the bad conditions of their medical equipment, the very bad transport conditions patients have to deal with and the extremely poor hygienic conditions.

On top of all of the above, the poor alimentary situation affecting most of the Cuban society, except a small privileged class, does not help to improve the health conditions of patients.

The overall bad conditions in which doctors and nurses live, which is rather similar to the one of the rest of the population, together with their small salaries and the lack of incentives, create a sense of frustration in these professionals. This frustration increases for most of them when they are sent abroad to fulfill missions assigned by Castro's Ministry of Health and they are separated from their families who have to survive with their miserable salaries that they collect back in Cuba.

The salaries that these medical personnel receive for their work in other countries, which includes the sacrifice of being separated from their families for long periods of time, are only a tiny fraction of what Castro receives in payment for their services.

The situation of these doctors and other medical personnel is very sad because they realize that are being exploited, but they cannot do much to avoid this unless they try to find refuge in other countries, and in that case, Castro would take revenge of this with their families in Cuba, which he uses as hostages.

It is obvious that these doctors compare their situation with the one of other professionals in those countries and they realize the bad situation in which they are, which includes not only their poor salaries but also their terrible living conditions and the total lack of perspective of any improvement under the system existing in the island.

The idyllic image of Cuban medical facilities, research centers, and hospitals presented abroad by Castro's propaganda is mainly based on the conditions existing in some institutions, not available to the general population, created to treat and operate people and leaders from other countries and members of the Cuban communist establishment. It has nothing to do with the facilities available for the Cuban people in general.

Castro for treatment in Cuba numerous people from around the world, especially from those countries that he has targeted for other political reasons. He brought people from Venezuela, for instance, to be operated of their eyes and he also brought numerous children from the former Soviet Union, from the region around the Chernovil atomic plant, which belongs nowadays to Ukraine, who were affected by radiations after the accident at that plant. These apparently Good Samaritan actions of Castro can be compared with the case of a criminal or a gangster, who makes large donations to his church, to try to buy some indulgencies.

I understand that the people who receive the benefit of this free medical attention in Cuba must be grateful and it is almost impossible for them not to be so, but unfortunately, we must explain to them that Castro is not a saint nor is he a new version of Mother Theresa. He was a man with an unlimited duplicity of character and a calculator, who did all this to gain prestige and recognition, by the way, using the resources of Cuba for this, not his own illicit richness, in order to improve his image and as a cover up for his multiple crimes and atrocities and also to gain influences and access in those countries. This is a good example of how elaborate the schemes created by the tortuous mind of Castro could be.

The mentioned use of these medical institutions by Castro for his political games cannot be considered as a noble gesture of him. When one considers the internal situation of the country, these same institutions represent the privilege of the ruling group and they are one of the best examples of the apartheid system the Cuban people suffer from and what Castro pretended with this kind of gestures was to hide this reality.

I have included in previous chapters the description of the conditions that any regular Cuban citizen has to deal with when needing medical services and I have inserted this within the overall context of the present Cuban society. This description is not the result of my imagination, but an accurate image of what exists in Cuba today.

One has to understand that, given the gigantic disaster in which the Cuban society has been immersed by Castro, it would be impossible that some large sectors of Cuban life, like health and education, were under different conditions and could exist as successful and well-managed ones.

The simple and sad reality is that they are in a state of total failure, like any other aspect of Cuba, even when the information on them is manipulated by Castro's propaganda, which needs desperately to improve the image of his system, which each day is becoming more and more decrepit.

In January 2010, there were some rumors coming from Havana explaining that more than forty old inmates at the National Psychiatric Hospital had died of cold and hunger during a week in which there were unusually low temperatures in Havana, brought by a cold front which affected the island.

After few days, Castro's government could not hide any more to the population what had happened and was forced to recognize these events and the fact that these inmates had in fact died of hunger and cold due to the lack of proper clothes to cover themselves from the cold temperatures and the lack of food supplies as well as the generalized pilferage existing in most medical institutions.

Several weeks later, some people managed to send from Cuba the images of the corpses of the inmates who died, which were kept piled, at the dirty and run-down morgue of the hospital, and showed that their bodies, in many cases, had numerous marks, which indicated that these men and women were regularly abused, which is a known and well-documented case at this and other psychiatric institutions in the island.

This is a reflection of the conditions in Cuban hospitals and the only reason why people are not aware of this is the total censure of information of these matters established by the government.

Terrible situations happen there every day in different hospitals of the island, and generally, nobody outside Cuba knows about this, unless somebody takes the risk and denounces some specific case. There have been numerous epidemics at Castro's hospitals and infections with new bacteria, which are able to resist antibiotics. There are regular cases of children without proper nutrition and cases of group poisoning in jails, but nobody is allowed to report them or include them in the statistics fabricated by the government for international institutions.

A valiant Cuban dissident doctor, Dersy Ferrer, who had been incarcerated several times, made very detailed denounces, which have been sent to international forums, showing the degradation and deteriorated conditions, as well as the extremely bad and corrupt administration of most hospitals of the island. They reflect a very different reality in comparison with Castro's propaganda.

There is also the case of Doctor Oscar Elias Biscet, who was condemned to 25 years in prison for his defense of Human Rights and his denounces on the terrible conditions of health in the island, as well as for trying to mobilize the Cuban people to protest for the inhumane conditions of living and the repression of the government.

Something almost never mentioned when people of other countries or even people in Cuba refer to the Cuban health services is the moral and ethical basis of those services. The system of health established by Castro is immoral, and it is the basis for all sorts of discriminatory practices, humiliations, corruption, bad administration, and privileges, as well as the generalize abuse of the population and all these factors result in the worst moral and ethical conditions that any health system existing in the island during all its history have had.

The first simplistic idea many people may have, especially if they are under the effect of Castro's propaganda, is that his government has been willing to incur practically in any expense, in order to carry on any effort in this field, something that, in a country like Cuba like in any other, should be welcomed and applauded. Well, this is not the case.

The health system established by Castro is, in first place, based in the enormous infrastructure and resources his regime illegally appropriated five decades ago and the exploitation of hundreds of thousands of people, who work in this sector in very bad conditions and receive miserable salaries, as well as in the imposition of administrative and unethical rules, which force the population to accept all sorts of irregularities and bad services and the manipulation of data on their own fate.

I believe that Cubans, indeed, are entitled to have a proper health system, but it is the duty of whatever government Cuba could have to administer it properly, not as Castro has done for fifty years.

Castro was not a doctor, nor he had any particular expertise in this field of health and he has not given much chance either to properly qualified people to develop and manage this large sector of Cuban society.

By the contrary, the materialization of Castro's ideas in this field, which as it happens in all the other main sectors, reflects his maniac personal conditions, and his unlimited ambitions of power and recognition have created an enormous waste of resources and produced very little in change.

Cuban health system is today a bad administered and scientifically backward one, which is unable to properly provide to the Cuban people the quality and amplitude of service they deserve.

Castro's statistics are designed in a way that makes impossible to properly study the economic side of all his social and political adventures, but it is very evident that the health system of Cuba, like many other sectors, is in bankruptcy and has been in this state for half a century.

Not only the resources dedicated to the health system by Castro and later by his followers have been insufficient, among the huge resources he has received, most of which have been dilapidated, when not stolen by him and his people, but the terrible and incompetent administration established by him to operate this system is something that the Cuban people have the right to object.

All those irrational plans created by Castro's fertile imagination, which include his ideas in regard to medicine and health services, are governed not by any noble reason, but by his political ambitions and they lack any sense of economic reality and scientific support, much less of ethics.

The result is that every step taken by him to develop something in this field, or to take some actions in regard to it, or to introduce changes in the way these services are provided, have been a total failure and a waste of resources and a better democratic government could have used these resources in a much more efficient way.

Castro mismanaged, with total lack of scruples and without any control, very large resources, without any proper rational knowledge about the most advanced existing techniques in the administration of health.

One thing is to present as a big achievement, for propaganda purposes, the allocation of newly graduated doctors in many Cuban neighborhoods and another much complex and demanding one is to guarantee that good and reliable medical services are provided at them, within a certain rational and balanced economic budget.

There is a big difference between both actions and this is one of the main problems created by Castro. His logic may be good for propaganda and to keep him and others after him in power, but it is a total disaster when analyzed from the point of view of rationality. What he presented as achievements are not so when analyzed under the light of their social and economic cost.

If the underdeveloped countries were going to copy the system promoted by Castro, they would get into the trap of a vicious circle, in which they would waste many years and resources, and at the end, they would have to come back to the same starting point, with a high degree of frustration. Any feasibility study of Castro's system of health would indicate that it represents an enormous waste of resources due to its low level of efficiency, backward scientific support, and bad administration, all of which indicate that it should not be copied by any new country.

It is derisory that some people in developed countries look at Castro's Cuba as the source of solutions for their countries in the field of health, education, or in any other field.

I would advise that they try first to illustrate themselves on the economic and social misconceptions existing in regard to Castro and his regime, which would allow them to overcome the effect of his propaganda. They will then realize the enormous human, social, and economic waste represented by Castro and his revolution, which in reality has had only one single big achievement: make Castro famous!

In the case of medicine and health services under Castro's government, it is useful to carry on a more specific and detailed analysis, to look at them within the context of the Cuban society in general.

Cuba, like any other country, has needs in every aspect of life and limited resources available to deal with as many as possible of those needs. A good government system should be able to balance both aspects; otherwise, there will be unbalances in the development of their societies.

It is not logical to have most of the population living in terribly bad conditions, with a perpetual scarcity or total absence of most products, including medicines and medical products, and to pretend a big achievement, when offering to them access to a doctor in every neighborhood. They could go to a doctor in a clinic and get a better service and it would be more economic, especially if the Cuban society functioned normally, as any other country and not were immersed in a catastrophic administrative disaster.

Some aspects of health are impacted by the very poor hygienic conditions in which Cubans live, which obviously must be considered also part of their health system. It would be better to have normal conditions of living than to afford all sorts of limitations.

This is obviously not mentioned by Castro's propaganda and unfortunately, many people in this world do not understand these simple facts.

Cuba has been full of prisons from one corner of the island to the other, during all the time Castro has lasted. It is unbelievable how many prisons have been functioning for a population the size of Cuba.

The people at those prisons have lived in the worst conditions and the medical services for them have been horrendous because they have been part of the almost unlimited repression existing.

I was in La Cabaña prison when there was an epidemic of hemorrhagic dengue years ago, and I witnessed how almost every prisoner got it, including myself, and we were there, with our red eyes, looking like dragons, when Captain Ortega, the doctor in charge of La Cabaña prison in Havana, oriented some prisoners to put lemon drops in their eyes! They had medicines available, but did not supply them to the prisoners and that monster, dressed as a doctor, enjoyed when many of them started crying of pain.

One has to ask a number of very elemental questions:

Why so many Cuban people and their families have to suffer all those humiliating conditions due to the situations created by the government of Castro? Is it worthy to sacrifice so much to keep something like this system and a man like Castro in power? Is it worthy also that so many Cubans go through all these aberrations to have a socialist dictatorship? And all those young people who have lost their lives at the Strait of Florida trying to escape from Cuba, their country?

In the past, the Americans liked to go to Cuba to live. The lives of each of them were millions times worthier than all the empty list of those supposed medical achievements Castro pretends to have. Are the Cubans receiving something so special in education, health, living conditions, human rights, or in any other aspect, to justify the existence for so long of such a failed system?

What are the so-called conquests of the revolution, that empty and exhausted slogan continually used by Castro and the main people around him, in their speeches and articles? Are those "conquests" by any chance the right to study, or the right to work, or the right to go to a hospital to receive medical attention, or the right to eat, or the right to be communist or a democrat, or the right of women to be treated equally, or the right of blacks to be the same as white people, or the right of children to grow, or the right to live in a house, or the right to be treated with respect no matter your economic status?

These mentioned rights cannot be those "conquests," because all those rights and many more, existed in Cuba for every citizen since many years before Castro took power and they were established in our Constitution.

Then, what are those "conquests" that they mention so frequently?

Would they be the obligation to accept the existence of the government of Castro for fifty years, always exonerating him of any responsibility for all the huge disasters caused by his system, or they are the fright of people to go to jail or to be tortured for showing any kind of dissent, or the mandate to suffer in silence all sorts of limitations because of Castro's bad administration, or the sacrifice to be killed by a fire squad for opposing this aberration, or the sadness of dying in the Strait of Florida, trying to escape from Cuba, or maybe they are the torture of suffering every day all sorts of intromissions in your private life by Castro's secret services?

Quite frankly, I do not understand what these "conquests" are or what they can be in the sick minds of Castro and his people, but I believe that Castro and his regime have not achieved any "conquest" for the Cuban people, but by the contrary, all this has been a huge disaster for our nation.

In the case of the health system, Castro and his propaganda repeat once and again that thanks to him and his revolution, the Cubans can have the right to medical attention and to be hospitalized and cured if one gets ill no matter who one is. I come from a humble family and all my family had all that as part of our lives, previous to Castro's revolution, without the need to have Castro there.

Castro achieved nothing in this field that was strange to the Cuban people, and fifty years after he took power, Cuba would have much more in this field than anything Castro represents, if he was not there and without the need to suffer his dictatorship.

CHAPTER VIII

~~

Some facts of the Cuban economy after fifty years of communism

I have referred before in this book to some main aspects of the economy Cuba had in 1959, when Castro started controlling all Cuban matters. In this chapter, I will get into some more details on this.

Almost thirty years ago, after I had finished lecturing a couple of postgraduate courses on planning and control of investments in the national economy, in Havana, I was preparing to start a new version of them, which included the addition of a new course on management of the national economy. Everything indicated that the new courses were going to be a success, according to the more than two hundred professionals from different ministries and other institutions who had registered for it, but unfortunately, Castro and his secret services had different views and one day, without further notice, my courses were canceled. Several months later, as I explain the preamble of this book, they put me in jail for six and a half years because of my intention to create a new political party in Cuba.

Some of the ideas I express in this chapter were to be explained at those courses and it is interesting to me that they are still valid, with some logical updating, after so many years.

It may look to some people that I may be exaggerating when I explain how Castro and his regime have created a disaster in practically every different sector of Cuban society. They may think that there must be something they had done well, and indeed, I must explain that, in my view, he has been extremely successful in a couple of things: he has managed to stay in power for five decades, something without parallel, at least in Latin America, and he has managed to repress the Cuban people in such a way that they have not been able to get rid of him.

These two facts are in my view extremely difficult things to achieve and certainly they may represent a success for him and his close followers, but unfortunately, they have meant a disgrace for the rest of the Cuban people.

The Cuban economy has been another example of the terrible results achieved by Castro, and certainly it, cannot be precisely considered as one of the myths of the revolution because it is very difficult to find anybody, with some knowledge in this field, who is willing to recognize some kind of success of Castro in it, the disaster being so obvious.

In 1959, Cuba had most of its economic indicators, if not all, ranked among the best three countries in Latin America, and in most cases, Cuban statistics and actual conditions showed that Cuba was a quickly developing country, which matched many developed countries in numerous aspects. It may look unbelievable to many people when they are told that Cuba had better indicators in many economic and social aspects than countries like Spain, Portugal, Norway, and Italy, for instance, but this was indeed the case.

The Cuban people ate much better than in most of the other countries in Latin America and its average rate of consumption of meat, vegetables, sugar, and cereals was the highest in the continent. Cuba also had a very high level of consumption of rice, fish, fruits, milk, and derivates comparable to other developed countries.

The Cuban people were used to the early and quick introduction of all sorts of new inventions, and Cuba had the highest rate per inhabitant of autos, buses, telephones, television sets, and radios in Latin America, which was higher also than in most European countries.

The indicators of miles of roads and highways per inhabitant were high for that time and the same happened with the railways.

As I explained before, Cuba had a very large number of excellent newspapers and magazines as well as long-established radio and television stations. The introduction of first of black and white and later color television followed immediately its development in the United States.

The artistic industry was very advanced and all the main figures visited the island while Cuban artists were well-known all over the world as well. The Cubans were used to have full access to all expressions of art.

The transport infrastructure of the island was efficient and satisfied the needs of the population, but it was also being developed at a very quick pace, following the standards of the United States. All the different transport means, roadway, railway, air, or maritime, were established in a way that satisfied the demand Cuba had for those services, but there were important new projects being developed in each of them oriented to develop even more these aspects.

Cuba had port and airport facilities according to its trade and passenger traffic and new modern ones were in process of development in order to meet the growing demand for them originated by the growth in tourism and commerce, mainly from and to the United States.

Any new developments in these fields in the world were immediately applied in Cuba. It is interesting to mention that the first flight ever of Pan-American Airlines, a pioneer of air transport, went precisely to Cuba.

The influence of having the United States as Cuba's main partner was enormous because the Cuban people were used to the same advantages of civilization the American people had.

It is interesting to explain that when the Russians and people from other communist countries started coming to Cuba after Castro took power, they were impressed by many products, which were of common use in the island but they did not know existed, because all these countries were rather backward in numerous aspects and did not have access to any of them.

Cuba had a dependency on sugar trade as its main export source in 1959, but an important portion of it corresponded to a large quota of that product established by the American government, which had privileged prices.

In 1959, there were a large number of industries in the process of development in Cuba, which were not only oriented to satisfy almost fully the internal market and to replace, on competitive basis, numerous foreign articles, but were also a growingly important source of export trade.

Due to the closeness of the huge American market, Cuban products could reach it in a matter of few hours and a fleet of ferries made this service very efficient.

The fact that Cuban labor was more qualified and educated in comparison with most other countries in Latin America, this including the widespread knowledge of the English language in the island, was opening the way for the development of many new industries in different provinces of the island, including several assembling plants for new American vehicles.

Cuba had very advanced and progressive labor laws, and in most aspects, these laws were far more advanced than the ones existing even in the United States nowadays. They gave all sorts of rights to the Cuban workers, which were among the best paid in the world.

The above was so much so that, in the case of some products, Cuba had difficulties to compete against other countries and there was a continuing need to increase the efficiency of those industries.

Together, the agriculture and national industry were able to satisfy the internal demand of food and numerous other products for the Cuban population, even when Cuba acquired a wide range of products from other countries, which helped to make more efficient its economy and to sustain a highly productive and reciprocate foreign trade.

No one in Cuba could even imagine having a rationing book, like the one Castro has established for almost fifty years and being forced to live with meager quotas of a very short list of basic products and the nonexistence of many other products, which used to be common in the island.

There could be people in poverty, like in any other developed nation nowadays, but in general, Cubans ate better than the people of all the other countries in Latin America and also of most countries in Europe.

The Cubans had also a tradition for dressing well. It was a long-established tradition and there were norms of elegance and behavior. One gets impressed, when seeing documentaries and pictures from the past, about how well the people dressed and how elegantly they behave. No one could imagine what Castro has done to destroy all this and to bring the population to wear rags as clothing.

Cuba also had very other advanced laws, on top of the mentioned labor laws, in comparison to most other countries at that time, to protect the equal rights of women, which among other many rights, had their right to compensation when they became pregnant.

I discuss the issue of race in another chapter of this book, but it is necessary to mention that Cuban laws clearly established the equal right of people of all races, without any kind of discrimination, this being another aspect in which Cuba was decades ahead of other developed countries.

As a note of interest, I must note that President Batista was a mulatto and was elected for his first period in that position in 1940, this meaning that Cuba was much more advanced than other countries in regard to this aspect.

The fact that Cuba is a relatively large beautiful island with friendly people made Cuba a developing tourism pole. The tourism industry of Cuba was growing very fast.

There are people who argue that some aspects of this tourism were linked to the gambling business, but there is no doubt that Cuba was already a strong place for all kinds of tourism and even the presence of gambling was not necessarily negative in the island due to the large source of income it represented, which could translate in many ways in the development of its economy. Also, the historical evidence of the United States and other European countries indicate that these countries managed to keep under control these activities in an orderly way while using them as an important source of income and the generation of new development possibilities.

This becomes evident when one considers the fact that the development of other highly productive tourism places like Las Vegas, Florida, Cancun, Bahamas, and the Caribbean was mainly due to Castro's destruction of the Cuban tourism industry and one can only wonder what Cuba had received in income and being able to develop if Castro had not been there all these years.

The level of development of the entertainment industry associated with tourism in Cuba is not matched, after so many decades, by most of the countries that are considered the main tourism centers of the world.

Cuba had all sorts of cabarets, night clubs, hotels, beach resorts, casinos, golf and sport facilities with established world-class level. Its cabaret shows were the top of their class in the world.

It was natural for Cubans to see important people from all over the world visiting as tourists to their country. The tourists Cuba received were among the most highly rewarding in the world, mainly coming from the United States and Europe.

If one considers the development achieved, thanks to their tourism industries, by other nations that were well behind Cuba in this field at that time, it is easy to reach the conclusion that Cuba would be by now a very developed country in this field and in general in all others.

Cuba still had problems in regard to some inequalities existing between different sectors of the society, in which unemployment existed, but the speed in which new possibilities of work were being created was very high and this evidently was creating the conditions for the enrichment of the Cuban society in general.

What Castro has done to the Cuban economy can be illustrated, using terms of the construction industry, as a demolition work. There is practically no aspect of the Cuban economy that has not suffered a total disruption of it.

Paradoxically, while all this has happened and the Cuban people have seen their standard of living lower to the level of some of the less-developed countries in the world, Castro and his family and some of his closest followers have seen their illicit fortunes soar and their well-masked overseas investments grow.

One has to reach the conclusion that Castro scared the Cuban people with the role of the mafia in the gambling business in Cuba, only to become, few years later, himself, a new sort of super Mafioso, who has involved Cuba in all sorts of illicit activities and vices and has exploited the Cuban people in the worst ways, much worse actually by far than anything the mafia could have done.

Like it happened with tourism, all the other main aspects of the Cuban economy have also been destroyed by Castro.

The sugar industry, which had been the Cuban pride for a whole century, has been reduced to the level of 1902 and with much more inefficiency, this meaning a 20 percent of the capacity of 1959.

The markets for Cuban sugar have shrink or have been lost and most Cuban sugar mills have been destroyed and abandoned. There is some evidence indicating that it is possible that Cuba does not have enough sugar to even satisfy the national demand, something that would be almost incredible.

The agricultural sector has become totally unable to sustain the Cuban population, even of the most elementary products, and its production has reduced in all major products, or has simply commercially disappeared, like in the case of fruits and the possibility that these products generate an additional source of export trade has simply been nonexistence because most new markets are too far in comparison to the close American market.

In the case of some products, like citric fruits, in which Castro at some moment invested important amounts of money to increase the areas of cultivation, they mean nothing to the population because most of their shrinking production is exported and evidently he has not been able to sustain the proper care of their plantations.

Practically all the traditional agricultural products, which were basic to the Cuban cuisine, are nowadays scarce and very expensive to buy. The same happens with most fruits, many classes of which have disappeared. Vegetables and salads are very scarce and almost nonexistent.

The tobacco industry, in which Cuba had a well-known fame, has decreased not only in terms of productivity, but also of quality and workmanship and must compete now with the production of several other neighbor countries, like Dominican Republic and the Center American countries, which have become important producers, after Castro's policies caused the loss of the American market and the migration of some of the best and most qualified Cuban producers and manufacturers, several of whom moved to these countries and developed new enterprises and plantations at them.

The livestock industry is a total disaster. Cuba has today half the cattle population that it had in 1959, but with less quality and weight and full of illnesses. Since Cuban population has almost double, the number of heads of cattle per person has become half of what it was.

Cubans practically cannot eat meat, which has been rationed to ridiculous levels within the rationing system established by Castro for the past five decades. Even pork, the traditional Cuban food, is very scarce and expensive. Ham is almost nonexistent and several Cuban generations almost know it only by name. The population of pigs has decreased to a level unimaginable decades ago.

Milk and derivates are only supplied for small children, in very limited amounts. Once the children are seven years old, they are not entitled to them anymore.

The very small and rationed supply of chicken comes mostly from imports because the national production is very low, and Cuba does not have anymore any production of corn to sustain it.

The main traditional commodities Cuba exported before 1958 were raw and refined sugar, nickel and other minerals, tobacco, fishing products, and varied agricultural products, which together with the tourism industry, were the source of Cuban income abroad, but there was another much more varied production of all sorts of agricultural and industrial products directed to the national market, which, as I explained before, satisfied a large portion of the population needs.

As I mentioned, all these industrial and agricultural sectors were full of potential, and they were in the middle of an accelerated process of expansion, directed to satisfy the needs and possibilities of foreign markets and also to replace those imports of numerous industrial products that could be produced in Cuba, from cars to textiles and including all sorts of commercial products, this also being supported by the high rate of increase of the local demand due to the growth of the Cuban economy.

Castro stopped all this process and after fifty years, all the mentioned productive fields are in state of abandonment and technological decadence, incredibly low productivity, and financial disarray.

There is practically no aspect of the Cuban economy that at this moment can be compared with any logical projection of what Cuba would have, if Castro has not been there, this despite the huge subsidies he has received and all the numerous debts his regime has contracted.

Castro has not been able to create any significant industry that was able to fully supply the national market of absolutely any product. Most of the few existing industries oriented to the national market are the ones still remaining of those that were confiscated by Castro in 1959, but since they have experienced a total lack of maintenance for five decades and they do not have any supply of the proper products that should be used in their production, most of them have become obsolescent and cannot compete with those of other countries.

At the time when the subsidies of the Soviet Union were at their peak, Castro tried to develop some agricultural and industrial plans in different regions, which he presented in his propaganda as his own enormous achievements, even before he could collect a single result from them.

Most of these developments, without exception, ended in a total failure, because of the lack of organization and capability of him and his regime. The amount of resources wasted in these economic adventures was astronomical.

For instance, Castro bought some of the most-priced cattle in Canada and other countries and tried to create new plans that he managed personally. He developed a huge propaganda around this and most Cubans even knew by their names the main cows and bulls. As soon as he started getting involved into this, he seriously announced that he was going to achieve new varieties that were going to produce more milk than any other in the world. He even erected a statue to one of his cows, which he said broke all the records.

He brought water buffaloes to Cuba from Africa and started mixing them with cows, and then one day, he announced that he was getting a new breed of animals, which was more resistant to the flooding of fields and were going to produce more meat.

Apparently, at some point, Castro reached the conclusion that he, like the pharaohs, was a god and then he decided to start producing new varieties of all sorts of species, from cows to horses, from geese to goats, whichever animal came to his aberrant mind. He created new research centers in which, under secret and classified conditions, he created large teams of professionals that worked under his direct orders in order to perform all sorts of strange experiments.

Most, if not all, of the above, obviously ended in disaster and nothing on this has never again being mentioned.

But even worse, at the same time he wasted huge amounts of money pretending to use these plans to show to the world that he was transforming the Cuban economy with his policies, he destroyed the traditional well-established Cuban cattle industry, which had been able to sustain the high consumption of meat the Cuban people had in the past, which was one of the highest in Latin America. This important sector of Cuban economy was arbitrarily confiscated by Castro, and after this, it was gradually destroyed by the same irrational policies and incompetence of his government.

The incredible result is that meat has become in Cuba a luxury, only available in the black market or in the supermarkets for foreign people, even when one can find obviously all kinds of it in the table of the main figures of the government.

The Cuban transport system is a whole disaster of incalculable proportions by itself and practically all transport means have been in state of crisis for decades. The administration of this important sector of the economy has been a disaster of enormous proportions, as a result of having in charge some of the most incompetent and corrupt people around Castro, who, one after the other, have been leaving their fingerprints of corruption and mismanagement.

Most roads and highways of the country are in terrible conditions due to the lack of maintenance and they have an almost total absence of any modern signalization means and the fact that their surface usually is in terrible shape, with potholes everywhere, makes them very dangerous.

There are very few cars in Cuba and most of them are so old that they look like antics, even when most of them have been modified with adapted engines. The number of private cars per capita is extremely low and they have become a luxury. Taxies are also a luxury and Cubans are using small bicycles and horse carts converted as taxies to deal with the shortage of transport.

Buses are scarce within all the main cities and the interprovincial services are very limited. All the main terminals are in state of abandonment and their workshops lack parts and modern tools.

For many years, Cubans had to use adapted trucks for their transport within Havana, until Cuba received recently a large package of new buses from China. The problem is that, as it has become evident before, due to the bad state of most roads and the lack of care of the people in charge of their maintenance and the bad treatment of the users, any new buses tend to last very little in the island.

The infrastructure of workshops for all the different means of transport is very inefficient and lacks modern means. The same happens with the remains of the network of gas stations, which are just a tiny fraction of those same ones that Castro confiscated during the initial years of his regime.

The railways are in a state of total abandonment as well, experiencing the lack of new equipment and spare parts, very antiquated workshops and very old and deteriorated terminals as well as crumbling bridges and other installations and all the lines are in very bad shape, something that represents an enormous risk for users.

The relatively few planes Cuba has are refurbished old models bought from the Soviet Union or later from Russia and some are chartered from other countries. They all lack proper maintenance and the service on them is terrible. Most Cuban airports have antiquated and underdeveloped installations, which provide inadequate facilities and the services to passengers are not good due to the repressive style of the people who operate their customs and security.

Cuban ports are all polluted and they have a shortage of proper modern facilities. Some of the old docks and piers, which Castro confiscated in the early sixties, still exist, but they are in very bad shape, like other new installations that have been built more recently and all of them lack modern equipments and technologies to handle efficiently the cargo, and as a result, the level of productivity is in constant decrease. The conditions of work at them are far from being good, and there is a lack of modern safety means, which forces the workers to perform their duties in very backward conditions.

The Cuban maritime fleet is formed mainly by few very inefficient, old vessels, which are in terrible conditions due to the lack of maintenance. Cuba bought more than one hundred ships, mostly of medium size, at the peak of the stage in which the country was receiving large subsidies from the Soviets, but these ships were gradually sold once it became evident that Cuba could not maintain properly them and they presented old sort of deficiencies. There are many speculations about what happened with the results of the sale of so many ships and there are indications that the money that was obtained from the sale of them may have ended in the private coffers of Castro and some of his people.

Since the Cuban fleet disappeared, Castro has been hiring their former crews to other shipping companies, and these people are forced to work most of the time in very bad conditions while they only receive as salaries a tiny fraction of what Castro receives for their services.

The salaries for most transport workers in general are very low and they lack any incentive for their work. As a result, the life of transport means, owned and operated by the government, has shortened, due to the lack of care and improper maintenance. This situation has also produced the proliferation of chaos within the industry and all sorts of irregularities.

At the beginning of his regime, Castro confiscated two existing American nickel plants, including cobalt as a byproduct, which had been built during the Second World War, with funds mainly provided by the United States government and had been in exploitation irregularly before he took power.

Considering that Cuba has one of the most important reserves of nickel and cobalt in the world, Castro has been trying for five decades to develop this sector, and he has managed to find a number of occasional partners, like the Soviets and the Canadians and more recently the Chinese and the Venezuelan governments, that have been willing, at different stages, to invest enormous amounts of money and other resources in it, establishing different kinds of joint ventures with Castro's government, to develop and exploit this mining industry.

As a result of the above, Cuba has been increasing the extraction of nickel and cobalt, which are converted, in the mentioned two plants and a new one built since, in sinter and oxide and then shipped for refining in other countries. The total output of production of nickel has reached more than eighty thousand tons.

Obviously, considering Castro's credit record, he never paid to the Soviets for their investment and it remains to be seen how much his relationships with the Canadians will last.

In these past years, the nickel industry has become the main source of exports of the country, surpassing the tourism sector, which had itself become the largest producer of foreign currency, once the Cuban sugar industry lost its relevance due to Castro's improper management.

The Cuban nickel industry, however, has had serious economic and market problems and the operation of these plants has not always being economically sound, especially at some stages, when there have been large drops in the price of this product in the world markets.

The whole results of the exploitation of these mentioned reserves of nickel and cobalt, which are a precious natural resource of the country, have not translated in any improvement for the country, because, as usual with Castro, they have been dilapidated and used to keep afloat his bankrupt regime, like it happened before with the sugar industry, during some stages in which the price of sugar was very high.

I have explained before the enormous damage created to the region around these plants due to the unscrupulous exploitation pattern established by Castro's government and its different foreign partners.

Those deals that Castro has negotiated with different governments and foreign interests, for the development and operation of the mentioned plants and the exploitation of the mines, have allowed him to obtain an important source of income, which has become precious for his regime in recent years, but they have also caused an enormous environmental disaster that implies a huge cost for the country and this must be quantified together with the overall results of all this.

Other important economic sector is the electrical industry, which has serious difficulties as well due to the advanced age and obsolescence of many of the most important generating plants. The actual capacity of production cannot meet the national demand and the productivity of the industry as a whole and its different plants separately is relatively low. There is a scarcity of spare parts that continually affect the industry, and due to the backward conditions of most plants, they have a very high consumption of oil, becoming very expensive to operate.

In recent years, Castro has been using his connections with Venezuelan president Hugo Chavez to get a cheap or almost free supply of oil, which has allowed him to keep the electrical infrastructure in operation, even when this is becoming a gigantic waste for Venezuela, like it happened before with all the oil Cuba received from Russia for almost thirty years, part of which was sold by Castro to third world countries.

The conditions of the electrical infrastructure are very bad and there all sorts of problems regarding the service to the population and also to the industry. Cuba would need to replace a large percentage of its electrical infrastructure and develop new modern plants in order to have an efficient and reliable system. There is a generalized waste of electricity established in the island at all levels and regions and Castro has not been able to change this.

There are strong indications that there are important reserves of oil under the waters around Cuba and even in some regions of the island and Castro's regime has been negotiating with many countries and large firms different drillings operations and the whole undersea platform of the island has been divided in parcels that are assigned to them, but so far this has not produced enough results.

After the dissolution of the Soviet Union, Castro incremented the resources to develop some biotechnological industries and his regime has been selling increasing quantities of medicines and vaccines abroad. This new industry has reached some importance and has become one of the main export trades the country has and seems economically more efficient.

If one considers the number of items of foreign trade that Cuba has not been able to develop at their full capacity and all the possibilities of businesses with the United States that have been lost during these past five decades in multiple sectors, the impact of Castro's policies on the potential development of Cuban foreign trade has been enormous.

The Cuban foreign trade, which used to be stable and represented a continuingly positive balance before 1959, has been incredibly unbalanced and have had a permanently negative result under Castro and his policies have not been able to even remotely correct this. All the financing and loans Castro has got to sustain such a situation has become accumulated debt of the Cuban government and must pay interests, even when Castro obviously, has not taken this seriously.

Castro's regime has also being sending Cuban graduates to work in other countries and some of these countries that pay to him for the services these professionals perform while others only receive this "assistance" as a way to promote his political agenda and to ensure other compromises.

Cuba exports only a portion of what it buys and this is so even when the population is not allowed to consume any of the most valuable products produced at the island, which are regularly exported, except some quantities destined to the top communists and for the tourism industry.

As a result of the terribly bad conditions of the economy of the island, there are many products that Cuba imported in the past, which are no longer bought, at least in the same quantities, but on the other hand, there were many products that were produced in the island and were already used to substitute imports, which are no longer produced in enough quantities and this has created a basic additional need of importing them.

Due to the percentage decline of its national industry, the range and variety of goods that Cuba needs to buy nowadays to satisfy even a minimum portion of its demand is wider and larger than in the past, even when the existence of open market conditions, before Castro took power, and the strength of the Cuban economy at that time, allowed the purchasing of numerous articles that are inexistent in Cuba now.

Cuba has one of the largest foreign debts of the world and this does not include the old huge debt to Russia, which comes from the times of the Soviet Union. It is interesting to note that Cuba received, during more than twenty years, a huge amount of subsidies and loans from the Soviet Union, which represented more than all the money Cuba had received for its commerce during all the centuries of our previous history, but Castro astonishingly dilapidated those resources, being unable to develop our country despite having had access to these resources.

In the middle of all of the above, the salaries paid to the Cuban workers are among the lowest of the world and they do not allow them to satisfy their most basic needs while many Cubans manage to survive thanks to the money sent by their relatives in the United States and other countries.

All of the above conditions, which are similar to those existing in other sectors of the economy and the society in general have created a situation in which most Cubans do not want to work, due to the total lack of incentives and the fact that they realize that are being exploited. Obviously, this is a situation that does not have solution while Castro's system remains in power. The construction industry has suffered, like other sectors, the incompetency of Castro, who managed it as a personal resource in order to implement his most absurd plans and ideas, in most cases mismanaging the resources available. The fact is that the construction industry has been unable to satisfy the needs of the Cuban economy and society.

As we have described, Cuba has an enormous shortage of housing, but it also has an enormous deficit of industries and of all sorts of facilities for the most varied aspects of Cuban life, and together with this, there is an almost total lack of capacity to maintain any existing installation within the island.

Any Cuban city or town, and in general any building in the island, look like a ruin, without paint and in a state of abandonment like if they had been bombed.

It is ironic, considering the above, that Cuba has been selling its construction services to some countries, this becoming another source of hard currency and influence. This has been the case of those brigades sent to Libya, Granada, Angola, and other countries, which have built roads, airports, and house programs at them.

For decades, Castro established a policy of sending most of the high school students, as well as other intermediate schools, to schools built in rural areas, something that allowed him to separate them from their parents and also use them for all sorts of agricultural activities. In order to do that, he oriented the construction of hundreds of facilities in the most isolated locations.

The above conception was a huge disaster from every point of view and many of those schools, usually built with very low-quality standards, must be shifted now to other uses while the former schools existing in all cities were totally abandoned and neglected.

Castro also used the construction industry to create huge networks of military facilities and prisons in practically every corner of the island. They each are the size of small towns and there are hundreds and hundreds of them. All this has become a new symbol of the disaster caused by his government.

All the commercial infrastructure of the island is in ruins and lack almost all kinds of products and the images of Cubans acquiring their meager rations of food and other products at them has been around the world.

Many aspects of the whole national infrastructure Castro confiscated, when he took power in 1959, are still the only ones existent in the island and he has not been able to renew or improve them, despite all the resources he has handled, due to his neglect and bad administration.

To analyze Cuban current economic and social matters is a journey to the past. It is something like visiting a prehistoric place due to the backward conditions and the main obsolete philosophical concepts established by Castro.

As I explain in previous chapters, after many years of almost total abandonment of the tourism industry, Castro was forced by the dissolution of the Soviet Union, his main support for almost three decades, to start developing it again, and his regime facilitated a number of hotel chains, mainly from Europe, to build new facilities and renovate others.

Some problems with this new tourism are that the income Cuba gets from it per capita is not even remotely comparable to what it got in the past, but also and most important is that, in a country with such a level of poverty and misery like Cuba has now, the presence of tourists becomes a source of discrimination and frustration for the Cuban people, who see how those people from other countries can come and go freely and then, spontaneously, compare them with their own conditions, in which they are not allowed to do any of this, due to the travel restrictions they suffer. At the same time the presence of all these tourists allow them to have at least a partial view of how these other people live and establish further comparisons with what the Cubans nowadays regularly have.

On top of the above, most Cubans realize that they have many limitations, which do not make easy to visit those tourism facilities, which actually, until only a year ago, were even closed for them.

Castro also used at different stages, depending on how serious the shortage of funds his regime has been experiencing, the travels of the Cuban community abroad to visit their relatives in the island. The amount of money sent or brought to the island by these "other" Cubans, who are not liked by Castro, has been an important source of income to him. In reality, he has used the population of the island as hostages in order to force their relatives to visit the island and to leave there money to sustain their families, which would be immersed in the worst misery if they were not receiving this help.

After decades considering the tenancy of dollars by Cubans an evil and punishable crime, Castro implemented a new monetary system within Cuba, with the existence of three basic monetary elements: the traditional Cuban peso, which is valued arbitrarily at approximately twenty-five units per dollar, the dollar itself, which after some years of experiment using it as a parallel monetary means, was again taken out from official transactions, and a new piece of monetary paper, created to collect those dollars and to facilitate the appropriation of them by Castro and the government, arbitrarily establishing a par value with the dollar, on which a 20 percent tax is imposed, at the time of change.

Castro criticized most of the governments Cuba had in the past for their corruption, which his propaganda magnifies considerably, but the fact is that, as I have explained, he and his family as well as some of his closest followers have been more corrupt and have stolen more money than all the other Cuban governments together, and Castro has become one of the richest men on earth, which is astonishing, when one considers that he comes from a small island he has converted from one developing nation in one of the poorest countries of the world.

With total lack of scruples, Castro used the sophisticated powers of his intelligence system, together with some elaborated channels of the Cuban banking institutions, to procure and hide the ownership of all sorts of fraudulently acquired assets in many different countries, as well as deposits of money and precious metals in many important banks.

The way he managed to do this has consisted in establishing an absolute personal control on all the government resources, including the full scope of transactions originated by all Cuba's foreign trade and banking services.

No former Cuban president or functionary could even think of doing that to such extend because, one way or another, there was some kind of fiscal control on the official government operations, but also because many sectors were basically private, while Castro has acted as the owner of the whole country.

The powers achieved illegally by Castro allowed him all sorts of privileges and a lifestyle that very few people on earth have been able to have. He had private marine units converted as personal yachts; personal, exclusive, and fully supplied residences in every province; government planes used as private ones; military helicopters for his private use; hundreds of people of the armed forces devoted to his personal protection and to all sorts of personal services; all the resources of the printing industry to publish his writings; all the radio and television stations open at any time for his personal use and obviously all the money, from the government, that he may need to satisfy his appetites.

As time passed, he found only logical to also ensure that, once he passes away like any other mortal, his family, who, by the way, were officially introduced to the Cuban people only few years ago, have all the resources to live economically safe anywhere in this world, well in Cuba, if they survive the changes after his death, or anywhere if they have to leave.

Castro devoted considerable resources and time to create a network of hidden treasures and properties, which were basically acquired with funds stolen from the Cuban patrimony and which, hopefully, one day may be discovered and recovered for the Cuban state.

Every new small or large piece of information that filtrates one way or another to the public indicates that this has been a long and well-planned operation, involving a huge amount of resources. With the same mega ambitions he has had to project his image, Castro has been one of the worst thieves the world has ever seen, and the innocent people who believed in his dramatic calls for honesty and devotion to a noble cause, at the beginning of his rule, could not imagine how much they have been cheated.

Another neigborhood, more trash

Former stores abandoned

A huge building fall

A penetration of water

A building in ruins

Destroyed houses in a good neighbourhood

A citadel at the center of Vedado

A Havana tunnel under water

A tree growing in an abandoned building

Abandonment

An unreal image

Another piece of art abandoned

Sewage waters running down the streets.

These are houses in Havana!

This is Castro's Havana

tourism vs reality

147

Swimming in pollution

House without roof since the last hurricanes

Long line for bread

Beautiful buildings have become ruins everywhere in Havana.

People use to sit on the steps of their home entrances

Photo of the disaster

Havana looks like a bombed city

The Malecon of Havana destroyed

Way of living under socialism!

Elders are hungry and suffering

The cementery

Jose Marti's base is damaged

Buildings at the Malecon

Nobody cares!

Old TV equipments

Inside a citadel

Another failed building

There are people living in this building!

This is no imagination

CHAPTER IX

The case of race under Castro's government

Race has been one of the most manipulated myths of Castro's revolution and the results his regime has achieved for this manipulation of historical and social facts, in terms of recognition and even more important, in terms of subordination of an important portion of the population, are astonishing.

When Castro took power, most of the population was considered white and were descendants of the Spaniards who colonized the island and sent more immigrants to the island than any other country while approximately 28 percent of the Cuban population was considered well mulatto or black, with a very small Chinese percentage. In this chapter, I am going to refer to all the mulatto and black people as black people.

The continuing exodus of Cubans to the United States and other countries for the past half century has been predominantly of white people, and as a result of this and a higher rate of birth among the black, the percentage of blacks has increased considerably and may be between 50 and 60 percent of the total population.

The situation of race in Cuba was still far from being perfect in 1959, but there is no doubt that there were substantial positive differences between how these matters were treated in the island and the situation of other countries at that time. In order to understand these differences, one must go back to Cuban history.

Cuba was an important base for all the slave traffic that took place in the Americas during the eighteen and nineteen century, and slavery played an important role in the development of Cuban agriculture and the incipient sugar industry. By the middle of the nineteen century, Cuba had an important black population, including slaves and others who had already reached their freedom.

When Cubans started its first war of independence against Spain in 1868, one of the first steps taken by the leaders of the insurrection, who were mainly Cuban-born owners of some of the existing sugar mills and plantations located in the Oriente Province, was to liberate their own slaves, who in most cases incorporated to the insurrection with their former owners. Other blacks, who were already free, incorporated as well to the fight and soon the bravest among them started ascending the ranks of the Cuban forces due to their courage, which made some of them heroic and well-known figures among the Cuban population.

At the end of the first war of independence, several of the main figures of the Cuban liberation army were black and they became symbols of military courage.

This important role of black fighters continued along the other two wars fought by Cubans against Spain during the second half of the nineteenth century, and some of them consolidated their prestige as generals and high-ranking officers of the liberation army.

Antonio Maceo, who came from a family of heroic fighters, became the main Cuban military figure of the war while his mother, Mariana Grajales, became the symbol of patriotism of Cuban women.

The admiration of generations of Cubans for Maceo, his mother, and other military leaders was later accompanied by the admiration and recognition for other respected black leaders and intellectuals who also played an important role in the development of the Cuban nation.

If certainly, mainly due to their different original economic situation, the Cuban black people had by far much less economic power than the Cuban white people and other foreign owners in the island, at the initiation of the republic, after Cuba achieved its independence from Spain, there was no doubt that the Cuban blacks were gradually improving their status within the Cuban society and were obtaining important social achievements that were unthinkable at that time in other countries including the United States.

During the first part of the twentieth century, the different Cuban constitutions were the basis for, at least in legal and legislative terms, establishing the same rights for Cubans of all races and different labor and social laws and regulations followed that line.

The Cuban society, however, could not overcome the influence of the times, and it could not achieve a full and equal integration of all the different races who lived in the island, at least in the way one could understand it today. The result was the development of two parallel societies of whites and blacks, which coexisted and lived together under the same government and acted according to some basic rules of mutual acceptance and a certain kind of understanding, which was not fair, but had a considerable degree of positivism, considering the way racial matters were perceived in the world at that time.

There is no doubt that the Cuban black population was improving its social and economic status during the years of the republic and many black people were reaching high levels of recognition in most fields of society, including the political arena. All the main books of history taught in Cuban schools referred to the black Cuban heroes with the same level of recognition as of the main white figures and this, no doubt, was a large difference with other countries.

Important artists, sport figures, musicians, intellectuals, and painters were black and some of them became idols of the Cuban people.

Blacks and whites were also joined by other important factors, one of them religion. The Cuban Catholic religion developed and integrated jointly important elements of the black and white cultures.

The fact was that the Cuban people were gradually progressing in the field of racial relations, with many decades of advancement in regard to other countries. In most neighborhoods white and black people lived together and Cuban public schools and most private as well were similarly open for all races. Despite this, there were sectors of Cuban blacks that still lived in bad conditions and the fact is white people were in better conditions than most black people. Cuba, like most countries at that time, had still limitations in regard to the integration of races.

When Castro took power, he saw the advantage of playing the racial card and introduced a number of demagogic gestures and measures in order to not only attract the black portion of the population, which until then had been in large extend sympathetic to the Batista's regime, but also to establish the presumption that the unconditional support of his government was the only logical and patriotic line the black people could follow, based in some sense of gratitude for the "possibilities" his government was opening to them.

This false propaganda scheme worked incredibly well, and Castro has managed to have a very large part of the black people supporting unconditionally his regime for fifty years. Even when there are important exceptional black personalities who have not followed this pattern and deserve to be recognized, the fact remains that Castro's regime has been able to keep most of the black population supporting blindly his government.

Following the same line he defined to deal with the Cuban blacks, Castro decided to project the same pattern of propaganda internationally, and soon he became an outspoken promoter of all sorts of liberation causes related with racial issues in the whole world.

Once he became known for these ideas, which, together with his opposition to the United States, brought him recognition at a worldwide scale, he was able to start another kind of actions and Cuban troops and intelligence services, supplied and supported by the Soviet Union, became involved in all sorts of wars and political events in Africa, which were presented as liberation efforts for blacks.

This scheme worked again so well that in a matter of few years Castro became an undisputed hero for many black people around the world, who innocently came to accept his views and actions as noble gestures of a man devoted to promote freedom principles, in the otherwise unjust world, something diametrically contrary to Castro's real motives.

Obviously, considering the dimension of the stature and pseudo prestige he had achieved at that point, the real crude details of many of his actions were easily ignored. The image of Castro, as a worldwide black liberator, served to hide the real image of Castro as an exploiter of Cuban blacks.

The stubborn facts, however, show a very clear picture of what Castro has been. While he was promising to the Cuban blacks all sorts of new rights and possibilities, in most cases manipulating the actual facts of the republic, the actual participation of them in important positions within his government or in key roles was minimized. The standard of living of the black population became incredibly poorer than under the worst conditions they had lived never before in Cuba and all these years have passed and they have not received any improvement in regard to this, other than Castro's promises.

Many black families saw how their young members were recruited by Castro for his army and sent by him to wars and political movements in Africa, where he, with total lack of scruples, represented the expansionist interests of the Soviet Union, and many of them died there for causes that they could never understand fully.

The way Castro recruited and used these black Cubans in order to facilitate the acceptance of his forces by the Africa leaders symbolizes his lack of scruples and tortuous mind.

I have described in other chapters the continued deterioration of the conditions in which Cubans in general live, but it is just fair to say that the Cuban black people live, in general, in much poorer conditions now than in any time before Castro, and that their standard of living is much worse than the one of the white people in the island.

There was nothing real or noble in Castro's promises to the black sectors of Cuban society, but just hypocrisy and obscure political intentions. I believe that fifty years later, it is obvious what his real intentions were since the beginning.

There was nothing noble in Castro's actions in Africa, Latin America, and other continents, but only crude personal political ambitions. He served as the representative of the interests of the Soviet Union as a way to pay for the huge economic and political support his regime was receiving.

He did not care how many people died in those countries as a result of his actions, and he was not interested in giving any sort of freedom and liberty to those peoples, but only to put them under an even worse system of exploitation than the colonial one against which they were struggling, which could use their resources for their new geopolitical ambitions at whatever human cost.

The component of Cuban blacks among the troops sent by Castro to Africa was very large because, as I explained in previous paragraphs, he pretended that since they were black, they should be accepted more easily by those peoples, but in reality, he used them like mercenaries, with little concern for their families, their lives, or well-being.

Those who came back alive to Cuba from those adventures never received any reward, but only returned to the same miseries in which they had been living. The families of those who died fighting for the most obscure of Castro's causes only received some brief notification and they had to keep going with their daily disgraces.

The families of the many thousands of African people, as well as those in other continents, who died due to Castro's military adventures, never received any explanation either about what really happened and why Cubans had to go there, so far from their own land, to kill their relatives and destroy their lives, while pretending to establish a good and progressive system, when in reality they were promoting communism and Castro and the Soviet Union.

Many of the new pseudo leaders imposed to those countries by Castro and the Soviets had been trained, indoctrinated, and prepared in Cuba and were people who had been injected in their brains the same sick ambitions of power and the same total lack of moral and scruples and were ready to work under the orders of the Cuban and Soviet intelligence services, helping to fulfill the geopolitical goals of a new and more elaborated kind of colonization.

The fact that Castro trained, supported, promoted, and finally positioned at very high levels of those countries a good number of those people he had brought to Cuba to be trained there and that, once in power, they became some of the worst leaders and dictators those countries have had, is just one aspect of what he had in mind with all those operations.

The meticulous details to which he went to select, prepare, and promote those people as new pseudo leaders for these nations, among the many he had recruited, was typical of his pattern of political corruption and ambition and it becomes astonishing, when one looks into these events in detail, how he was able to do that with total impunity.

As time passed and some of these pseudo leaders consolidated their power, they became his unconditional supporters in the United Nations and in every international organization, and they were, and some still are after so many years, those leaders who are always ready to, in silence or openly, allow Castro's intelligence services to operate freely within their societies and those who have become his accomplices in all sorts of obscure deals.

All of them knew, however, that they owed their own positions to Castro and they had to obey his orientations because, otherwise, they could suffer the consequences no matter who they have become. They were at the end part of Castro's international political mafia and poor of those countries where this scheme was established.

The case was that, incredibly, while all these grave events occurred in the international arena, nobody in this world really cared, for sixty years, about what was happening to the Cuban blacks, until some people started to realize of their mistake recently because the accumulated evidence is so overwhelming that it has become impossible to hide anymore the terribly bad conditions in which black people have lived under Castro's government and the internal repression they have suffered.

The social and economic problems of the increasing black portion of the Cuban population have aggravated to very dramatic and terrible levels and this has caused all sorts of new problems to them, unthinkable in our previous republican history, the main one being that a huge number of blacks have been for many years suffering all sorts of atrocities, illnesses, corruption, aberrations, and abuses at Castro's prisons, where hundreds of thousands of blacks have not only being forced to live for many years like animals, but have been also exploited to work like slaves, for long daily journeys, with no remuneration and without any chance to achieve any proper education and working skills, with no access to religion or proper health care and separated from their suffered families.

The savage conditions in which hundreds of thousands of blacks, at one time or another, and for varying lengths of time, have lived in those terrible prisons created by Castro during these past fifty years are comparable in most cases with those of the times of slavery, which I have seen, reserved for illustration of visitors, in some Caribbean islands and should be considered a crime against humanity. If his crimes were only for this, they would be enough for Castro to be considered one of the world's worst criminals.

As I explained, the majority of the more than a million and a half Cubans who have left the island to live in the United States and other countries, running away of Castro's policies and oppression, have been white, and due to this, the percentage of blacks and mulattos within the Cuban population has increased considerably; however, this has not translated or reflected in any increase in the level of participation of blacks in the positions of leadership around Castro or in any other key role within the Cuban society.

The current racial discrimination in Cuba, under Castro, is worse, more absolute and elaborated than anything seen in Cuba before.

Even those well-known achievements of some Cuban black athletes in international events, or those of black artists and musicians, have intrinsic and another kind of goal, which is to be used by Castro for his propaganda.

This is why they are forced subtly by the managers of Cuban sports to present their awards to Castro when they return to Cuba, as if he was the only one responsible for their achievements and sacrifices.

The conditions in which these talented people have to train and compete, the way they have Castro's agents always vigilant around them, do not allow any kind of freedom to them, and they are exploited with total lack of scruples and like everything Castro does, this is another part of his megalomaniac ambitions.

The achievements of these athletes do not represent any improvement for the Cuban black community or for the Cuban people because those relevant figures practically do not get any remuneration for their effort, and they return from those events to live in the same miserable conditions in which they have lived with their families all their life.

Once they get older and lower their rankings and results, they are not usable anymore for Castro's purposes and they regularly disappear from the candle lights and finish living under the worst conditions of poverty and abandonment.

The stories of many of the best Cuban black athletes during these past decades are really sad because it is obvious how they have been used by this regime to represent their achievements as Castro's achievements, only to become, few years later, abandoned human beings who live in the total disgrace.

It is less known how many of the best black athletes Cuba has produced in these past fifty years have been vetoed by Castro because he has felt that they were too independent and how this destroyed their lives.

Cuba always had good athletes and several of them achieved world titles before Castro like Jose Raul Capablanca, the World Chess Champion, or like Kid Chocolate and Kid Gavilan, both black, in boxing, or so many good baseball players, or Ramon Font, in fencing, to mention few of them and the increase in the number of medals obtained by Cuban athletes during these years of Castro's government does not mean necessarily that Cubans were not going to be able to get also more medals if Castro had not existed.

The fact is that no medal obtained during these past years can compensate the degree of degradation and exploitation suffered for so many Cuban athletes, black and white, due to Castro.

On top of the above, another enormous problem exists because, while the percentages of blacks in the universities, in most professional fields, and in positions of responsibility within the government and the armed forces are relatively very small, black people are almost 80 percent of the huge population of Castro's common prisons and the black Cuban families have suffered to unbelievable levels because of this.

It is impressive, however, to observe how, during all this long time, Castro has managed, using his propaganda and the resources of his machinery of repression and intimidation, as well as its censure of information, to make most black people accept the concept that they have to support and follow his regime because they have no better option.

Even a psychiatrist, especially if he is not familiar with Cuban matters, would find difficult to understand how is possible that many Cuban black people, who have been in jail in Cuba for many years and subject to all sorts of abuses and humiliations and have seen their human rights violated in every sense, can continue saying that they support Castro and his revolution.

I have been witness of this numerous times while I was in prison, and the explanation of this strange phenomenon seems to be in the effect caused in their minds by the combination of the continuing propaganda of the regime with the terror in which these people have lived all their lives while they have at the same time been immersed in the worst conditions of living.

The black sector of the Cuban population, which in the past was usually hardworking, noble, happy, with good manners, and respectful, was integrated within Cuba's society with its own style of life and was always willing to accept progress.

It had a lower standard of living as a whole than the white people in the cities, but this happened as well with the predominantly white rural population, which had lower level of living than those white people living in the cities, and both social groups were improving their conditions very quickly.

Castro not only disrupted all the process of development of the black Cubans, but confronted them with a huge machinery of repression and oppression, which has impacted and destroyed the lives of many of their people with total perversion.

It is difficult for a person, who has a normal life anywhere in the world, to even imagine how is the day-to-day life of those black people in Cuban prisons, and the fact is that, after many years in those conditions, this has become their way of life and they have come to accept those conditions as almost normal.

How is it possible that, during all the republican years, the number of prisoners in Cuba, both white and black, in the few prisons that existed then, was minimal and Castro has needed, in order to be able to govern, to build this huge and monstrous prison network in the whole island and condemn there so many black people?

The mentality of these men, and also women, because Castro has created many prison facilities for women as well and they are full of black women, is a reflection of their conditions of living there and they are not normal anymore. Most black people who have lived for so many years in those prisons have in their brains the accumulated damage caused by the conditions in which they have been immersed.

It will take many years of serious professional psychiatric treatment, based on an overall medical policy, to alleviate the deep damages in the minds of all those people, who have suffered this side of Castro's repression.

For most of these black people, immersed in the corruption and violence of Cuban prisons, all sorts of vices are their day-to-day reality. The destruction of the moral values of these human beings has been total.

On the other hand, Castro has recruited many people to work as guards in those prisons and many of them are also blacks, who have been trained to be the repressors of their own race, and these people, who have spent also most of their lives in this environment, are also affected by the same conditions in which they work and the rules they have to follow, losing all sense of moral and principles.

It is easy to imagine the effect this situation has had on the Cuban black population, not only of the repression under which they have been forced by Castro to live, but also the sacrifices all this imposes over the black families in general.

It is difficult to estimate how many black mothers have had their sons, husbands, daughters, and relatives in Castro's prisons and what this situation has imposed on them, in the middle of the miserable conditions in which they live.

It is a very sad image that never is erased of my memory, to watch those long lines of women, under the rain or sun, waiting for hours, to see their relatives in prison, during the few sporadic visits they are allowed according to the stringent conditions and rules of Castro's prison system.

Castro's prisons are regularly located in very isolated places, where the rest of the population cannot see them, and in order to make it easier for other people to forget about their existence; to get to them, these mothers, because usually the mothers or the prisoners' wives are the only one visitor regularly allowed, must overcome all sorts of transport difficulties, and they must, before that, look for weeks for something to bring to these prisoners, in the middle of all the scarcities and without means to live and feed themselves.

This criminal Castro's policy has produced a social impact of immensurable proportions because a huge portion of Cuban population has grown up in the middle of this subculture.

These people have come to accept anything as normal and they lack all the moral, patriotic, and social principles; they have lost any sense of labor discipline or any principle of orderly family existence and they lack any real hope for a better future.

Most of them do not have any kind of capability and they are vulnerable to all sorts of vices. Their character has been crunched by the society in which they have lived under Castro's rule and they have to simulate every minute of their lives.

How a future Cuba is going to be able to solve this situation is something that will require a lot of imagination and the allocation of huge resources.

To me, the only way this is going to somehow change positively is if important portions of the black population finally react to the dramatic suffering they have been condemned by Castro's system.

It is for me encouraging to observe that there are few signs indicating that the above situation has started to change because, not only the evidence produced by the new events in the world is too obvious and Castro cannot hide any more to the Cuban blacks the advance of other proud black people, in all sorts of worldwide functions and events, but also because the black Cubans are increasingly more and more open to compare their real status with the one of other people in the world and within Cuba and this forces them to recognize that they have been cheated by Castro and to wake up to their realities, after fifty years of his rule.

Castro procured with his propaganda to create the image that his government had some black figures among its top leaders, but a detailed analysis shows that this has not been the case. The few black people around him at the top of his regime have just been real clowns or parasites and have become accessories for his propaganda, with no real power and without the capacity to be real leaders. They have been chosen for their unconditional support and their corruption and lack of scruples, not because of their talents and capabilities. They do not represent the Cuban people, but on the contrary, they represent what Castro has wanted the Cuban blacks to become.

When Castro appointed a person like Esteban Lazo, the most noticeable black figure because of his physical size, to the politburo, or sends him to the United Nations, he was laughing of the Cuban blacks and of many people in this world, and he was not sending there a real representative of the Cuban blacks.

He knew how abject this man has been and how much he has ignored the suffering of his own people in order to escalate to these positions he holds and the degree in which he has been accomplice of many of Castro's crimes.

During the past fifty years, Cuba has produced a large number of prominent black people, from intellectuals to military leaders, and they have all well vetoed by Castro or what is the same, their lives have been deviated, in one way or another, to eliminate any possibility of their surge as real black leaders.

Curiously and still little known by most Cubans, the most prominent black figure within Castro's revolution, the commander of the revolution Juan Almeida, who was also member of the politburo and vice president of Castro's government, who died some years ago in strange circumstances in Cuba, has been mentioned, in a recently published book, which is based in confidential sources and declassified documents, released from the National Archives a short time ago, as the main element, in a never before disclosed conspiracy to eliminate Castro and reorient the revolution toward its original democratic ways, which was promoted by President Kennedy and his brother Robert in the early years of Castro's government.

Whether this was true, and according to what has been described in this book or not, will require many years of further research, and it may become an extraordinary event, shedding new light on many of the obscure and tortuous corridors of power of Castro's revolution. Until now, officially, Almeida has been considered an important accomplice of Castro, who followed him in all his actions and participated in the most conspicuous events.

After what I have witnessed in Cuba, I am convinced that Castro hates the black people and he has designed, in his elaborate mind, a political scheme to use them for his political ambitions and, at the same time, damage them, with incredible levels of sadism, and I am convinced that Castro deeply enjoys doing this monstrosity.

The same way that one cannot find a single real and serious black leader among the top people, who have been controlling Cuba during the past half century, it is very difficult to identify any real decent and competent leader among those who Castro has supported and helped to ascend to high positions of leadership in Africa, and it is important here to note that a similar kind of situation exists with his policies in Latin America, where he has tried to similarly use and manipulate the conflict of races within the continent to his political advantage with total lack of scruples, promoting a number of corrupted figures in different countries.

In Africa, Castro supported for many years people like Mengistu Marian and Robert Mugabe; in Latin America, he has supported Daniel Ortega and Hugo Chavez; in Asia, he supported the Red Kramer's regime; in Europe, he fully and unconditionally supported the Soviet Union and he was in excellent terms with Erik Honecker. None of those regimes and the many others he supported has represented anything good for their countries.

But things do not stop there, Castro also tried to use the racial card in the United States, where he tried to promote a number of black leaders whom he found acceptable for his purposes of destabilizing the American society, most of which were invited to Cuba at some moment and offered or given advise and resources, including intelligence support.

Castro was never been really interested in supporting a certain type of black American leader, who characteristically possesses a combination of cultural, moral, and religious values with a valuable kind of intellectual prestige, because these people are difficult to manipulate, and with their deep understanding and experience of the society where they have grown up, they in general want to improve it because that society is where they and their families live and will continue living.

He preferably tried to promote disarrayed people, interested in destabilizing and if possible destroying the best values of the American society in one way or another, well by violent political activism, by gang activism, or by the introduction of drugs.

Castro's intelligence services have procured to keep good records of black American figures for all these years and he and the people handling these matters within his regime know that they cannot afford any kind of conflict with black American leaders because this would be extremely dangerous politically for his regime due to the potential ideological impact any conflict of this nature could have on the Cuban black population, who tend to look with interest to what happens among the American blacks and is eager to proudly adopt any of their achievements as its own.

The problem for Castro and his followers in this regard may be that, the situation of blacks in Cuba is so terribly bad that once the reality of it is fully discovered, it will be very difficult for them to avoid the whole disclosure of the abuses and atrocities that have been in existence for fifty years in the island.

I have observed how, after recent demands expressed in a letter sent to him by some prominent and well-known American black leaders, Raúl Castro immediately responded with a well-elaborated short speech, in which he demagogically accepted some of the real facts condemned in the mentioned letter and qualified the existence of those facts as a real shame. Of course, he forgot to mention that, only few days before, he had oriented some of the most corrupted intellectuals, members of the euphemistically called Cuban Union of Writers and Artists, to write a document expressing their deepest condemn to the mentioned letter.

I can only establish a historical comparison between the above and how it had looked that Hitler or Stalin, at some moment, had made a speech saying that it was true that their concentration camps had been just a mistake and promising that that situation had to be corrected and they pretended to continue in power as if nothing else had happened. Just like that!

After sixty years of crimes, abuses, and aberrations, the other Castro recognizes that the policy of the revolution toward the black people has had "shortcomings" because not many blacks are in high positions. It looks like a lack of respect for the intelligence of those American black leaders and also of all the Cuban blacks. This is just another example of what Castro has always been ready to do, or simulate to do, in order to avoid controversy and stay in power. Obviously, they prefer not to have any embarrassing conflict, which could alter their status quo. After all, they may think that, after a while, they will be able to go around this situation with those American leaders, like they have done in the past with other similar situations and following in their same style, they must be looking for ways to use those among them who have accepted to work with them in the past to alleviate any tensions.

I sincerely hope that, sooner or later, the people of developing countries and also of many developed countries will come to realize that Castro is not and has never been what his propaganda has made them to believe he is. Once Castro disappears, the development of a new democratic Cuba must require a total revision of the racial situation in the island and black people must be really given the same possibilities to fully achieve their potentials.

CHAPTER X

$\rightharpoondown$

The case of Cuban women

Right since the beginning of his government, Castro defined a strategy to deal with Cuban women, who represent close to 50 percent of the population and who were and obviously always will be a very key element of Cuban society, trying to integrate them within his political plans to dominate Cuba.

Castro's strategy consisted basically in altering the traditional structure, customs, and values of the average Cuban family, replacing the responsibilities that customarily a large portion of women had within their families for new activities associated with the revolution.

The pattern of the traditional Cuban family, which had been developing spontaneously through Cuban history and was according with the degree of development of the country and the advance of its society, was probably one the most important moral elements of our nation.

Castro started using his propaganda and his frequent speeches to promote a number of demagogic slogans, which contained the basic elemental concept that Cuban women were being exploited because a large proportion of them were housewives and this activity was limiting their potential.

In the case of all those women who, contradicting that simplistic image, had jobs in all sorts of activities, he generalized the fact that some of them were receiving lower salaries than men and therefore he considered they were receiving less opportunities, something that according to his views was unfair. He started repeating that this situation was going to be solved by his revolution.

This simple vision was also touched with references to the case of women who worked as maids for the upper economic class and those who worked at bars or were prostitutes, because, in 1959, prostitution was legal in Cuba, like in most of the world. No need to say that it was Castro's revolution that was coming to the rescue of Cuban women!

He established the above slogans as the basic elements of his policy toward this important sector of Cuban society and gradually he started incorporating some other more elaborated elements to it.

He created a number of organizations, like the Federation of Cuban Women and the Committees for the Defense of the Revolution, which could facilitate and control the incorporation of women to the activities of the revolution, even if they were still housewives.

He also created the militias to "defend" Cuba against the Yankee imperialism, and this was supposed, according to Castro's propaganda, to create another opportunity for women to assume a new more independent role and the same happened with the huge expansion of the armed forces, in which a large number of women were recruited.

Since, as I explained before, most people of the upper economic layer of Cuban society started leaving Cuba due to Castro's policies and repression, soon Castro started offering to those women, who worked for them as nannies or maids, the opportunity to "study" or work in other activities.

Not many people in the island really cared, however, when most of the main leaders of the revolution, and very specially Castro himself, started using all the people they wished for the same tasks in their own homes, in contradiction with this predicament.

The above, in fact, has been a pattern that has continued along all these decades, in which the rules and concepts applied to criticize the rich class do not apply to the privileged class within the Castro, who can use the people they wish for their personal matters, with the aggravation that they are paid by the funds of the government.

Simultaneously, Castro started a campaign against all sorts of activities, which he considered incompatible with the new airs of his revolution. Gradually, his government started closing casinos, bars, and all sorts of entertainment centers, except few, like the famous Tropicana, which were left operating for the use mainly of the few tourists and diplomats who went to the island, and all this left many women, who worked at them, without work as well and they did not have other alternative than incorporating to the new duties the government offered to them or simply leaving their country.

At some point, Castro had to deal with the brothels that existed in certain areas of the main cities and especially in Havana, which in few years were gradually disappearing, and his government again offered new employment possibilities to the women who worked at them.

Castro's propaganda magnified the relative importance of these cases and converted them in a symbol of the possibilities the revolution was offering to women and presented as a great achievement the elimination of vice within the Cuban society.

Many people in the world, who were ignorant of the real situation of Cuba, got the idea that Cuba before Castro was a country in which most women were forced to be involved in all sorts of vices and Castro had been their savior.

With all the power of Castro's propaganda behind it, the enrollment of women in the so-called activities of the revolution continued across Cuban cities and gradually also in the rural areas.

Castro appointed his sister-in-law, Vilma Espin, who was the wife of his brother Raúl, as the president of the Federation of Cuban Women, and with her as their perpetual leader, until her death few years ago, he established an elaborated mechanism to involve Cuban women in all sorts of activities designed to support unconditionally his regime.

Castro subtly established the concept that in order to be equal to men, women had to incorporate to the activities the revolution was offering to them.

Since the new government was getting control of every branch of the economy and every piece of society, everybody had to work for the government and the propaganda of the regime was omnipresent.

He created new mechanisms of persuasion and pressure to force the incorporation of more and more women to those activities the revolution he said was opening for them. He called this the "liberation" of women.

During the past fifty years, coincidental with the time Castro has been in power, most developed nations, and also numerous developing nations, have experienced a gradual transformation of the role of important sectors of their female population in their societies and more and more women have gotten involved in all sorts of professional careers and every kind of working activities, which were usually performed by males in the past, or can be considered new activities created by the technological development of their societies.

Practically every university in the world has seen a huge increase in the number of women studying all sorts of careers. All this social phenomenon has come parallel with the expansion of their economies, which has created the possibility for the incorporation of women, as a relatively new productive sector of society.

In the case of Cuba, the same process was already happening, with some years of advantage in regard to most countries and there were numerous indicators showing that important numbers of Cuban women were already developing careers in the most diverse fields and getting involved in all sorts of new important functions within Cuban society, but this was happening in an orderly and gradual way, according to the pace at which Cuba was developing.

What Castro did was to alter the normal development process Cuba was experiencing in this field, as he also did in most others, replacing it by the chaotic new institutions, slogans, and concepts of his revolution.

In order to understand well the effect of all these changes on Cuban society and the impact they had on many traditional family values and in practically every aspect of life, it is necessary to look at them with the perspective of these past fifty years and this requires the honest answering of some questions: What advantages have the Cuban women gotten after fifty years of Castro? Have they improved economically and socially as a whole? Evidently, all the main parameters of Cuban standard of living reflect that Cuban women, and in general the Cuban people, are not living better. Most Cuban women live in a state of permanent frustration because they see that time keeps passing and they do not see any improvement in their conditions of life and this is just part of a disastrous situation in regard to the existence of their families, including their marriages and children, as well as their condition of work.

Most women continue dealing with most duties regarding with the care of their children, as well as with the activities of the house, but also they have to deal additionally with their jobs because the miserable salaries of people do not match with the cost of living and every basic product is scarce, expensive, and difficult to find in the parallel market, and the men alone cannot keep their families, as was the case in the past.

On top of this, the deteriorated conditions of living and many other limitations brought by the disaster that Castro's economic policies have imposed on them have created a burden that is unbearable and women must devote a lot of their energies to simply help their families to survive.

The role of women in regard to the education of their children has become limited due to the lack of time they experience, after having to deal with all the other existent problems.

The accumulated impression, which has been valid for several generations of Cubans, is that Cuban women have now more problems than never before in regard to family matters and every aspect of their lives.

The rate of divorce in Cuba, which was very low before Castro, is extremely high now, and even the existence of marriage as a stable traditional component of Cuban society is being seriously challenged by the harsh conditions imposed by the new way of life established under his regime, as well as by the new parameters of social behavior, which have established, as a priority, the participation of women in the activities oriented by the government, over the duties and obligations of marriage and motherhood.

Young Cubans frequently leave aside marriage because they find the conditions in which they live unstable, and they do not want to fully commit to the responsibility a marriage means.

Meanwhile, the rate of births in Cuba is the lowest of the continent because people feel they cannot raise children in the conditions they are living.

In present Cuba, it is seen as absolutely normal that people are sent to all sorts of tasks, assigned by the government, that can be in Cuba or abroad, with little concern about the separation of the families, and marriage has become somehow secondary in regard to numerous events in life.

It has become frequent that people trying to leave the country simulate a divorce in order to make possible that one of the partners "marry" some foreigner, which makes this partner eligible to travel without the restrictions imposed in the island and then to try later, possibly after many years, to reunify the family. There is no need to say that most of these experiences end in family disaster, but many people, especially young, do not care, because the links of traditional marriage, like other family values, have been diminished due to the pressures of the system and the lack of spirituality in which the new Cuban generations live.

In general, the participation of women in the most diverse activities within the Cuban society was changed dramatically in order to adjust it to Castro's strange concepts and megalomaniac vision of society.

An example of this was the case of carnivals. Cuba had a long-established and rich tradition of carnivals, which every year served to show the beauty of Cuban women, who regularly have a smart sensuality combined with a sense of elegance and passion, who enjoy music and like to be recognized for their beauty as well as to allow everybody to have some time of distraction.

The main carnivals were in Havana and Santiago de Cuba, the second main city, which were very large and luxurious popular parties, but there were also smaller versions in most other cities.

Each of these carnivals started by the election of a queen, elected for her beauty and sympathy. They were a good occasion for people to enjoy a good time and express their happiness, with long caravans of beautiful and elaborated carriages and convertibles with beautiful women onboard, lots of music and fireworks, and all sorts of foods and drinks.

Castro participated in some of these carnivals during his early years in power, but soon he prohibited them for many years, not before leaving some bad memories which exemplify the corruption that characterizes everything this man does, when he forced behind curtains the election of a participant he liked, whom he brought afterward to a hotel in Havana, to celebrate her election.

Years later, when he allowed the carnivals again, it was in his "revolutionary" version, which consists of selling cheap beverages to the people in the streets and playing some music in few spots. He eliminated the selection of the carnival queens, showing with this the paranoia he has always had for the surge of any new popular young figure, who could upset the rituals and false values adopted by his communist youth organizations and could become attractive and distracting for Cuban youth. The new carnivals became a symbol of the poverty existing in Cuba and the devaluation of taste and customs as well as the lowering moral and educational values.

The above may seem strange for a man with such a huge power, but apparently, Castro had a strange side regarding women, which forces him to take actions that degrade them.

The same way in which he prohibited and finished the long-established tradition of electing carnival queens in all Cuban towns every year, he forbade the participation of Cuban women in any beauty tournaments around the world, and he limited the promotion and development of young Cuban singers and actresses. The result can be seen in the fact that very few young Cuban singers have succeeded in becoming a recognized figure during the past fifty years, and there has not been any Cuban among all those beautiful women from many countries who participate in the well-known beauty tournaments that many people in the world watch every year.

Under Castro, Cuban women have been repressed of having access to new fashions and beauty products and Castro's educational system has avoided teaching them good manners and moral parameters because he considers them reminiscent of the past.

Cuban women have no access to modern clothes, and practically the only ways in which they can acquire them are if they have relatives living in other countries, or if they get related to foreigners.

They do not have any kind of access to information on new modern furniture and decoration or of new appliances, which are nonexistent in Cuba, and they have no hope about getting a new home because the possibility of getting any of them simply have not existed in Cuba for five decades!

More than this, the number of women who own something as common as a car in Cuba is incredibly small, and this has become a symbol of frustration, not only for all those who have achieved careers and professions but for all women in general, especially since they know about the conditions of women in other countries and among this, the Cuban women in the United States.

Those young women, who decide bravely to have children, do not have access to any of the many products existing everywhere in the world to feed and take care of children and also for their own care during pregnancy. It is very difficult for them to buy even a used cradle and bed clothes, and even more problematic, they usually have a total lack of space for their new baby because their homes are already full and there is no hope of expanding.

These limitations impose on the new parents all sorts of hardships and force children to grow up in the middle of very disadvantaged and underdeveloped conditions, in which they are ignorant of most advances of civilization that one could expect to exist in a country with the degree of development Cuba had in the past.

Some of these limitations involve the almost total lack of proper food for children, who may live their whole lives without even tasting products that are common everywhere in this world.

The almost total lack of milk, fish, cereals, and meats, for instance, implies that Cuban children grow up without a proper supply of needed minerals and this reflects later in the health of their teeth and in the structure of their bones and body.

On top of all of the above, Cuban women do not have access to any modern cleaning and washing products, nor can they buy new washer and dryer machines, which are nonexistent in the island except in the stores that function with dollars. Their cooking appliances are very old and obsolete and all the other kitchen tools are primitive. They also lack most modern health and sanitary products for them and for their children.

In a country like Cuba, in which, in the past, everybody was used to the immediate introduction of all sorts of new advances of civilization, it is unreal to realize that practically nobody knows nowadays what a microwave appliance is. The vast majority of several generations of Cubans who have lived under Castro, have never seen a dishwasher or a digital high-definition TV and even less a personal computer with access to the Internet. This, in a country located ninety miles from the United States, where new year models of cars used to run there the day after they were brought out from their factories!

New parents in Cuba must live with the fact that their children most likely will grow up and live all their young years without access to any modern toy because Castro also eliminated the religious tradition of the Three Magic Kings, an equivalent to Santa Claus for Americans, and Cuban children do not have any kind of equivalent traditional celebration in which they could receive presents. Castro attempted for some time to sell toys on the yearly celebrations for his attack to the Moncada barracks, a political event, but this was later eliminated due to lack of resources motivated by the perpetual economic crisis in which Cuba lives.

To make things even worse, since most Cuban stores are empty and they do not sell toys unless people have access to dollars to buy some limited models at the special shopping centers, parents cannot buy children any new toy!

Obviously, all the Cuban children who have grown in the middle of all these limitations imposed by Castro have not known the experience of learning at an early age about many new advanced games and modern toys, even less about computers and Internet and interactive means, which adds to the total lack of education they suffer regarding manners, moral values, and other basic knowledge, which Castro also decided to eradicate from the regular curriculum. Even when Cuban children are regularly smart, they have a handicapped education, which affects them in many aspects all their adult lives and their mothers suffer from this.

I must confess that, being under the impression that there was something diabolic in Castro's mind and actions, as I have explained before, I am convinced that he enjoyed all the damage he has created to the Cuban people, but within this, I certainly believe that he, specifically and for some unknown reason, hates even more women, like he has proved to hate more the black Cuban people and that he enjoyed the suffering he caused to them in the island.

Maybe some of this comes from the way he was grown up or from something that most people do not know, but there may be some reason for this.

It is interesting to observe how Castro hid the existence of a wife and a number of children he had with her from the whole world for several decades, until few years ago, when, mainly due to his illnesses and the possibility of his death, one day he surprisingly introduced them indirectly, through the Cuban press, to the population, contrary to what is a normal practice everywhere. Even for a man obsessed with his safety and security, this part of his life becomes a very strange piece, full of aberrations and ghosts.

During the very long time he was in power, he kept doing things that are very strange in this regard, showing disregard for his family, as if he was above all that they represented and they were something he had created to be used by him in case of necessity. For some reason, in every act of his life, Castro showed very little respect for the family institution.

It has been illustrated by several of his, at some time, close assistants, who apparently became disenchanted and decided to desert, how selfish he behaved in regard to other women in his life and how selfish his life with his own family has been. The more details people come to know about this concealed side of Castro's life, the more similar to their concept of a bad person this man becomes for them.

Even in the case of his brother Raúl, which he kept close to him all these years and used to his advantage due to his similar criminal orientation, one can note a strange relationship with him.

Castro's paranoia was omnipresent in all his family ties and connections, and the way he has handled the lives and existence of his wife and children is good example of that. The same happens in the way he managed women matters during his long stay in power. He was a hypocrite all his life in this regard.

A man with those conditions and so many aberrations could not pretend to be a role model for any society, and the bad influence of his presence, for so many years in absolute charge of Cuba, will cause a very bad damage to the Cuban society for many years to come. This is very easy to say, but it will be very difficult to deal with in future years.

Considering that approximately half of the Cuban population is female, this means that there are approximately 3.75million adult women in the island. They have been employed by Castro's government in all sorts of political, productive, and social activities, from the Communist Party to agricultural work to scientific work. Even those who are young students have been employed in voluntary labor activities.

Paradoxically, all this new pattern of employment has kept women busy, but it has not produced any improvement in the overall productivity of the country, which on the contrary has been totally unable, during Castro's years, to satisfy the needs of its population and is in total bankruptcy, or in any other aspect of its life, which is absurd and represents a huge waste of effort.

I have described before the really very bad conditions in which Cubans nowadays live and the deteriorated conditions of practically the whole housing, industrial, and commercial infrastructure of the country. This is in contradiction with the large increase in the number of people, especially women, who have been employed for many years in all sorts of activities by Castro's government.

One finds it strange how such a large number of economic and social activities could have been neglected during all these past decades, causing a generalized state of abandonment in the country, when so many people were supposedly available to perform them. There must be something, obviously wrong, in the way Castro has ordered this society that does not work!

In recent years, it has become more obvious that a large percent of the population does not have any recognized source of regular employment despite the many activities in which they could find work.

They usually make their living by dedicating mainly to unproductive activities associated with the procurement of all sorts of scarce products and this shows how things have increasingly got out of control in Cuba.

The stubborn facts show that Castro and his regime have more than failed in fulfilling the promises contained in all those slogans of the initial times of his revolution.

Women everywhere in this world have advanced considerably in their development and in achieving full equality with men, and Cuban women did not need to go throughout all the sacrifices Castro imposed to them and the rest of the Cuban people to have the chance to study or work.

Even more, Cuban women did not need to see their families disrupted and all the moral and educational principles, traditional of Cuban society, perverted by a materialistic regime like Castro's version of communism in order to advance within Cuban society.

They did not need to accept the dogmas of Castro's revolution, or the many injustices of it and even less the repression of any sign of dissent among them.

People who support Castro and his regime tend very easily to forget that, when more than two million and a half Cubans were forced to leave their country, going away of Castro's policy and oppression, almost half of them were women, and they suffered the same or more the separation from the rest of their families and the loss of all their patrimony, which was confiscated by Castro at the time of leaving.

Those mothers who lost their sons and husbands in front of Castro's firing squads, or those who saw their relatives sent to prison for many years, were also primarily Cuban women, who experienced in their own flesh the criminal nature of this inhumane regime.

The Cuban revolution has represented for them the worst disaster of their lives. There is no demagogical slogan, or false promise, that could replace what they have lost and there is no possibility of improvement that can overcome the enormous loss that Castro's revolution has caused among most of the Cuban families.

Many people in this world, including many Cubans of younger generations who have grown up under Castro's rule and are affected by his indoctrination, show very little interest in knowing about the sacrifices that that many men and women had to endure in Castro's prisons.

It is as if they do not want to hear of those events because they refer to an inconvenient political truth, or in cases, as if they do not want to hear of politics anymore, but those facts are part of Cuban history and they must be narrated and preserved for future generations.

People must know that, among his many crimes, Castro developed a large network of women prisons in Cuba and they operated under his direct management, especially those for women involved in political causes.

Castro's women prisons have been, without doubt, the worst the American continent has seen, comparable in some aspects to those of Stalin and Hitler, but more sophisticated, because Castro procured not to kill massively people and thousands of Cuban women were condemned, with the same hatred, to long sentences at them, due to their political opposition and dissent to Castro's policies.

In all these prisons, women experienced the limits, suffering all sorts of humiliations, abuses, lack of medical care and depravations, on top of extremely bad living conditions.

Castro showed at them his hatred for women and his aberrant personality and these women reciprocated, showing to him and his regime that, at least, some Cuban women still had the courage and temper to oppose him despite all what has been done to demoralize this sector of our society.

The narratives and recollections of many Cuban women political prisoners whom I have known show the level of terror applied to them, describe the many different tortures practiced by the guards at them, the elaborated techniques employed to try to break them, and the inhumane prison infrastructure created by Castro.

There were women prisoners and women who Castro recruited and converted to guards for those prisons, giving to them the worst role he could have found. Some of these women became real monsters following Castro's repressive policies. During all these years, Castro has put in charge of managing these places the worst people he could find.

The lack of scruples that he has manifested to orient the torture, alienation, and abuse of all those women whom he has sent to these prisons is absolute. As a symbol of this, one must mention that he ordered that all the women political prisoners were sent to the same prisons with other women common prisoners, in which they have suffered and they have been under the same regime of imprisonment.

Why a man with so much power has needed to do this is beyond my comprehension. The fact is that no normal man would be able to do all this to any woman. Castro was an abuser and a man without class.

These women political prisoners have been only a small fraction of the tens of thousands of Cuban women who have been in common prisons during all these years, including a large of proportion of black women, who regularly come from the poorest sectors of Cuban society. The conditions in which all these women have lived in those prisons are abusive and humiliating.

Most of these mentioned women have been sent to prison due to activities associated with the poor economic and moral conditions in which they grew up and have lived all their lives and the deteriorated status of their family housing conditions and their increasingly poor neighborhoods. They have also been victims of Castro's political disaster.

Never before in Cuban history has any government needed to incarcerate so many women to be able to govern. The Cuban society had problems, but there was no time in our history in which women did not continue improving as a social class, without any need for this kind of oppression on them.

All former Cuban presidents, even those who showed signs of authoritarianism and responded violently to any opposition to them, respected women, and this was so until Castro took power and altered this tacit rule.

The whole legal establishment created by Castro, which totally overruled the former Cuban legal system, which was professionally well elaborated and, has been based in abusive practices and abnormally high sentences, showing a total disregard for human being and women have not been an exception.

Women prisoners have been exploited in all sorts of activities, without proper compensation. They have been separated from their families, their children and husbands and their lives, independently of the crimes they could have committed, have in general been destroyed. The violation of human rights is a day-to-day practice in every aspect of the prison system created by Castro for Cuban women.

The conditions in which women have lived in Castro's prisons were never pretended to be corrective. They were designed to destroy these human beings for the rest of their lives.

Cuban women have been one of the main losers within the Cuban society as a result of Castro's policies because they have received very little if any improvement in their lives during these past decades. They have been exploited and used and they have been forced to experience all kind of sacrifices.

Women have had to work several times more than what they were used to, because of their multiple role within the new kind of society Castro has created, first in their regular eight hours of working activities in any sector of the economy, later for many more daily hours in their homes, including the care of their children and the effort required by the procurement of foods at the difficult supply stores operated by the government, and finally they have had to work voluntarily in the many organizations in which they have been enrolled by Castro's policies, all this to, at the end, receive less than what they usually had, before Castro said that he was going to "liberate" them.

On top of the above, women have been forced to accept blindly an ideology that is strange and surreal to Cubans, leaving very little ground for their own thinking and independent development.

Finally, they have seen how their living conditions deteriorate to unthinkable low levels. They have seen how the concept of marriage, the main basic social institution in the traditional Cuban society, sinks to lower and lower levels of respect, due to moral crisis created by the revolution and they have also seen how the principle of motherhood, something traditionally very special among Cubans, has lost most of its traditional bright due to the decomposition of Cuban society.

Many Cuban women now feel that they have been moved to work for a government that only uses them without scruples and with no real advantage, and they would prefer to be able to attend their children and family better than undergoing so many activities without any practical result. In many other countries, women develop a more balanced schedule, but not in Cuba, where Castro needs to keep the time of everybody tied and under control to avoid any possible subversion.

What can an average Cuban woman who has been incorporated to the activities of Castro's revolution expect to have after a life of sacrifices devoted to this regime? The answer is very simple, nothing.

Most women find that they have wasted their lives, like most of their countrymen, for something that does not go anywhere.

They have not been able, as a result of their work, to acquire any kind of assets or means, even less to accumulate some richness, that they could pass one day to their children, or to keep themselves economically safe, during their elder years. Families in Cuba usually have the same deteriorated pieces of furniture that came from their parents, or even grandparents, and they live in their same houses, obviously in much more deteriorated conditions. In other words, they lack everything that could show some generational material progress.

With his absolute lack of scruples, Castro cheated and laughed at Cubans in general, but he did this more on women.

When he sends young girls from the Communist youth, or recruited by the Security forces, to "attend" to those foreigners who live in special neighborhoods devoted for foreigners and high officers of the government and their families, he does not care.

When confronted with the fact that, many young women, frustrated by the total lack of opportunities, prefer to sell their bodies to tourists, in all the main cities than to suffer all the limitations of life in the island plus having the control of working for the government, Castro, philosophically, explained that, at least, Cuban prostitutes have a higher level of education than those in other countries. He forgot his slogans of the first year of his so-called revolution.

When each of the main figures of Castro's government has a small army of maids, drivers, bodyguards, and cooks and on top of this, they can use as many people as they need to deal with their personal and family living, all this paid by the coffers of the government, and when they facilitate good housing facilities and all sorts of privileges to every member of their families, they do not care how regular Cubans live and this include women among them.

While the above occurs, most Cuban women lack everything, from beauty products to modern appliances, from normal housing conditions to clothing, from food to cleaning products.

They cannot even dream of having a vehicle of their own, or some inexpensive jewelry, unless they inherited them from their parents.

They cannot travel abroad as they would like, and even traveling and vacationing inside Cuba has become difficult because transport conditions are limited and expensive and most hotel facilities must be paid in dollars or CUC.

Those women who have studied professional careers find very limited good employment opportunities because of the stagnation of Cuban economy, and they have very limited chances of improving their living conditions.

They lack access to all sorts of modern means, which are nowadays normal for women with similar educational standards in other countries. Their average salaries are ridiculous, equivalent to those in the poorest countries of the world. Considering all this, one wonders if it was worthy to devote so many years to support something that has proven to be a total failure and a fake promise. Evidently, the answer is too obvious.

Castro's regime has left without basis any moral criticisms about the role of women in Cuban society. Most of the main figures of the government and the armed forces are notorious for their numerous affairs with younger women and the lack of respect for their families.

They have their secluded and well-supplied housing facilities, usually hidden from the regular citizen view, where they can live discreetly and enjoy most of what is forbidden for the rest of the people, with little concern for any critics. After all, there is no free press in Cuba able to check what they do or not do, and they know that other people at the top levels mostly are used to do the same. Unless they had some kind of discrepancy with Castro or one of them, nobody was going to disclose the way they lived.

They have become a demoralized class of political simulators, who keep their corrupt system by the use of their repressive machinery. They are accomplices in the task of destroying Cuba.

It has become an extended and well-established practice for these pseudo leaders to enjoy their lives with little or no concern for anything that happens around them in Cuban society. After all, they compare themselves with Castro and his family and all the privileges they have had for so many years and they feel they are only getting a small chunk of the big pie.

They can pick young women from all the organizations or from the universities and other schools, based on the ostentation of their power, their cars, and all sorts of resources and they facilitate to them access to apartments and all sorts of means not available for most of the people. They are introduced into a privileged lifestyle. Since the whole moral of the system is empty, nobody really cares.

Frequently one finds that women, who have reached high positions within the regime at some stage, have previously been involved in romantic adventures with Castro himself, when he was still younger, or with other people around him. With so many privileges available and very little overseeing, it is easy to understand that everything within the main circles of power of Cuba is corrupted.

While all this occurs, many members of the families of most of these figures, who have been able to witness what really was going on around them, tend to become disenchanted at one point or another, and it has become frequent to see the children of them, or their former spouses, leaving Cuba as well to establish in Europe, the United States, or other countries.

When some of them narrate their stories, some people open their eyes, but it is surprising to see how little concern for all this exists in this world. Apparently, the world has just gotten tired of Castro, his people, and his revolution and is only waiting for them to pass away and they do not care anymore for something that everybody knows is a disaster.

CHAPTER XI

⟋

The Cuban youth: The generation gap

One of the factors that contributed to the attraction many Cubans felt for Castro and his revolution in 1959, was that he and most of the other main leaders within his movement were relatively young, and many people, who were ignorant of his background, developed some kind of illusory hope in the idea of having a better government that was formed by younger personalities, who were not connected to many of the problems the Cuban republic had experienced in the past.

When Castro started to introduce a different kind of speech to address the main topics of Cuban politics, many Cubans believed in him because they were convinced that the new young figure he represented was being honest and they could not see behind his appearance the bad intentions he really had.

When some of the main political figures existing in Cuba at that time realized, almost immediately, of Castro's real intentions and tried to alert the Cubans, most people could not accept that a young man like Castro was able, with all premeditation, to do what these other experienced figures were denouncing. It was some kind of fascination, comparable to the one many people develop for pop artists in our days.

The Cuban revolution was introduced to the Cuban people and to the world, with the invaluable assistance of some national and international press, as a movement of the Cuban youth, created to eradicate all sorts of illnesses, real and imaginary, the Cuban society and political system had. This proved to be one of the most elaborated and fraudulent acts of political sale the twentieth century saw.

In reality, what Castro brought with him was an old model of corruption, autocracy, and hatred, which was copied with some tropical variances from the ones that had originated in the Soviet Union and Germany, earlier in the century, and had nothing to do with the illusory hopes of people in the pure values of youth.

Castro was exactly the opposite of the young pure ideals many people insisted stubbornly in seeing in him. Why so many people adopted such an idiotic posture is a very long topic to discuss.

The case was that, once in power, Castro almost immediately prioritized a number of actions designed precisely to eliminate most of those among the other young leaders, who were present in the new government and had shown brilliant personalities in the short time they had accompanied him, during the first stage of his fight.

There is no doubt that they could truly have represented the real interests of the Cuban people and this represented the first consummated action against the Cuban youth of the many Castro has committed since then.

One after another and in different ways, those new leaders were eliminated from his government and the rebel army. Some even died in strange circumstances, others were imprisoned and killed by Castro's firing squads, after spurious trials, and there were cases in which they were forced to leave Cuba. Those among these described valid young leaders, who remained in Cuba, were neutralized by the mediocrity around them and absorbed by the process and never again played any key role.

At the end, very few of them survived. The ones who replaced them were neutral, anodyne, and docile elements, without the imagination, courage, dignity, and intelligence to become in any way competitors to Castro.

The way Castro has dealt with Cuban youth along these past five decades is characteristic of his modus operandi and a copy of what he learned in his readings about some European notorious figures, like Stalin and Hitler, who represented the communism and fascism models.

He created a number of organizations to recruit and enroll as many youngsters as possible, and he defined a continuing number of activities to engage and keep busy them in a way that facilitated their indoctrination and control and ultimately guaranteed their support for all sorts of actions.

From the secondary schools to the universities, from the armed forces to the working places, he created a double set of organizations, one with a wide participation and less ideological commitment, the other much more strict in its commitment to the communist system, both with the joint purpose of forcing the enrollment of every young man or woman in the activities oriented by Castro. Thus, one can find in one side the Federation of University Students and the Association of Students of Secondary and in the other, the more deeply politicized Union of Communist Youth, which has more severe requirements of commitment. The leaders imposed by Castro to all of them are selected with the clear purpose of establishing a political machinery that can allow Castro to orient and control this very large number of young people with a close grip.

The Federation of Secondary Students and the Federation of University Students (a caricature of the one who existed before he took power) are the equivalent of what the trade unions are for the workers, all based all on the communist model.

The former student organizations that existed before Castro were totally refurbished, according to the new requirements established by him, in order to enroll every student and facilitate their mobilization and control, while the Union of Communist Youth, under the guidance and control of the Communist Party, was conceived as a more ideologically selective one, dedicated to implement Castro's policies and guarantee the total control on this huge sector of Cuban society.

In the improbable event that something could eventually get out of control, he also recruited some of the most unscrupulous among those youngsters. He started to recruit as soon as he took power or that came with him from the Sierra Maestra, for his secret services, to ensure that he could oversee in another manner what was happening, and if necessary, he could use his repressive machinery to put everything under control.

Obviously, such an elaborated scheme, supported by the whole machinery of the centralized state, allowed the manipulation of millions of young people according to Castro's political ambitions.

However, it was practically impossible that in a country with the traditions of free thinking that Cuba had, this scheme could be easily accepted by all of the young people, even considering the enormous pressure on all of them created by Castro's political machinery and he could not avoid having numerous problems with this sector of Cuban society.

Cuban youth normally were used in general to be independent and liked to have their own freedom and space, and they did not like the imposition of ideas and certain patterns of restricted behavior and it is not surprising to see that Castro had enormous difficulties in dealing with Cuban youth.

No matter all the meticulous efforts he developed trying to neutralize and manipulate the Cuban youth, he has not been able to achieve a total control of this sector of our society.

Apparently, the traditions of independence that the Cuban youth have inherited have been too strong, even considering the imposing force of Castro's ideological machinery, and he has not been able to eliminate them.

The gigantic machinery of repression created by Castro, established to eliminate any kind of dissent against his regime, has had numerous problems when dealing with the young portion of the Cuban population, and this reflects in the fact that they have been the largest group within the prisons of the island and among those who have lost their lives at sea, trying to escape from the island.

Soon after he took control of the new Cuban government, Castro started promoting a set of slogan campaigns and enrollment activities conceived to procure the separation of many young people from their families in order to facilitate the quick indoctrination of them, this including young women and men, many of whom were really still teenagers.

He organized, for instance, the Campaign of Alphabetization and surreptitiously appointed many old cadres of the former Socialist Party, to be in charge of the main distribution center, created for the supervision and training of those youngsters who were recruited, who were then sent to the rural areas of Cuba, with the idealistic hope of teaching the people who were illiterate how to read and write.

The mentioned training basically consisted in explaining to them how to introduce to their future students the new booklets, printed in a rush by Castro's incipient propaganda machinery, to be used as textbooks for the campaign, which introduced a number of political concepts that were obviously according to Castro's political vision, and in reality, they were more a work of propaganda for the regime he was trying to consolidate than any educational activity.

For nine months, those young people were separated from their families and brought to live in the rural areas, dressed with a uniform and under the control and guidance of Castro's Ministry of Education, which was already under the guidance of one of Castro's closest followers.

The whole personnel of that ministry, including most Cuban teachers, were simultaneously oriented by the same political rules and incorporated to the same campaign.

Castro also developed a quick campaign to recruit a legion of youngsters for a newly created rebel youth organization, and he created several brigades with them, which were sent, already under a military structure of command, to escalate the mountains of the Sierra Maestra, in order, according to Castro, to be trained as future military cadres. They were called the Five Peaks because they had to climb the five highest points of the mountains while on their way they were quickly indoctrinated and disciplined.

As I mentioned, Castro did not lose time either in promoting a number of young people, among those he found easier to manage, to become the new pseudo leaders of the student movement within the high school institutes, and more relevant, he backed some figures of his preference in the elections for the main positions within the Federation of University Students, which had been a very important organization for many years. In most cases, Castro manipulated the results to guarantee the election of those he supported.

There were other young people with better leadership conditions, who were vetoed by Castro and this created a number of conflicts and caused that some of these other leaders were later imprisoned, and one of them, Pedro Luis Boitel, became a legendary figure within the Cuban political prisoners.

Boitel was killed in prison, when his cell was fully blocked, following Castro's orders, depriving him of water and medical attention, while he was in the middle of one of many hunger strikes he had declared to oppose the repressive measures the prisoners were suffering. This was an extremely cruel act, which showed the criminal nature of Castro, as well as that of the main accomplices he had in charge of his Ministry of Interior.

Many young leaders, who opposed Castro's measures and policies, had to leave the country and continued fighting against Castro from abroad. Some of them decided to take again their arms and went to the mountains of Escambray, to try to recreate a guerrilla war, this time try to overcome Castro's government; others participated in the short-lived urban clandestine movement that followed Castro's assumption of power and his establishment of new rules of government, and in many cases, they lost their lives in those actions.

After a few years, Castro had already established a great deal of control on all the student movement and the Cuban youth and had positioned a large number of anodyne figures to all the main positions within the youth organizations that had been created or redefined as I described earlier in this chapter.

Castro continued introducing different variations of the same scheme in the following decades, and this way, he moved to the rural areas most of the secondary schools, to force again the young people to be separate of their parents and their influence.

With the pretext of employing them in all sorts of crazy and unproductive agricultural plans, in which, by the way, they did not get any monetary compensation, he procured to divert them from the traditional values of the Cuban families and keep indoctrinating generation after generation. The social and economic consequences of this abnormal policies had been enormous.

As we have mentioned, the Cuban armed forces became, during this time, a huge machinery, and young people were massively forced to participate in them, something that allowed Castro to use this large force for whatever irrational purpose he developed in his mind, well in Cuba, or in other countries where he sent his forces with the support of the Soviet Union. Many of these young Cubans found their death in those adventures.

The percentage of the youth within the Cuban society has been decreasing rapidly during these past decades because, due to the limitations in which people live, the rate of birth has been lowering to become the lowest in Latin America, but even considering this factor, approximately 40 percent of the Cuban population is under thirty-five years old.

Several generations of Cubans have lived all their young years under Castro's government. The only thing that Castro has offered and given to all these generations of young Cubans, many of whom have already become old men and women, are empty promises, which have never been even close to materialize, and absurd sacrifices, which have consumed their lives, with no logical purpose.

It is really sad to see how so many people have wasted their best years and even their whole lives, under a failed and irrational system, with no chance or remote possibility of achieving the common sense goal of simply living in a climate of freedom, dignity, and real opportunity, some values that generations of Cubans sadly have not known.

There is no doubt, considering one by one the humiliations and limitations that millions of Cubans have suffered, that the level of frustration accumulated by these mentioned generations have to be extremely high. Castro managed to hide this reality, with his repression and his propaganda, but there is no way that this does not exist.

But Castro's actions and their consequences go much farer than the frustration caused to several generations of young people within Cuba. Due to his policies, hundreds of thousands of young people have been forced to migrate, and one can measure that, according to their achievements in other countries, they represented an invaluable treasure for the development of Cuba, which was dilapidated by this regime.

It can be said that the energy and entrepreneurial power that Cuba could have had for several generations has been annihilated or wasted by Castro and this explains the enormous decrease of the Cuban conditions of living and its social and economic progress.

The suffering caused by Castro to several generations of people and specifically the damage caused to their lives in their best years, when they were still young, cannot be compensated with anything.

It is not only that all these people have grown up and spent their lives living in each day more and more primitive conditions and under more astringent and irrational rules, but the fact that they have not known most of the main conquests and developments the Western civilization has achieved and consolidated, at worldwide scale, during these decades, from freedom of speech to religious liberty, from free enterprise to the ability to travel without restrictions, from free elections to internet services, to mention just few examples, the Cuban youth have not had the chance to experience them.

Even when many Cuban young people seem to accept Castro's system and pretend to live normally under its astringent rules and institutions, this is not necessarily their real thinking. They have grown up conscious of the repression around them, something they have learned to coexist daily in their lives, but they are not idiots. Every young man and woman in Cuba has, in the depth of his or her mind, a will for a different life that could fulfill their dreams of progress and freedom.

The degree in which they keep for themselves their frustrations is explained by the fact that Cuba has become a country in which a simple critical word can represent many years of prison, or the separation of their careers and activities, but this does not mean that they are satisfied with what they receive from Castro and his regime, or that they accept the limitations imposed during all these decades to every young man and women by this government that has growingly become the dictatorship of an obsolete group of totally immoral and eroded figures on the rest of the Cuban people.

Cuban young people, white and black, asked themselves, in precautious silence, why they cannot assume the key positions of leadership within their society and have to afford for five decades the same ignorant, demagogic and manipulative corrupt regime, represented by a quasi mythological and irrational structure of power, in which a man without real patriotic or moral merits, with his gang of criminals, pretend to be eternally in charge.

One of the main sensors that can be used to measure the level of frustration of the Cuban youth, as well as the degree in which the young people are simply tired of the heavy load the Castros imposes on them, is the sad fact that a very large number of Cubans, most by far young ones, have been all these years trying to escape from the island in primitive rafts to go to the United States and other countries, a very dangerous and brave decision, considering the enormous risks they have to take in the treacherous waters of the Strait of Florida, which is full of sharks and is well-known for its changing weather conditions.

A person has to be totally desperate to assume such a level of risk; however, hundreds of thousands of Cubans have decided to take this risk before remaining under Castro's rule. This should speak by itself.

One must consider how is it possible that the number of foreigners who went to live in Cuba before the revolution was much higher than the number of Cubans who went to live and work abroad at that time, when they were free to do so, and under Castro, a situation totally opposite like this could develop? There is only one answer: Castro was a nightmare and young people want to live their dreams of freedom, no matter what the price, even if it cost them their lives. It shows their disposition to assume the upmost sacrifice in order to be free. They prefer to die than live under Castro.

The number of young Cubans who have lost their lives trying to escape from Castro is not exactly known, and the regime keeps secret these statistics, which obviously Castro is not interested to present, but the number is for sure in the many tens of thousands.

Only for this, there would never be a justification for Castro to remain in power. It is the cruelest sign of the failure of his system. But Castro has supinely ignored the meaning of this message, in the name of his unlimited and sick ambition of power.

The fact is that, with total lack of scruples, Castro has ignored the implicit call for freedom behind this tragic result of his wrong policies, which should have been enough for any government in the world to renounce and dissolve and their members to be put in jail for life, but on top of this, he has also brutally repressed these young men, with all his power, which is an indicator of the barbarity of his regime and himself.

Castro ordered repeatedly that units of the Cuban navy attack and destroy the fragile rafts and boats of many of those caught at sea while trying to leave Cuba, and thousands of young people have disappeared for this cause, leaving behind no sign of where they went.

Castro tried to keep their deaths secret, but frequently, somehow, details of many cases have reached their relatives, who have had to remain silent with their sorrow due to Castro's repression, until one day they manage to leave Cuba themselves and tell their stories.

Many other young people have not died or been killed, but have been captured and put in jail for many years, accused of trying to leave illegally the island. The legal processes against them have followed a well-formatted farce.

In recent years, due to the international pressure, Castro's followers hypocritically changed the laws, saying that these intents to leave the island were no longer going to be considered a crime, which has not been the case in numerous occasions. Those who are captured are punished and checked by the police and the secret services.

How is possible that such criminal actions of this regime have remained almost ignored by the international press and by so many political figures in this world? Some of these are the same people who enjoy Castro's favors and many of them discredit with their actions those governments and international organizations, which have made their policy look to the other side, indirectly becoming Castro's accomplices in these crimes.

There is no doubt that only honest explanation for the above is that they have lacked the moral capacity to defend the right of the Cuban people to be free.

The significance of this disgraceful result of the Cuban revolution is such that it cannot be ignored even for a person that is under the effect of all the propaganda that Castro develops to try to distort this.

Those young people who have died, as well as those who have successfully reached other countries to restart their lives, have their relatives and friends in Cuba and they are remembered and loved. They would not be dead or away if Castro was not there.

The component of young people within the Cuban society in the island has been shrinking for many years due not only to the continuing exodus to other countries, but also because the young couples, as I explained, are avoiding to have babies due to their desperation in regard to the difficult conditions in which they are living and the lack of housing and other means to raise their children. This situation tends to aggravate and it is not clear what will be the situation of young people in the coming years, if the system is not changed radically.

There is a permanent trend, in some media and political circles, to express an almost innocent hope in the surge of new younger political figures in Cuba and this usually comes associated with the impression that, even if they are contaminated by their role within the present regime, people feel that new figures cannot be as bad as Castro and they should probably become more open to a more modern and logical political system.

Castro's regime response to these mentioned hopes has repeatedly been the same. One after another, all those younger figures he has promoted and used for some time, after regularly having selected them among the most unscrupulous within his political machinery, one day are denounced and dismissed of their positions, whichever they were, and this has been used to prove to everybody his immense power, which has been able, in each case, to vanish in one second, with a stroke of his pen, all the imaginary or real power these new younger figures may have had.

The sick, paranoiac mind of Castro could not accept competitors, and even less if they are young and could represent a negation of him and his generation of leaders. One wonders how a man like this can govern a country if he is not able to deal with the natural evolution of the world.

In my view, what Castro wished, and he may have been very carefully planning for many years, is to guarantee a continuation of his regime when he disappears, but in a different sense of what many of even his own people would think.

I am convinced that he wants to preserve the power he has accumulated, not necessarily under the same system but through his family, and he has been protecting some of his sons and other members of it, avoiding as much as possible that they are overexposed and mixed in violent actions.

He has patiently tried to introduce them to the highest levels of power and provide them with all sorts of means and connections that not many other people of their age have in Cuba at this moment, and he may be planning that when he and his brother cannot command anymore and the conditions are ready, they can jump safely to positions of power, that is, if things happens as he would like.

The above would have a curious side that is precisely what this means to other young Cubans, including those who have sacrificed to ascend within his own organizations.

Castro pretended, in my view, to try to overcome whatever role other older people at the top of his regime could aspire in case of his death and after his brother Raúl cannot continue in his role of protector of Castro's establishment and legacy, but even more, he wishes to implement a process, in which these younger members of the Castro family can supplant with little effort their elders, leaving aside also all the other young cadres within the party and the armed forces, who could have legitimate aspirations to the most important positions.

If they need to use the power of his secret services and a new campaign of terror for this, they will not vacillate.

One must wonder how the internal process of transition in a country like Korea and places like that must have been, in order to understand that, in Cuba, everything is possible.

There are a number of facts regarding these younger Castros, which people usually do not give much attention, in part because they have been kept outside the day-to-day exposure and isolated from any regular observation.

These facts seem to define that Castro carefully prepared a sort of contingency plan, to try to ensure that his main young relatives have, at least, a real good chance of getting some key control, after his death and that of his brother, within the future structure of power, with all what this means in regard to political and economic matters.

The sons, daughters, and grandchildren of Castro and his brother Raúl have had access to all sorts of means and connections, which are unthinkable for practically any other young Cuban of their generations, even those few who have been in relatively high positions.

They have had plenty of money, which has allowed them to keep a lifestyle prohibited to all the other youngsters in Cuba and they have been allowed to travel as much as they want, having a different kind of training and education. They have been oriented to establish links with all sorts of people in other countries, and they have been involved in all sorts of transactions made by Castro, including investments in different countries, designed to ensure that, in any event, his family will be safe.

While practically all the other young people within the ranks of Castro's system have had to work and fight hard to get promotions and to achieve some usually basic improvements in their status, the members of the new Castro generations have not needed to do much to have infinitely more.

Curiously, but not casually, most of Castro's young siblings have not been identified with the repression of the regime, including even those who have been given high military ranks already, something that has allowed them more natural connections with many people abroad, who may look at them in a more acceptable way than other figures within the top levels of the political machinery.

These younger Castro have become used to dealing with a more real world, at a high level, and they have been placed in positions that facilitate their compatibility with a possibly different future situation, something that is not the case with most of the other young cadres who have grown up and operated within the crazy structures and mechanisms of the regime and have been wrapped by its empty slogans and precepts and the absurd controls on their whole lives, having remained mostly ignorant of the actual conditions of the rest of the world.

While most Cubans have been mostly isolated from the advancement of the world in practically every aspect, ideological, cultural, or material, these other young members of Castro's family have grown up used to them and all these mentioned elements could give to them an enormous advantage at the time of defining who and what comes after Castro.

Even more, most of these young members of Castro's family have become familiar with all sorts of strange handlings in business and commercial transactions, as well as in the methods and procedures used in a machinery of corruption like the one Castro has freely operated by so many years.

On top of all this, they have been able to witness, from privileged seats, how Castro's revolution operates, learning all the methods of betrayal, corruption, and intimidation. They are used to the low moral values and the lack of scruples, which have been implemented by Castro as part of his basic order and they have even been able to practice their learning, under the protective aura of their parents, which want to make sure they can assume other roles when the time comes.

For Castro, a man used to see things in a way different than the way others see them and used to plan much farer ahead than most other people, who are used to deal with the immediate events, it apparently has became extremely important to ensure that his family is well positioned, to, at least, have a very good chance of keeping control of his regime, when he was no longer in this earth.

The above may even consider the possibility of introducing a number of basic changes to make the system more acceptable and compatible with the rest of the world, something that, among other things, will help not only to preserve what he considers his legacy, but as important or more than this, will allow them to keep all the assets and monetary resources stolen by him, including those he enjoys in Cuba as well as those he has surreptitiously acquired in other countries, which he considers would allow them, in any scenario, to survive whatever it happens after his death and that of his brother.

It will be a serious challenge for the young Cubans, and in general for the people of Cuba, to disrupt these contingency plans that may have been prepared in detail by Castro's diabolic mind, based on his corruption and sick ambitions, with which he may try to extend and perpetuate beyond his life, his current powers.

Most people have come to believe, based in the evidences gathered after all these decades of Castro's absolute power, in which nothing seriously challenged his power, that Cubans will have to wait for his brother Raúl's death to start seeing changes in Cuba and they do not venture much about what kind of changes they can expect, considering the kind of system existing in the island and the existence of other people within the party and the government who could attempt to continue the system on a similar pattern.

I believe that the Cuban people, especially the young ones, can have a better hope and that they can overcome Castro and his regime before his brother pass away.

There are many relatively young people in all sectors of Cuban society, from the military to the exile community, who do not like what is happening in their own country and can promote a serious challenge to Castro's people.

A good example of the resolution that young people may be reaching to remove Castro's system from power was the hunger strike of Orlando Tamayo, a humble dissident, who preferred to die than accept Castro's oppression, which has served as an awakening to many people in the world about the state of things in Cuba. Castro and his brother and all his acolytes left Tamayo die, trying to show to other possible followers that they would not vacillate to kill as many people as necessary to stay in power, but this may back fire on them. It may be that other young people start thinking that a more violent approach is their only solution to end this dictatorship.

Cubans must convince themselves that the Castro's regime is not invincible and that they can be free. They must understand the feasibility of changing the system. If they start trying to do so, even if logically, they must assume their risks, like other generations have done and at that point. They must be very conscious that, in order to be able to recuperate the real Cuba, they must get rid not only of his brother but also of all this bunch of parasites and corrupted figures, who have grown up under him.

CHAPTER XII

~

The Cubans in exile

It is well-known and recognized that the Cuban exiled community, formed by the Cubans of several generations, who left Cuba to come to the United States and other countries during the past five decades, has been able to reach a considerable high level of prosperity and has been able to show numerous achievements in practically in every branch of society and everywhere they have established.

It is also a fact that most of these Cubans and their families were forced by Castro to leave the island with only the clothes they had on and they had to start their lives all over again, in many cases at mid age.

Obviously, the effort that these generations of Cubans had to make in order to be able to succeed in the countries they have established has been enormous. There is no way this can be ignored.

For many years, Castro procured to focus a great deal of his propaganda in presenting the Cuban exiled community as a sort of corrupt and violent social entity, which only dreams of reestablishing the past order in Cuba. This, of course, has not mean for him and his followers to refuse the dollars the exiled Cubans bring to the island, when they go to visit their families, or the continuing stream of money they keep sending to their relatives, to try to sustain them in most of the cases.

Many authors have tried to describe and analyze the main events and achievements of the Cuban community, some with more success than others, and I feel that it is not necessary that I get into details on this in this book; however, one thing that calls my attention is the fact that one must wonder what these generations of Cubans, generally lovers of freedom and an entrepreneurial kind of people, would have been able to develop in their own country, if they had lived in a Cuba without Castro.

Their success seems to be an indication that, in general, the people who left Cuba represented the most entrepreneurial class within Cuban society, those who, as an average, had the strongest force of character, will, and independent spirit to create, organize, and develop all sorts of productive activities and were willing to work and struggle against all odds, until they achieved their goal.

There is also the fact that, on top of the above, one of the reasons for the success the Cubans have had, especially in the United States, which has made their community one of the most successful, among the many nationalities living here, is the fact that they found, in their new country, a stable system of law and economic rules, which evidently allowed them to develop their efforts, within a better-established and organized order than the one existing in Cuba, and this facilitated to them to canalize their sane ambitions of progress and energies, in a highly productive fashion.

Apparently, Cubans are made for democracy and freedom because when their achievements are compared with the disaster created by Castro and his system in the island during these past decades, the results are appalling.

The fact also emerges, when analyzing the average success of Cubans compared with that of people from other countries, that they have been apparently better prepared to adapt to the American society than other people, maybe because they had, in their background, the influence of the way in which the Cuban society, before Castro, followed the lead of America and tried to replicate its economic achievements, by incorporating all sorts of technological and organizational advances, within an environment of freedom and opportunity.

Considering the above, one can reach the conclusion that Castro's policies destroyed the normal path of development the Cuban society had and introduced it into chaos.

If Cuba had continued its development, under what logically should have been a sort of improved democracy, in comparison with what it had, in which numerous social and economic conquests, as well as new products and methods that came with the advance of civilization during these decades, had been introduced, the level of development of our country would be very high now, and most likely, Cuba would be a very developed nation.

Many of the most relevant figures, who participated with Castro in the revolution, were democrats, who had a clear vision about what Cuba needed and they wanted to improve the way Cuba was governed, in order to facilitate the conditions to bring Cuba to a higher stage of economic development. They came from all sorts of professions, from lawyers to civil engineers.

These men, in some extent, were kind of visionaries, who could foresee a better and developed Cuba, in a short period of time, by having an honest and dedicated government that could help in the development of all sectors of the economy and use in Cuba's favor the characteristics and resources of the island and its closeness to the United States.

When Castro betrayed and sacrificed those ideals of the original Cuban revolution in order to satisfy his political ambitions, most of these men opposed him almost immediately and, with their enormous energy and potential, took different avenues to resolutely try bringing back to its track what they considered their own movement.

Many of these people and their families decided to leave Cuba to continue their fight against Castro from the United States, and due to their capacity, courage, and energy, they were very quickly connected to the highest levels of the American society and government, who found in them a natural ally against the communist forces, which were trying to establish in the continent using Cuba as a base and Castro as its promoter.

During the initial years of Castro's revolution, when the spirits and energies of those mentioned people were still fresh, after having fought against Batista, many of them tried very actively to promote all sorts of movements and actions against the new regime Castro was trying to establish in Cuba, which was exactly the opposite of what they wished for their country.

They found that Castro was a different kind of enemy than Batista and that he lacked any scruples and was willing to implement a level of repression never seen nor known in Cuba to stay in power and that he had a extraordinary capacity to manipulate and mobilize a large portion of the Cuban people against them, which was paradoxical, considering that they were risking their lives to try to save precisely their country.

This original first wave of democratic revolutionaries, who came to the United States still having close connections within Cuba, were also willing to do whatever it was necessary to recover their country and they gave to the Cuban exiled community an impromptu of ideas and energies, focused in the liberation of Cuba, but also able to serve as an introductory statement for the American society, which opened its doors to them and all of the other Cubans who were coming to the United States, showing the same love for freedom and resolution to oppose Castro and his communism, which came from the bottom of their hearts.

The years passed and the dreams of all those people, who represented the first wave of exiled Cubans, did not materialize and Castro consolidated his regime, showing a visceral hatred for those who opposed him.

Castro and the exiled community became the opposite antagonistic poles of the great disaster to which the island was brought.

After many failures in their attempts to overthrow Castro, including some disgraceful events, among them the defeat of Bay of Pigs, as well as the defeat of the movement against Castro inside Cuba, including those people in arms at the Escambray Mountains and those operating clandestinely within the cities, the possibility of continuing that kind of actions started to diminish and they became more difficult to materialize and with this any real chance of producing a movement to liberate the island started to decline.

There have been many critics of the role of President Kennedy in regard to the failed expedition of Bay of Pigs, but it may be that history gives at least some attenuation in regard to his actions related to these events.

There is no doubt that the critics to the wrong handling of all the events that culminated with the attempted invasion of Bay of Pigs have merits, however there are other aspects of Kennedy's actions which deserve recognition. It may well be that even his death may have been associated with the actions he was planning and executing in regard to Cuba.

Many new pieces of information that remained secret for almost half a century are slowly coming to light and researchers are finding on them all sorts of evidences about the resolute will of Kennedy and his brother Robert to overthrow the government of Castro, describing their involvement in actions that were extremely risky for them, considering the political situation within the United States at that time and the risk these actions implied for their own lives, considering Castro's animosity, as well as that of other powerful enemies they were dealing with.

There are important elements within the whole complicated set of events surrounding the assassination of President Kennedy, which could associate Castro to it, even when recent authors and researchers have put more emphasis in describing the existence of a conspiracy, with members of the intelligence community and the mafia participating in it, together with some important political figures and even including some members and figures of the Cuban exiled community.

The assassination of President Kennedy had an immediate and enormous impact on the cause for the liberation of Cuba and most operations designed to overthrow Castro, that were being planned at that time, including the participation of figures and resources of the American government, were postponed and ultimately cancelled.

Kennedy was the last American president who tried to implement a military and political action against Castro that could be considered viable to overthrow his regime.

After Kennedy, all the other presidents, even those who were deeply and sincerely sympathetic to the cause of liberating Cuba, have not been able to go much further than expressing their support to the exiled community and the Cuban people in general, also implementing some regulations to make more difficult to Castro the access to the American products and to financing from American banks.

One can appreciate every positive action of support, but it is just fair to recognize that the cause of Cuba is mainly nowadays something that Cubans have to start all over again.

Most of the main leaders of the exiled community during those initial years are already dead and some of the most prominent among more recent ones have also died. Some of those men were hunted by Castro's secret agents in Miami and other countries and others died in strange circumstances.

They could feel, in the years following Kennedy's assassination, the change in the perception that other American and world politicians had on their cause, and at some moment in their lives, they could realize as well that conditions had changed and they could not mobilize anymore the huge political and military energies, which were needed to effectively oppose the Castro.

They were also witnesses of all the efforts of Castro's propaganda to try to destroy their reputation and all the hatred and misinformation against them inoculated by him among the Cuban people and in international political circles.

They could even see how, as a result of the extraordinary economic success that many Cubans have had in the United States and other countries and the level of influence this has brought with it, in regard to American politics as well as in the way Cubans in general are considered within the American society, this has been sometimes been used to generate wrong feelings from other communities, or even among people within Cuba, who tend to ignore the enormous sacrifices behind these achievements.

They also had to accept a much more limited role and the reality of the almost total lack of resources to carry on their cause, even when they kept their hope for a free Cuba and tried to do what they could to this end.

Most Cuban organizations have existed mainly in paper and they have been very limited in the resources they have had to develop their activities and this has made them almost inexistent and unable to produce much impact.

Most Cuban organizations, like the Cuban Patriotic Board, an umbrella of many small political organizations and a number of exiled personalities, have had for many years a very small budget to carry on its activities and there are only a small group of organizations, which are those that include among their members some successful business leaders, that have the capacity to promote activities that can have a real political weight, which can translate in the achievement of political influences and effective support.

As time passed, those leaders had also to deal with the reality that the much-needed new generations of Cubans within the exiled community, including those who grew up in the United States and also many others who have kept coming from Cuba, became subject to the complex realities of the world in which we live and devote more time to their work than to patriotic activities, in part because they have to keep their families, this gradually diminishing their role in the continuation of those efforts to free Cuba.

There are important exceptions to the above and some brilliant and enthusiastic young Cubans, especially those who belong to the Cuban Democratic Directory, have developed important initiatives to oppose Castro, which have been successful, but in general, the new generations of Cubans in the United States sadly seem to be more interested in other things, including those activities associated with their professions, than in fighting for the freedom of Cuba, even when they usually show obvious signs of their attraction and love for Cuban values.

Due probably to the fact that they got tired of so many political pressures in Cuba for many years, other young Cubans who have been coming from the island during the past two decades, generally also avoid in large extent participating in political activities to oppose Castro and they do not seem to be interested in devoting their time to them. There are exceptions again, but this is in general the rule.

Several times during these past decades, Castro has decided to allow the migration of important numbers of former political prisoners, well, because they had finished their usually long sentences and he did not like them on the streets in Cuba, or because they were still in prison and their liberation was negotiated with him by different world leaders, governments, or organizations of human rights. Most of these men and women have come to the United States because they could not stay in Cuba.

Each wave of political prisoners that has come from Cuba has brought new impressions and experiences to the exiled community. Many of these men and women are already old, after sacrificing their best years for the cause of freedom, but they keep alive the sentiments of love for their country and remain an invaluable source of dignity and resolution in their opposition to Castro and continue participating in the different political organizations, most of which are each day smaller, due to the crude reality of the deaths of their members.

The case of those former political prisoners deserves honor and recognition because they suffered all the force of Castro's repression against them and their families, and despite this, they are still present in every way they can, to show their resolution, no matter their everyday worse conditions of health, because of their age, and the many ailments they inherited from their years in prison.

They have had to work very hard and with honor for their living in their new country, despite their usually advanced age, and after so many sacrifices in their lives, they remain resolute in their hope to see a new free Cuba.

There are many Cuban organizations in the United States, Spain, and other countries, that have remained active in one way or another in their opposition to Castro all these years, and they regularly denounce the violation of human rights and the repressive conditions in the island while they try to give support to the many regularly small groups of opposition that have been created there during the past two decades.

The support to the Cuban dissidents and the denounce of the situation in Cuba have become the most important functions for most of them, which all deserve recognition and are extremely valuable, but unfortunately, they mostly represent a drop in the sea and their chances of overthrowing Castro, which should be their ultimate goal, have become remote.

If certainly all these organizations have an important role to play, trying to denounce in front of governments, the media, and international organizations the terrible conditions in which Castro has kept the Cuban people, their chances of actively promoting a real widespread movement within the island have been limited because their resources are based more in their moral and endurable spirit than in the actual means they have to carry on their activities.

Castro tried to vilify with his propaganda the exiled community in front of the population of the island in order to create a separation of interests and perceptions and he has tried hard with his secret services to destroy any possibility of coordinated and effective actions to create a solid and effective movement within the exiled community, which could at least serve as the initiator of a wider movement within the island oriented to oppose effectively the Castro's regime and bring his system down.

There is an enormous unbalance between the resources that Castro was able to use, including his propaganda machinery, his money, and his secret services, even in the worst economic moments of his regime, and those of that the existing Cuban organizations within the exiled community can mobilize, no matter the economic and social status of their members.

Even when many Cuban personalities have achieved high political, social, and economic positions within the American society as well as in other countries where they live and the Cuban exiled community has become a recognizable economic and political element, something that reflects in general in some important political influences, it is not easy to mobilize the numerous different interests, which coexist in these countries, to denounce Castro's actions and even more difficult is to obtain an effective and full support for the fight to free Cuba from him.

Even more difficult has been to simultaneously mobilize the Cuban people in exile and that of the island, by the creation of an effective integrated movement that could change things in Cuba.

I am convinced, however, that the creation of a movement to overcome the Castro's regime is possible and the role of the exiled community within this is fundamental.

I tend to believe that it is outside Cuba, within the exiled community, where better conditions exist for the creation and development of a political movement that can expand its opposition activities to Cuba, but this is not necessarily so because there are a number of situations in Cuba that can produce a sudden spontaneous popular explosion, and if this happens, the role of the exiled community will be to follow this movement, to try to bring down Castro and his system.

There is also the possibility that something happens within the Cuban armed forces and a group of officers somehow can successfully produce a movement to overthrow Castro, or that, if there is a spontaneous popular explosion, this could create the conditions for the former.

There is no doubt that the Cuban people living abroad have the capacity to organize freely, to travel anywhere they need, and to collect funds and request cooperation while the Cubans within the island are extremely limited in regard to all this due to the repression under which they live.

There is no doubt either that the own existence of the many Cuban political organizations created within the exiled community has required an enormous amount of energy and dedication, but due to innumerable reasons, they have lacked the capacity to mobilize the whole spectrum of the Cuban exile under one single and well identified political party, in some extend due to the many superficial conflicts of personalities and the infinite number of small and large interests and conflicting political ambitions existing. Unless something happens, that can serve as a catalytic of patriotic emotions and energies, this situation is not easy to change.

Any person, who is familiar with the main attempts to develop some kind of integrated organization of exiled Cubans to oppose Castro during the past decades knows how difficult it has been to put together, even for the simplest and most elemental political actions, any group of individuals and organizations, people, and organizations that otherwise have been active to show separately their fervor to oppose his regime.

It seems that at some point, the Cubans, the same who have been successful in many other fields, cannot leave their egos and interests at home and become conscious that, if they do not follow a more practical approach and a more disciplined and modest attitude, they will never be able to overcome those formidable enemies that Castro and his regime represent.

Castro always knew of these, at times almost ridiculous, political rivalries and has been the most interested one in inducing and provoking them, using its secret services and other resources, to stimulate their growth.

Unfortunately, even when everybody seems to know this, among the political sectors of the Cuban community, very few people have been willing to sacrifice the tiniest part of the status they consider they have, to put together a real cause and movement for the liberation of Cuba.

Many leaders have been satisfied when they have organized a big parade, or a crowded event, to denounce the policies of Castro, but after this, there has usually not existed enough energy to continue with real actions.

The applauds of those present have been gratifying for most leaders, but they have not meant much for the cause of the Cuban liberation.

In large extent, there have been incredible and almost innocent illusions in most of the attempts to do something effective to fight against Castro during the past two decades, and unfortunately, politics in the world in which we live can accept everything, except that sense of innocence.

I was a participant in some illustrative events, which show clearly the problems the exiled community has had to create a real effective movement to oppose Castro. At times, there have been situations that had even their funny side, if they had not been so dramatically frustrating for all of us.

I remember when, in the early years of the decade of the nineties, there was an attempt to create a new coordinated entity in which a large number of Cuban organizations were represented like a new umbrella, but with more participants than in other existing similar organizations, to try to give a sense of unity to the political movement opposing Castro.

As a result of this effort, there was a declaration, signed by representatives of each organization in a large event organized in a theater of Miami, and there was some limited collection of money to support the patriotic activities that were being theoretically discussed.

One night, there was a call for a meeting to discuss some details that had to be decided, to create a unified approach, and some more specific actions. For some reason, the late Dr. Manuel Antonio de Varona, who was the president of the Cuban Patriotic Board and had been selected by the participants as one of the main leaders of the new unified entity, could not go to the meeting and asked me at the last minute to represent him at it.

The meeting started under the direction of several of us, who were seated in front of the rest, and almost immediately some of the participants, who represented different organizations and actually were known and respected by all of us for their bravery in different actions in Cuba and their dedication to the cause, passionately brought the discussion to the definition of one specific and crucial aspect, this being what to do with the funds that had been collected, which he and some other people insisted, were better invested in buying arms!

The discussion became really moved, with all sorts of arguments in favor and against that crucial issue and time started passing. The case was that, more than two hours later, we were still dealing with this issue and some people were really upset and even angry.

At that point, suddenly, the person who was in charge of finances and accountancy interrupted the discussion and requested that he was allowed to speak, because it was getting too late and he had to go home as he had to get up early in the morning to work.

The discussion was put on hold and he was given some time to present his report about the state of finances of the newly created entity, which showed that we had a little more than two thousand dollars in total!

No need to say that few minutes after he talked, the meeting was called to end and everybody returned home with anger and frustration and a sour taste in our mouths.

The above represents a contrast with the situation existing in the early years of Castro, when, at least some of the different movements working to free Cuba, which were mainly established in the United States due to the obvious reason that the majority of the exiled community lived here, managed to have access to important funds from many different sources, including the American government and other governments also opposed to Castro, they also having some effective support from important American and foreign political figures, who were seriously committed and interested in the liberation of Cuba.

A recent version of the book *Ultimate Sacrifice*, written by Lamar Waldron and Tom Hartmann, describes, based on new documents declassified by the American government, a number of plans that were in process simultaneously, to try to overthrow Castro, including among them an important plan that had never before been disclosed, which was in its final stage at the time of President Kennedy's assassination. Other books, written in the United States and in Cuba in recent years, also give, from different perspectives, account of other plans that were in process at that time with the same purpose.

The mentioned authors describe how the mentioned recently declassified plan to overthrow Castro was backed by the late President Kennedy and supported and organized in total secrecy by his brother Robert, according to the declassified documents and what makes it completely different is that it included the participation of some important Cuban figures within the island, who were very close to Castro in his government and also the participation of several well-known figures within the exiled community.

According to the new information that has been made available and is analyzed in detail in the mentioned book, apparently, after some contacts, an agreement was reached between some figures of the exiled community, who were very active in the fight against Castro and had a close relationship with Robert Kennedy, who had for this the full support of the president and Commander Juan Almeida, who was one of the main figures within Castro's movement, to produce a coup and overthrow Castro.

Considering that many of the main people who fought with Castro against Batista were not communist and they did not like the idea of the Soviets intervening in Cuban matters either, this may have been possible. If this was so, probably many aspects of the Cuban history of these years will have to be revised, especially considering that there may be many other events that may still be kept classified.

According to the logic of the mentioned events, it seems that there were other important people around Castro who were also ready to participate in this operation and there is speculation about the possibility that Che Guevara, who was close to Almeida, was also a participant beside him in all this.

There are a number of situations that happened in Cuba afterward involving these two figures that could indicate that they had some kind of problem with Castro at that time.

The strange situation in which Guevara left Cuba to fight in other countries seems to indicate that there were important differences behind doors involving him and Castro, and most likely the real history was substantially different than the official and redecorated stories presented by Castro's propaganda about those events, including the novelized accounts of some of Castro's people.

According to the mentioned book, those declassified records also indicate that some close relatives of Almeida went to live in Mexico at that time, as part of an agreement with him, and received money from the American government for a long time.

When President Kennedy was assassinated, the mentioned actions were in their final stage and just few days of being implemented and this tragic event stopped the whole advanced process of preparation.

Commander Almeida managed to remain being a very important figure within Castro's government for the past five decades, even when he experienced some notable ups and down at some stages, and this plan was kept classified and secret for close to forty-five years. It was considered by some participant people, one of the closest secrets that have existed in the past century in American politics.

Commander Almeida passed away recently in Cuba, in some strange circumstances. The way his funeral took place and other details of the whole treatment given to it by Castro makes suspicious this event.

It will require some time, and a new situation in Cuba, to establish more detailed facts on this and other events, including the possible participation of other important figures, also close to Castro, not only in this, but also in other events.

The recently announced and apparently large new release of documents by the National Archives may also bring more light on these little known events.

After the dismiss or failure of a number of plans, including the mentioned one and others equally designed to overthrow Castro, during the early nineteen sixties, the conditions of the world and some key aspects of American politics were gradually changing and later American leaders found increasingly difficult to give a full and open effective support to any movement or action oriented to overthrow Castro, other than expressing their sympathy for the cause of the liberation of Cuba, something that has become a regular ceremony in the visits to Miami of every American leader, as well as in their support of a number of rules, laws and regulations oriented to keep the Cuban regime isolated, at least in regard to the United States.

The resources and capacity of the different Cuban political organizations within the exiled community diminished considerably as a result of all of the above, and they experienced as well the erosion produced by the long time that has passed since Castro took power, this no doubt making very difficult to organize a new serious movement to change the course of things in the island.

I remember that, during the decade of the nineties, I had the opportunity of going to Center America with Dr. Manuel Antonio de Varona, president of the Cuban Patriotic Board, where we explained to a number of leaders the conditions existing in Cuba and discussed the possibility of getting some assistance for our cause.

We learned during that trip that, at that time, after the different wars that had taken place in the region during those years, there were important quantities of arms that had been left by those conflicts, which were not being used, and also that there were some radio facilities that remained unused there since the time in which the United States was supporting the intense struggle of several governments against the Marxist movements promoted from Havana.

We received a very encouraging support from several important political and military figures, but other than that, when we came back, we had to accept the reality that there were not enough people or means available, at least in our organization, to sustain any operations involving those resources, which was a clear sign that most of the movement to liberate Cuba had become essentially political and very limited in its means and goals.

The late Jorge Mas Canosa, president of the Cuban American National Foundation, was able to integrate a much more powerful organization, which was able to reestablish a considerable level of influence again within the high circles of American politics and this gave support to many important activities, including the operation of Radio Marti, to confront Castro's propaganda and denounce the situation of human rights in Cuba, including the liberation of political prisoners, as well as a large program to assist the new immigrants from the island.

The influence of the Foundation, as it is known, was also essential to keep in place a number of measures oriented to limit the capacity of Castro to do business with the United States, among other measures.

The Cuban National Foundation was able to operate with a larger budget than other Cuban organizations and developed considerable influence, showing a more serious Cuban presence in the American political scene and also within Cuba, where they were also active in their support to dissidents and new political organizations, but the conditions of the world kept changing and the possibility of organizing a movement to change the regime in Havana was not reached.

After Mas Canosa's premature and strange death, the Foundation unfortunately divided, and from there on the influence of the two organizations that resulted of this, the Council for the Liberation of Cuba and the Foundation itself, has not been the same, they becoming less popular and less influential within the circles of American politics, even when both organizations keep considerable economic strength, in comparison to other groups, mainly because some of their members are successful businessmen who give their financial support to them.

There have been other organizations created in recent years, mainly to try, once again, to renew the efforts to unify the political spectrum of the exiled community under one umbrella and to try to develop more and larger activities, but their role have unfortunately been very limited and their presence diffused.

One important organization created in recent years is the Cuban-American Pack, which is mainly formed by successful Cuban personalities in numerous fields, including politics and business, which develops its actions within the core levels of American politics, trying to influence those policies and regulations that have to deal with Cuba. This organization has been successful in stopping numerous attempts to open new conditions of trade and political openness with Castro.

There have also been a small number of organizations, which have become branches of international political tendencies linked to the social democracy and Catholic movements, but their role has also been limited probably due to their limited membership, even when they have some distinguished personalities among their leaders, who have been effective in their denounce of the situation in Cuba, specially at international level.

The participation of people from the large exiled community within all the Cuban organizations that exist has been decreasing through the years and it has becomes obvious that, apart from few large events that have very sporadically been organized with varied degree of success, the large population of Cubans in Miami and other cities remains mostly ignorant of their activities and do not show much interest for them, which causes that they do not contribute monetarily to them.

In many cases, the only knowledge most of the people have about the activities of these organizations comes from the participation of some of their members in a number of radio programs, but even these programs are also reducing their ratings and their audience is mainly of older people.

Many people precisely see most of these organizations as groups of elders, who basically meet periodically to talk about Cuba and organize social events, which is unfair, because, if certainly the average age of their members is elevated, each of them has the merit of not only trying to preserve the Cuban legacy, but also, despite their age, they try to continue the political opposition to Castro.

One of the issues that have influenced this mentioned decline in the participation of people in the political organizations of the exiled community is precisely the age factor. The world has changed dramatically during the past decades, and the younger generations of Cubans have been fully and successfully immersed within the development of the most advanced country in the world, in which they are used to deal with all the new technological and organizational advancements, and accordingly, they have a different interpretation of many things, which I believe we have to respect.

The cultural gap between most of the people who participate in the different political organizations of the exiled community and those young professional people, who work in all branches of the American society where they live, or those even younger ones, who are at the universities, is abysmal.

In some extent, this process keeps some similarities in regard to the age factor with what happens in Cuba, where the younger generations have the same problem when dealing with Castro and so many old people in the government, who they feel want to impose or convince them about what they must do.

There have been some attempts in recent years, among young professional Cubans, to try to develop activities related with the cause of Cuba, basically from their own perspective and with their own methods, but the fact is that they are usually very busy in other things due to the demanding conditions of the fast world in which they live, and this has made them very limited.

It is a polemic matter, but most young Cubans consider the situation of Cuba as a secondary issue, when they establish their priorities in life and this has some obvious logic, because they must first study, work, and survive in the society in which they live in order to advance in their lives.

The Cuban factor remains in their mind and probably will become more alive only if the situation of Cuba could change and they would again have the possibility of doing something practical in regard to it.

I believe that one of the factors that has influenced more the way in which the political movement to change the system in Cuba has become neutralized, and this is valid within the exiled community but also in the island, is the fact that there has not surged any new leader who could catalyze the dormant aspirations of the different sectors and age groups of the Cuban people and make them to move, to try to change the obsolete system controlling Cuba.

Castro used his many resources to deviate or eliminate the possibility of the surge of any new leader in Cuba and within the exiled community because he knows that our countries are not like some other European countries, or even the United States, in which there is a complex structure of organizations, laws, and methods, which provide continuity and control for the development of the society.

The Cubans, like the people in Latin America, are used and required to have leaders, whom they can identify and follow. After sixty years of having Castro as their wrong leader, this is even more so.

In my view, a huge mistake of the political organizations within the exiled Cuban community has been that they have not been able to accept or elect a leader, among the many valuable people who exists, who can be identified and followed not only by the exiled community, but also by the people in Cuba and at the same time can be identified and recognized by other political forces and governments.

The above does not mean that this leader has to be an isolated figure at the top, because obviously there can be a group of people around him, to assist and cooperate in the development of things.

The chances that Castro allows the surge of a new leader in Cuba have proven to be extremely low, or nonexistent, and unless somebody decides to take the risk of trying to assume that role, this is not going to come spontaneously from the system. However, outside Cuba, the only impediment to allow the surge of new leaders is in the difficulty to reach a possible agreement between the many different organizations and people who are interested in the cause of Cuba, but this so far has proven to be a real challenge, because there have been so many little interests and conflicts of personalities, rivalries, and envies, on top of Castro's secret services actions to avoid this, that there has not been practically any one that could be identified and followed.

It is interesting to me, why the Cubans have been able to elect their senators and congressmen, which give to them a participation in the

American government that no other minority has, and they have elected commissioners and mayors for some important cities and counties and have also been appointed to all sorts of positions of one American government after another, while they have not been able to select or elect a single person to be their leader in the movement to get back their country.

I remember that many years ago, during a short time I contributed some articles to the *Miami Herald*, after I was liberated in Cuba, and I wrote an article in which I said that, in my view, it was necessary to have some elections within the exiled community, to elect a leader among us and to do this periodically.

It was incredible to me the reaction I could see in many people of different organizations against this, which in general was totally out of base and could not be justified. Some people even saw in it some kind of mysterious wrong purpose to diminish their organizations, which anyway were really each formed by a small bunch of active members. They reminded me of a character of Cervantes, in *The Quixote*, his masterpiece, who had an imaginary property.

Not only has there been no way to identify a unified elected leadership, but in the case of most of these organizations, the main people running them have not changed for many years, because they have lacked any kind of real internal elections to democratically renovate regularly their leaders and create an influx of new ideas. The result is that most of these organizations of all sizes and scope have become mostly ankylosed.

On the other hand, I could see that many people on the street, who were not related to any of the existing organizations but loved Cuba as their country, had a different view on this and agreed that this could be good, and this made me feel that, somehow, the cause of a free Cuba may have been involuntarily limited by these organizations, which even now do not understand that they go nowhere if the whole structure of them does not change.

The above gave me the feeling that most of the fault for the exiled community not to have been able, after all these years, to achieve considerably more success, as is required in reaching the goal of changing the system in Cuba, can be identified with the stubborn way most of the political organizations of the exiled community and many of their leaders have not been able to accept the reality that they mean very little separately and one cannot pretend to oppose a monster like Castro with such a divided and fragmented force.

It is interesting to mention that at some moment, during the early years of the revolution, the American government found serious difficulties to deal with the organizations of the exiled community, because they wanted to work together with the Cubans to overthrow Castro, but there were so many hundreds of them that they got confused about with whom to deal.

Unfortunately, the above has not changed much and the main factor that has contributed in some extend to the reduction of the number of members in many of them is that they have passed away and their tiny organizations have become virtually nonexistent.

The above has been another obstacle for the participation of young people in the political activities opposing Castro. They do not understand this strange way of doing things of the older generation within these organizations and they feel that their way of thinking and acting is not compatible with theirs.

The Cuban exile represents a large and important power, which can become the engine to support an effective movement to change the status of Cuba and to participate actively in the future development of the island, as one of its most important elements, but it has still to find a way to channel this potential.

CHAPTER XIII

$\smile$

The persecution of free thinking under Castro

Fidel Castro was a strange man and he has problems with many things, especially if they represented something that could, even remotely, contradict his interpretation of events, or his orders, and obviously, this makes extremely difficult for him to accept that other people may have different criteria and ideas.

This is especially more so when they refer to something he considered that could interfere, somehow, with his status as an absolute leader, that is, a leader that was like a god, above everyone and everything around him.

Even when his propaganda tried to present him as an open and progressive man, worried by all sorts of causes of social justice and a promoter of good values, the reality was completely different. He was a dictator to the full extent of the word, who has managed to be in power for half a century using his violence and repression against anybody that he did not like or distrust.

Right since the beginning of his revolution, he started eliminating people around him, among those who had been part of his movement in the opposition to Batista, but had different views than his. No matter if they were good and intelligent people, he simply could not accept that they had the slightest different view than him because, in the bottom of things, what he wanted was to achieve total control of the government of Cuba and not to govern according to any sort of democratic and civilized rule.

Evidently, after eliminating from the revolution, in one way or another, all those who could represent some kind of challenge to his ideas and ambitions, the only people who remained beside him were those who had a much lower level of intellect or those who, even having the intellectual capacity to interpret things differently, were too coward or too opportunistic to do so.

The result of the above process was not only the elimination of most of the best and more competent people the revolution so far had, but also the destruction of all the enormous potential capacity their intelligence, energy, and intellect represented.

Those men had positive and valuable initiatives that were ignored and put aside and they were replaced by Castro's singular views about practically everything that could exist in our society and economy. Like Mao Tse-Tung in China, who published a red book to guide every citizen in all what they did, Castro developed a cult to his personality that extended to every aspect of Cuban life. There was no red book like in China, but the official press and the rest of the government controlled media assumed a similar role in Cuba.

Once he established the limits and rules for the way things had to be carried on in his government and introduced the repressive measures that would eventually be applied in case of any digression from his orders, the people who were willing to participate with him at all levels of his political and administrative machinery knew that the main thing that mattered, from there on, was that they showed, at all times, the most unconditional support and acceptance to his orders.

Cuba, from there on, took a downward road and has not stopped falling until present days. The intellectual freedom, in its broadest sense, was annihilated and the smallest sign of free expression or even original thinking became mutilated.

While in prison, I met a Jehovah's Witness follower who had been sentenced to many years in jail, because one day his wife had commented to a neighbor that he had dreamed the night before that the minister of interior had died. There was also the case of another prisoner who had jokingly, after being challenged by a couple of friends in his work, said "Abajo Fidel (Down with Fidel)" in low voice in front of two others and one of them mentioned this to other people, this causing that he was sentenced to five years.

When most historians and researchers of the Cuban revolution analyze the situation of the writers and artists in the island, they usually refer to the words and concepts expressed by Castro in his speech to closure a meeting of three days that was organized by his government with a selected group of artists and writers, at the Cuban National Library, in 1961. One notices that, during all these decades, Castro has avoided to have much participation in meetings of this kind; therefore, there is no doubt that most cultural and artistic activities carried on in Cuba for the past half a century have been developed under the narrow and strict framework established in that meeting and especially in that mentioned speech by Castro, in which he defined, in the middle of a long demagogic diatribe of strange concepts, the limits within which all artists would have to develop their work under his regime, by using the following words: "With the revolution all, outside the revolution nothing," which meant, in more precise terms, "With Castro everything may be okay. Against Castro, nothing will be accepted and a serious problem will follow."

When one reads that speech, it becomes obvious that all those writers and artists, who were present at it, must have felt an electric current coming down along their backs, because each paragraph of it represents a subtle menace, which, coming from a man in his position at a moment in which violence was everywhere, must not have been easy to digest for most of them.

In reality, the policy he established, regarding not only artistic and writing expressions, but practically all intellectual activities, was established earlier and had a much wider scope and interpretation than this mentioned one, but probably most intellectuals at that time could not identify themselves with these other moves of Castro.

During the period of two years prior to the mentioned meeting, Castro had already literally eliminated from the leadership of the revolution almost all the most talented and brilliant men, who were those able to express openly their views on all sorts of Cuban matters, with the backing not only of their intellectual capacity, but also of their own merit within the revolution and he knew that the rest of the intellectuals in Cuba were going to have no option other than accepting his terms or leave the country and this is why he called the most notable and independent of them to the mentioned meeting, of course, accompanied by a number of other intellectuals that were already working for him, to facilitate what he wanted to establish.

One of the problems with the interpretation given by Castro is that, despite what he said, even the most loyal and opportunistic intellectuals have never been able to be completely sure, when they produce some piece of work, about whether Castro is going to like it or not, because he has a very peculiar and narrow way of interpreting artistic works and especially the "interconnection" of them with what he considers the realities of his revolution.

Another problem of the mentioned definition is that the meaning of *all*, in the context it is used, obviously was something demagogic, and Castro has never given a very wide meaning to it. In reality, most intellectuals can expect relatively very little reward from servicing unconditionally him and his revolution.

Of course, there have been some exceptions to the above, as there are people who have received all sorts of special treatments and have lived very comfortably in Cuba, but most of them have been those who have given an invaluable service and full support to Castro, having burned their ships in the process.

If one considers all the problems that have existed in Cuba during these past decades and also the repression that has existed, it becomes obvious that it has been extremely difficult to be an intellectual there during all these years, not only for an artist or writer, but also for any person, in any profession, with the overall capacity to analyze things and events with a higher degree of understanding. Even the most abject among the intellectuals of other countries who have become notorious for being great defenders of Castro and his revolution and for looking to the other side, to avoid seeing the crimes of the revolution, find very complicated to demonstrate that, under the rules established by him, anybody could find full realization.

One of the main aspects of the human mind since the early times of civilization is its capacity to produce an interpretation of things and events, which is different in any person, and this process is the one that opens new ways to define the world in which we live and allows us to develop better criteria.

The above is impossible in Cuba, unless somebody decides to cross the thin line established by Castro, assuming the serious risks of doing it.

All Cuban intellectuals and professionals are aware of these risks and they know what their limits are. There have been many who have tried to cross those limits and have paid, without exception, a heavy price.

The repression of ideas under Castro and his followers, a dictator in body and soul, has been something almost absolute and no intellectual activity has been able to escape of it. The limitations this has produced in all branches of knowledge have been astonishing and have altered the traditions of progress existing in the island.

As I mentioned, not only the artists and writers, who, without any doubt, all feel a closed vigilance on them, but practically anybody, with the intellectual capacity to analyze and interpret the situation in which they live, knows that his or her ideas and expressions are being observed, and if necessary, they will be censored and even punished.

The above has a logical outcome, especially for the younger intellectual generations, because these rules create an environment in which it is extremely difficult to create something really original.

These conditions are rather similar in many aspects to those established in the Soviet bloc. The pressures on top of those working in cultural activities force them to the production of pamphlets, which represent the views of the government or some bureaucrats acting as censors, but lack literary quality. Thus, the number of books describing the success of the secret services in their operations against the "imperialist enemies" has proliferated, as well as pseudo historical books, in which totally altered interpretation of events are presented and Castro's actions are magnified and decorated, to show him as a hero.

Castro created three main organizations to deal with the world of art and culture—the Union of Writers and Artists, the House of the Americas, and later the Ministry of Culture—and has tried during all these years to keep in charge of them people who cannot represent a problem to him, no matter if they are good artists or not, even when he has always tried to find some artists to use as decorative figures, which allow him to present a good show to the rest of the world. Obviously, he has been more interested in keeping under control this important sector of Cuban society than in producing works of art and the real people operating this mechanism work under the guidance of his secret services.

Cuban writers and artists in general are considered a potential problem, because of their capacity to express critical views in regard to the political and social realities happening around them, and this kind of suspicious approach to their activities is something that has been present during all this time.

In the same way that this happens within the artistic world, one finds that most intellectuals in other branches of society are also oriented to do research works according to the terms and conditions established by bureaucrats, who work as censors at higher levels of the administrative apparatus.

It may be that an engineer, who may be studying the development of highways, is forced to accept the concept of Castro that an eight-line highway is necessary, even if Cuba does not have cars and it does not have the means to maintain such a highway either, or it may as well happen that a doctor doing research on the hospitals of the island has a portion of his work vetoed, if it makes some references to the terrible state of them.

In the remote event that an intellectual manages to create a genuine valuable and original piece of work, despite those repressive conditions and escaping the official controls, it will be very difficult that his work is properly recognized, unless Castro and his people got some advantage from it.

No need to say that all this represents an arduous process for each creator, making almost impossible to become a recognized figure, with the character and individuality of the ones existing in other countries in any branch.

The intellectual world of Cuba is a rather enclosed one, and the regime, through a number of demoniac structures that exist within the different levels of the government and the numerous organizations and associations that have been created, which are all full of secret services agents, bureaucrats and opportunists, is the one that decides whether or not any new work is published, exposed or represented.

Any artist or writer reading this can imagine himself, after finishing some work, whichever it can be, going to the police station to see somebody there, to see if they like it and then, from there going to see somebody else within the government of the city or state in which they live, to get their approval also, and then to wait for some time until the governor of the state gets the information and gives his view on it and finally, if the work deserves this, of course, to wait some time more until the president decides if it is good, after getting the advice of his chief of staff, who must analyze all those views received from the lower and local levels of government. Believe it or not, this is the case of Cuban artists under Castro's regime.

Metaphorically, one can say that the intellectual creativity of the island has been incarcerated and crunched for fifty years, only this time the jail is not made of blocks and steel bars but of repressive ideas, slogans, and the paranoia of Castro and the anachronism of his system.

It is not a coincidence that most of the important artists and writers Cuba has had during the past decades, among those who have been living in Cuba, were people that had already reached a level of maturity before Castro took power.

Alejo Carpentier, Jose Lezama Lima, Virgilio Piñera, Amelia Pelaez, Wilfredo Lam, Rene Portocarrero, Alicia Alonso, Cintio Vitier, Fernando Ortiz, Dulce Maria Loynaz, Tomas Gutierrez Alea, to mention some among many other important figures in different fields of art, who lived at least for many years in Cuba during the past five decades and are well-known and recognized, all came from the stage previous to the revolution.

In fifty years, the large portion of the Cuban society who have grown up and lived in the island should have had more than enough time to produce many other younger recognized figures comparable and at the same level of the mentioned ones, who lived in the island, however one must ask what happened that this has not been the case.

In the case of numerous good artists who were born in Cuba during these years, a huge percentage of them have had to migrate, as others did before them, because obviously they reached a point in which they could not live any more under that system if they wished to reach all their potential and as important or more than this, if they were not willing to be accomplices of Castro.

By far, most of the artists and writers and all sorts of intellectuals of younger generations that Cuba has produced during these past decades, have had to develop at least a large portion of their main work outside Cuba, and the same happened also with a large number of the older ones, those who came from before the revolution, who were forced earlier as well to emigrate from Cuba because of the lack of freedom existing there and the persecution they suffered.

There have been a relatively small number of artists from younger generations who have become well known in other countries and have lived all these past decades in Cuba. The problem with most, if not all, of them, is that in order to be able to reach that status, they have had to accept a number of conditions and become instruments of Castro and his regime, something that was not the case in artists and writers and intellectuals of all kinds of previous generations.

When one of these mentioned artists or writers connect their work to the ideology and objectives of the system Castro has established in Cuba, they automatically become accomplices of a number of irrational and most likely criminal events, even when they were not direct participants in them.

They do not need to be torturers of the secret services of Castro to know about what has been going on for fifty years in the prisons of the island, or about all the repression existing in every aspect of Cuban life, and once they know all this and pretend to be ignorant of these facts and keep defending the same concepts Castro developed, in order basically to try to get a number of privileges and become better known, they are selling their souls to the devil.

The above kind of artist can become well known, especially if they have the support of Castro's machinery and propaganda, but even if they are good as artists or writers, there is an immense difference between them and other important artists of Cuba in the past, because those were genuine popular figures and people loved them, without the need of being accomplices of any wrong thing and they did not need to accept being used by anybody for other political purposes.

In large degree, these people become singing puppets, who are used by the regime to try to improve and soften the image of his monstrous system and to indirectly try to convince people about the "noble" intentions of it.

Some ingenuous people want to protect these characters and pretend to read hidden interpretations in the letters of some of their songs or in the images of some paintings and they even scratch their heads, looking for a different significance or resemblance in the character of some book, but in reality, at least in regard to the case of those who have served Castro so well, I prefer quite simply to consider them a more sophisticated class of opportunists and I place them in the same position of those artists who supported Hitler or Stalin, who had indeed many similarities in their actions and ideas.

When one of these singers or artists gives a concert in a Latin American country, in Europe, or in the United States and they receive their script and orientation in Havana, from those who organize and control these activities in the government there, what is that they represent and who is going to get the main profit if people like their message? Obviously, they represent the interests of the regime and this is the one who is going to get the profit of misguiding many of the assistants to those events, with their songs of ambiguous meanings, which all ignore the realities and barbarity the Cuban people suffer.

For many people in the Western world who have grown used to the independence and individualism of artists and writers, as well as that of all sorts of political, professional, and academic figures, it may result difficult to believe and understand that many of these pseudo artists are able to have different faces, depending on where they are, and the same they become nice and progressive when they are in the United States than become the worst kind of jackals when they are in Cuba, or among Castro's allies, and it may be even more difficult for them to accept that most of them have worked efficiently for decades for the secret services of Castro and in many cases have been involved in activities that have nothing to do with their art, when fulfilling their most important role as agents of him.

As I explained before, the case of the lack of freedom for all sorts of intellectual expressions goes beyond the cultural world, to cover all sorts of activities of professionals in every branch of the Cuban society. The consequence of this is that the concept of progress is dead and everything remains stagnant in the island or goes backward.

As I explained before, one may be a professional, in any field, who is looking for a solution to a problem and there is a huge chance that one can find very soon some kind of obstacle, which ultimately may result in your work being vetoed, especially if it represents any kind of conflict or contradiction with incompetent people within the political system and the stupid way of managing things there.

This may not be logical because the solution that is being looked at could benefit everybody, but the degree in which Castro's system has become unable to advance is such that the system cannot accept changes and even less, if they come from somebody that the bureaucrats in the main positions, somehow, identify as independent or intellectually competent, because this kind of people are seen differently and become suspicious very easily for those within the ranks of the political machinery.

The process by which all people, in every branch or activity of the country, who are considered able to think with some degree of independence and can express their own criteria on any matter, are seen with suspicious, extends also to all those who have religious belief, who through the years have become marginalized, which has represented a massive intellectual hunt and a frustration of enormous proportions.

It is well known that Castro used in his favor and even promoted all the contradictions of his political and ideological adversaries. There is perhaps not better example of this than his relations with the Catholic

Church, which clearly show how far Castro was able to go to repress his ideological opponents.

Cuba was, during all his history previous to 1959, a predominantly Catholic country, in which all the main religious traditions were followed and people were used to go regularly to church and express their belief in numerous ways. The main moral teachings of the Catholic faith were respected and priests were an important element of our society.

Castro, who went to a Jesuit school himself, eliminated all this during these past fifty years, in his pursuit to establish communism in our country, leaving the Catholic Church in a state of almost powerless defense, with lack of strong figures in charge of it and subject to a very severe limitation of their influence, this on top of having suffered the powerful animosity of Castro and his secret services.

To make things worse, there has been a lack of proper and effective actions against Castro by most of the high hierarchy of the Vatican and this has no doubt disoriented the way the Cuban Catholic people see the church.

During all the time, since he attacked the Moncada barracks in Santiago de Cuba in 1953 until the beginning of his regime in 1959, Castro received an invaluable support from authorities of the church and members of Catholic organizations. The archbishop of Santiago de Cuba, Enrique Perez Serantes, who years later became critical of him, interceded for Castro after he was captured in the aftermath of the attack, saving literally his life, and church authorities played a role later in obtaining that he was sentenced to fifteen years of prison, instead of the death penalty requested by the prosecutor for his criminal acts, and later they also played a role in his liberation, after only fifteen months in prison.

After he took power in 1959, Catholic organizations in Cuba including some important Catholic authorities in the island, initially gave a strong support to him, even when other Catholic figures almost immediately, after he took power, had alerted about a visible communism trend, and for a short time Castro used that support while he tried to consolidate his regime.

Once Castro felt that his position as head of the government was strong enough, he showed his real intentions, and in a short period of time, he closed all the private religious schools, confiscated a number of churches and church properties, imprisoned some priests, expelled from Cuba to Spain more than one hundred priests, and forced another five hundred to leave Cuba while he incited the masses against the church and in general against all religious citizens.

Not satisfied with the above, Castro promoted a breakup within the Catholic Church, promoting the development of a new movement identified as the Theology of Liberation, which caused considerable damage to it.

He used his secret services to recruit and promote a number of priests and authorities of different religions, especially the Catholic, which, as I explained, was the most powerful in Cuba, and soon a number of these people started proclaiming that Castro was a saint and the church had to be transformed, to put it more in line with social problems, some of these characters even enrolling in the numerous guerrilla movements organized by Castro in Latin America.

Some of this people whom he recruited and planted cautiously within the Catholic Church during those years and many more who have followed the same process since then have been ascending the ranks during these past fifty years, and there is strong indication that Castro may have his secret services operating very high within the faith.

The same he has done in most other religions operating in Cuba, with some of their main figures being almost openly members of his secret services, and also in other countries, including the United States.

Castro's secret services have tried their best to blackmail the church, by devoting considerable efforts to the surveillance of every priest and church figure in Cuba, not only gathering all sorts of information and keeping a dossier on them, but also by trying to use their character weaknesses in every way he has wished.

The Catholic Church in Cuba has had the same problems than in the United States and other countries, but the difference is that Castro stimulated these problems, in order to use the results of his secret service surveillance as a tool of blackmailing, in order to facilitate the penetration of the faith by them.

Most Cuban churches currently are in a state of abandonment and decay and many others have disappeared, especially in provincial cities, but the number of followers who attend mass, which had reduced to a tiny fraction in comparison with the figures before 1959, seem to finally have stabilized, and there has even been an increase in the number of people attending mass in recent years, perhaps as a result of the state of desperation in which the people are living and the overwhelming disastrous conditions of the country.

Castro played with all this and one day he sent a hoard of his most savage people against the people who are meeting in a church and another he received with all solemnity an envoy of the Vatican or a Pope himself.

The Cuban society has suffered enormous moral consequences as a result of sixty years of communism and Castro's systematic attacks on the faith, which are obvious, despite his frequent demagogic gestures toward some important religious figures, something that was no more than a another sign of his hypocrisy.

One can only imagine the consequences of prohibiting and censoring all sorts of ideas and beliefs, simply because a man does not like them. It is the equivalent to pretend to stop all the forces behind the advance of civilization and prohibit any new progress. This is what Castro has done.

During the past decades, there have been numerous attempts in Cuba to develop some kind of opposition to Castro and his system by a wide spectrum of people, who have tried to find ways to express different views than those established by his system. Outside Cuba, they are called dissidents, following the concept that was applied to the writers and intellectuals who opposed communism in the Soviet Union, but I am not sure if that term is accurate in the case of Cuba and this may be a philosophical matter.

The fact is that of all them, as well as their families in most cases, have suffered the repression of Castro with full intensity. Most have been incarcerated for many years, in extremely bad conditions, usually in isolation cells, and their families have only being allowed to see them very sporadically.

In many cases they have suffered attacks and all sorts of abuses by the prison guards and they have contracted illnesses due to the bad conditions in which they are kept while they are not allowed to communicate with their relatives nor with other people. Their sentences have been arbitrarily high and without any legal basis and they are all subject to an increase of them for whatever reason.

These prisoners of consciousness are evidently used by Castro to intimidate the rest of the population and to show the rest of the world that his system is ready to repress any opposition.

Some people have denounced the situation of human rights, which has been obviously terrible and has become a vulnerable aspect of Castro's policies and this has served as a base to promote the ideals of freedom and free expression in the country. Many of them have also been imprisoned and they have continued their battle of ideas from those prisons and once some of them have been freed they have continued defending those who have remained behind.

Other people, including among them the group of us who participated in the World Conferences on the Environment with the Environmental Cuban Association, have tried to denounce the grave situation of the environment and the enormous damage caused to it by Castro's disastrous administration and their reports have been presented in numerous forums.

There have been a number of attempts to create new political opposition parties, one of them the one that we tried unsuccessfully to create in 1981, which I mention in the foreword of this book and consisted in trying to present to the national Assembly a request for the inscription of a new political party. We tried to organize a number of people in different cells and start collecting signatures but Castro evidently did not like this idea, despite the fact that this was allowed by the existing constitution and I ended in prison

There have been other attempts to create also a number of new political organizations and also to try to unify them under a single umbrella that could work coordinately.

One of the main efforts to try to open a space for the opposition in Cuba is known as Varela Project, promoted by Oswaldo Payá, which consisted basically in the presentation to the National Assembly of a formal request with ten thousand signatures to allow the participation of people of other political ideas in government matters, this including the possibility of the existence of an independent political organization. Castro this time allowed them to collect the signatures and to prepare their documents and their effort was widely covered by the international press, but their petition was simply ignored.

These attempts suffered a big setback, when Castro incarcerated, with long sentences, seventy-five people, many of them intellectuals, in what has been named the Black Spring, in 2003. All of them suffered abuses, isolation, bad treatment, illnesses, and offenses, but all kept their firm position against the dictatorship of Castro.

Few days after the above happened, a number of wives and mothers of those men created a movement called the Ladies in White, which have been fighting all these seven years for the liberation of them and have become very well known and recognized due to their bravery and tenacity. These women have been attacked and humiliated by Castro's forces numerous times and they have persisted in their effort, becoming a symbol of freedom and love in front of the Cuban people and the whole world.

In Miami, another group of women created, in 1994, a movement under the name MAR por Cuba (Women against the Repression in Cuba), which is presided by Silvia Iriondo and they have been present all these years in numerous actions of opposition to Castro. They dress in black as a sign of their mourning for what is happening in Cuba.

A new kind of movement appeared recently, which is represented by bloggers within the island, who express their criticism of the system openly and the main figure of that movement has been Yoani Sanchez, a young and brave woman, who has become a serious challenger to Castro's repression of free expression.

All the people, who have tried to oppose Castro within the island, in one way or another, deserve our respect and recognition, over any possible political differences that is natural that exist, because they have had to confront a huge machinery of repression, which is infinitely more powerful than them and despite this, they have been willing to assume this enormous risk, which no doubt has affected all their families the same. They have sacrificed the best years of the lives, in the name of freedom for their country, and this must be appreciated and honored.

Some people who try to defend Castro's system use the argument that the overall number of people who have been sent to political prison in the last decade in Cuba, due to their opposition to Castro, is relatively small compared with the size of the Cuban population; however, this is misguiding. Castro incarcerated numerous people, who were opponents of his regime, arbitrarily masking their political causes under other kinds of common causes, trying to present them as common prisoners. One cannot compare the case of Cuba with other countries because one finds that the number of political prisoners in Cuban prisons is considerably more than in any other.

On top of the above, one can see that Castro's policy of repression and abuse is still the same and the mechanisms he created to apply it remain in place and functioning. The Cuban people live under the repressive boot of a cruel regime and an abusive machinery of intimidation and corruption.

It is almost unbelievable how, in the beginning of the twenty-first century, a system so repressive as the one Castro established, which has violated all the principles of human rights and every norm of decency and democratic rule can still allow itself to continue its repression on any manifestation of free thinking, but unfortunately, this is still the case.

The communist system established by Castro in Cuba has become a compendium of all the most retrograde methods of political and social organization that have been conceived during the past several centuries by the sickest and most irrational minds and this has resulted in an aberration of gigantic dimensions, which is difficult to classify.

In order to remain in power for half a century, Castro needed to repress all valid ideas and concepts of progress and the people behind them, making no case of the fact that they represented the engine for the advancement of Cuban society and economy.

To replace this enormous intellectual force, formed by the best minds the Cuban society produced during seven or eight decades of our existence, to whom he literally pretended to annihilate one way or another with his repression, he tried to use all sorts of incompetent people, who have proven to be totally unable to perform that role, only basing his decision in their capacity to accept being manipulated by him and their lack of courage to represent any opposition.

But not being satisfied with leaving aside the most qualified people, Castro went further and he replaced also all sorts of those functionaries and people he appointed, at all levels and in all kinds of functions, every time one of them gave the simplest opinion that could represent even the tiniest difference in comparison to his views, which created a system of incompetent human robots that had to wait for Castro's instructions to take the simplest decisions.

The same could happen that he replaced a minister, simply because he expressed his view that it would be difficult to produce and process ten million tons of sugar, an obsession of him during the sixties, something in which the minister was totally right about, than he practically expelled from Cuba, after offending them with all sort of epithets, some of the best known authorities of the world in the field of cattle raising, because they differed with his views on something in which it was probed later he was totally wrong.

It may be look funny, but Castro considered himself simultaneously the best baseball manager of baseball in the world, the most talented agricultural scientist, the best fisher of sail fish, a world level expert in economy, a military genius compared to Napoleon Bonaparte, and the best cane cutter; and he sent away or disappeared anybody who tried to explain respectfully to him a different view. It has been evidently impossible that, with such a maniac in charge, Cuba could progress.

Castro's irrationality was proverbial. One day, the Cubans learned from him about his plans to make Cuba the most important producer of pate in the world, because somebody showed him some geese and he immediately started multiplying them in his imagination, and the next day, he delivered a speech about the production of milk in which he described, with all seriousness in his face, how he literally "invented" a super cow able to produce more milk than any other cow in the world while it ate less grass, and people learn, some months later, that he even built a statue for the cow!

The only comparison that I have been able to find with the case of Castro and his relation with those around him, which no doubt keeps many similarities, is the case of Caligula, the notorious Roman emperor. Since in this case, he used his propaganda during the early years of the revolution to make the people call him *el caballo* (the horse), the similarities are even more striking and the fact that he has represented the same intellectual capacity of the famous horse of Caligula while managing Cuban matters is an incredible coincidence.

The real obsession he had for persecuting and repressing any kind of manifestation of free expression, in all branches and activities of society, and the perversion he used to destroy and disappear any person, who had shown the intellectual courage and capability to disagree with him, cannot belong to a person that was well of his mind.

There have been numerous typical cases of people he appointed to high positions, who almost invariably started appearing in the newspaper every day while they were engaged in the development of some kind of irrational plan elaborated by him, until one day, unexpectedly, the people read a little note in the same newspaper, which regularly said that they have been demoted for their mistakes and or or bad attitudes. Castro, of course, could not assume any responsibility, because the failure is due to the incompetence of the mentioned guy, who had all sorts of deficiencies.

The degree of irrationality of Castro was contagious and it was a good breeding ground for the most ambitious opportunism, which to this day is the specialty of all those unconditional and abject people around him, who learned to profit from following whatever crazy orders they received from him, at the same time cautiously giving all the credit to him. This way, when the disaster comes, there won't be anybody around except Castro and he obviously is not going to be blamed for it; therefore they will be there, ready to fulfill his orders in another task, as if nothing had happened.

There have been a number of notorious characters who have absorbed so well their roles that they have come to believe that they are important, and they can, indeed, perform the disparate tasks assigned by Castro to them and have tried to show off and this is something Castro did not tolerate. Very soon, rumors started flowing and the people learned that the guy had been sent to work at a pig farm in the most remote location because he had the audacity of trying to take from Castro some of the exposure, which in reality was the most important for him. Whether he was successful or not seems to be irrelevant. In his mind, people tended to forget easily those kinds of things, but in the meantime he had always to have his show going. That was the most important thing.

The above means that his own people who are at the high levels of the party or the government were also restricted of expressing their views and thinking and had to be afraid of Castro all the time.

However, the above is not an absolute rule. In the case of his brother Raúl and few others whom he apparently found crucial to protect his back and became a sort of last trench of his defense to keep others away, he procured to avoid any serious conflict with them, no matter what disaster they created by their own or how much corrupted and vicious they were.

To me, Castro was a maniac, whose sick mind was full of aberrations, but somehow, he was able to canalize his madness and impose it on others, by using all sort of violent methods, forcing them to accept the irrational ideas produced by his imagination as if they were irrefutable truths.

It is very sad that he was able to find many people in Cuba and in the world who have been willing to recognize him as their prophet, and even more sad that so many people accepted to become his puppets, including very specially all those he used to fill the ranks of his apparatus and have been ready to abandon all their scruples only for being allowed to enjoy for some time the honey of power.

CHAPTER XIV

~

Repression as a way to govern

Human beings meant nothing to Fidel Castro and apart, maybe, from some of his closest relatives, I do not think that Castro cared much during all his life about any person; it would seem that the affective portion of the mind of this man has been completely busy, implementing all sorts of schemes and plans, oriented to achieve glory and fame for himself.

The lack of scruples of Castro has been absolute all his life and this may have been his best arm to deal with all sorts of situations and characters in Cuba and the world arena. He has ordered so many criminal actions, has killed and destroyed so many lives and families, and has caused so many irrationally violent events, without losing his sleep, that I do not think there is anything that could affect this strange man.

The level of hatred and malevolence Castro possessed allowed him to have a place among the worst characters of recent world history, and it has been a great disgrace for all of us that he was born in Cuba, a paradisiacal and beautiful island of the Caribbean, populated by people who always were friendly and enjoyed life and music and whose only dream was to achieve progress and being free.

The world, however, must be grateful that Castro was born in Cuba, a small country with relatively limited resources, as this has made impossible for him to implement in full extent the sick ideas of death and destruction he continually conceived during all his life, which, at times, have been so incredibly bad, that many people have found it difficult to believe they could be real. Those are the ones, who cannot believe he was talking seriously when he expressed his will of using the nuclear warheads he had borrowed from the Soviets against the United States in 1962 and pretend to convince us that he was just bluffing!

Castro considered violence and repression something natural and he became used to live with them and he learned very early in his political life to use these as his favorite tools, to keep under control other people.

It is very strange, however, when one follows all the different stages of his life, how this man was able to commit all kind of crimes and violent actions without having any serious punishment, which gives the impression that he has had some sort of license to kill and to violate all rules and laws at worldwide scale.

One could say that there has been some kind of special law for Castro, different to the laws that rule for everybody else. The case is that Castro, once and again during his life, was able to do all kind of atrocities and crimes, which are not normally allowed to anybody and he not only did not experience any serious punishment for them, but what is more incredible, he has been recognized for this as a paladin of liberty, not only in Cuba but also in the rest of the world.

He designed and implemented a new kind of repressive system for Cuba, in which he combined his own fanatical ambitions with the terrible experiences of other countries and former dictators, in order to subjugate the Cuban people, without any notion of limit and with no concern for the deaths and damages he caused. While this has been happening for sixty years, Castro has been able to establish a wide range of relationships with all sorts of people, governments, and institutions from around the world, who have considered Castro a great leader.

Violence and repression were for Castro a way to manifest himself; they are products of his tortuous mind and the main elements he used to govern. He could not live quietly without them and there is no single political event in his life in which they have not been somehow present. For some strange reason, his crimes have always been ignored, at least by many people, and he managed to keep going, without much trouble, despite the seriousness of his actions. Why this happened so easily, during all his life, is to me one big mystery.

Since his early student days, Castro has been associated with murder, when every existing element indicated, that he was involved in the assassination of a university leader, who had become his rival, something that was never investigated in detail, even when the police at that time had numerous indications to support an investigation of his involvement in the case.

Something even more strange happened, when he became the main responsible of the death of numerous soldiers of the constitutional army, after he organized a failed surprise attack to the Moncada barracks in Santiago de Cuba, in which many of his followers also lost their lives. Even when all this was one of the most serious crimes existing under Cuban law, he and his people received a very benign punishment from the Batista's government, which allowed him to continue his activities with total impunity a few months later.

After the failed mentioned attack, Castro and his people disbanded, trying to reach the Oriente mountains, looking for a place to hide, but few days later they were captured by the army and then they were brought to trial and judged under full legal warranties and sentenced to prison.

Despite the grave crimes he committed, during all this time, as I mentioned earlier, he was first saved and then protected by no other than the archbishop of Santiago de Cuba, Msgr. Perez-Serantes, the second authority of the church in Cuba at that time, who paradoxically became his critic years later, when he expelled many priests out of Cuba.

There is no totally clear explanation to this day about why, despite the serious consequences of their actions, Castro and his men were given all sorts of attentions and penitentiary privileges during their short stay in prison, which contrasted with the harsh conditions in which he kept so many political prisoners during all these past decades.

Incredible as this may now seem, it was the case that, after being only a few months in prison, President Batista decided to liberate Castro and his followers, despite the tragic consequences and the hatred and violence behind his actions and ignoring the enormous criminal responsibility he had in the death of so many constitutional soldiers.

Whoever were the people, or whatever the interests, were behind these almost magic circumstances, which allowed Castro to escape punishment, so easily, from his crimes and continue his path to political stardom and dictatorship belongs to the many obscure chapters of his life. Evidently, the stars, the sun, the moon and the planets had to be aligned for this to be happen!.

After he was liberated, he was allowed freely to travel, without any limitations, to the United States, where he started to collect huge amounts of money and recruited openly people for his movement, making arrangements to buy all sorts of arms while he promoted his ideas in different cities in which there were Cubans living. From the United States, he later went to Mexico, country in which he also openly organized, armed, and trained an expedition to go back to Cuba.

Curiously, he did not have much serious problems to carry out his conspiring activities in Mexico either, even when he was preparing a new uprising in Cuba and another serious attack to its institutions, in which he was going obviously to cause many new deaths again among his fellow citizens. Apparently, Castro, for some reason, was above the law, not only in Cuba but in the United States and Mexico as well.

If any citizen of the United States or Mexico had done just a small fraction of what Castro was doing, I am absolutely sure, he had ended in prison for many years, that is, if he had not had a worse end. Why Castro did not have any problem is something strange.

While he was in Mexico, Castro continued with total impunity living his dreams of violence and death and he organized training camps in front of everybody's eyes, in which his people practiced shooting and got familiar with guerrilla actions. There are well-supported accounts, by close associates of him at that time, about how he killed in cold blood, in front of all his men, one man, just because he thought he had differences with him, which, by the way, was not the case, and how he used this to enforce his authority among that group of men he had recruited to go to Cuba.

After he disembarked with his yacht expedition in Cuba, he established with a small group of followers at the Sierra Maestra mountains; there are also many well-documented accounts describing how he and his followers continued killing people there, among those he considered were cooperating with the government or even those who simply disagreed with his views. Evidently Castro felt that he had some special power to decide like a god about the life or death of others.

Curiously, despite his background of violence, a very positive and exaggerated account of Castro's actions was presented by some of the most important American news media at that moment and this introduced him as a new kind of hero to the rest of the world, who fell in love with his image.

In the meantime, in Cuba, important sectors of the media, which had a very high level of insight, also became his candid supporters and politicians of all ideologies gave him also their support.

As a result, he soon had a good number of men and women fighting beside him, some with lots of experience and political culture, who decided to leave their homes and families to fight against Batista in the mountains and accepted the leadership of this young man, who all knew and considered a sort of apprentice of gangster during his years at the University of Havana.

But the above was not all. While he was in the Sierra Maestra, many other people in Havana, Santiago de Cuba, and some other large cities organized a huge urban revolt, which included the explosion of bombs, the organization of strikes, the collection of money, the organization of an underground movement within the army, distribution of propaganda, and many other actions, and all of them accepted without much trouble his leadership.

Following the "magic," after just only two years, he had defeated President Batista, who decided to leave the island, following some "pressures" from the United States, despite having almost untouched most of the forces of the constitutional army, the navy and the air force.

Of course, Batista did not leave Cuba like many other people. He had a huge fortune of several hundred million dollars, which obviously was more than what his salary as president and head of the armed forces would allow him to save. He was forced to go to Dominican Republic but he had a lot of his money safe in the United States and other countries and nobody presented any claim against it.

After some time, Batista, who was the most powerful figure among all the people who became in only few months the opposition to Castro, was forced to move from Dominican Republic to another paradisiacal island, Madeira, in front of the coasts of Africa, where he stayed until he could go to live his last years in Spain.

There are all sorts of theories about Castro. Some say that Castro was recruited by the CIA in the early years of his political career and that all that followed was a well-orchestrated political show guided by obscure powerful interests.

Others refer to a kind of existing predetermined human path, which includes aspects like the meaning of the names of people and the symbolism behind each of them.

There are also those who talk about some pact between the Soviet Union and the EE.UU to protect Castro, which obviously cannot be explained on the light that the Soviet Union disappeared thirty years ago and the Castro's regime is still in power.

There are even references to some magic witchery "protections" Castro supposedly got years later during his travels to Africa, which leaves without explanation what protected him during his early years, and there are many more theories. The fact is that this man managed to get in power, under almost unbelievable circumstances and stayed in that position against all odds, doing practically all what he wished, including all sorts of crimes and he did not experience even the slightest harm or scratch.

Contrary to what the propaganda says, the main triumphant actions of the revolution were not really military, but by large facilitated by the corruption of some high officers of Batista's army, who accepted kickbacks to surrender their forces or got into strange compromises, which again are difficult to explain, but the reality was that the constitutional army was still a large and powerful force when Batista decided to leave and it is very difficult to explain why this man, who was used also to violence, so easily decided to leave Cuba, betraying many of his followers, toward an uncertain future, without first giving at least a final real battle against Castro's forces.

After Batista left, Castro saw himself embraced by the most unthinkable popularity and the incredible stupidity of so many Cubans of all classes, who were ready to support him for the strangest of causes, many of them without even knowing who he really was.

Obviously, considering Castro's character, the first thing he ordered to his followers, once he took power, was to start killing more people, his passion, and he targeted those among the commanders of Batista's army, who had been practically the only ones who had fought against him, not accepting money to surrender their forces like other corrupt officers did.

All the existing Cuban newspapers and magazines, as well as the international press, soon were full of extremely violent photos of those that were executed in front of the fire squads, following Castro's orders, while the television showed life crude images of the shootings. And incredibly, many educated people in Cuba, who had never killed a fly, accepted magically all this without much concern.

When Castro could not find any pretext to kill more people among the former members of Batista's army, he started looking for more people to kill and soon he deviated his attention to those around him, who could represent some kind of rivalry to him in the future and he started meticulously to plan and design, for each of them, a different version of death.

He showed an enormous criminal talent and audacity to arrange strange "accidents" like the one in which Camilo Cienfuegos, the most popular commander of his forces, disappeared in a plane, leaving no sign, and also to represent as if it was a "confusion" the assassination of Cristino Naranjo, one of the high officers closest to Cienfuegos, few days later, when he was arriving at the barracks of Columbia.

He did not vacillate when he brought to a prearranged trial his former close follower Commander Humberto Sori, who was brought to the fire squad a few hours after Castro had promised to his mother he was not going to be killed. Sori had been the man Castro appointed as prosecutor in the trials of those mentioned officers of Batista's army a short time before and he also had been the main author of the law of agrarian reform, which he implemented as Minister of Agriculture, only to apparently change course months later. According to Castro, he had become a conspirator against his government, but in reality, he was captured and accused under unclear circumstances. Being a man who knew so many facts and details about Castro's actions of those initial months of the revolution, it results very suspicious the way he was captured and accused, and even more the speed with which he was executed.

Many of his followers could not imagine at that time that all these mentioned early cases were simply samples of what those around him could expect years later if they decided to change course.

Following his criminal instincts, when he considered that he had eliminated enough of those people around him and conscious that he had already assembled and tested a formidable criminal machinery formed by his secret services, his revolutionary tribunals and prosecutors, he looked for new victims to feed them and soon he started killing right and left all those who opposed his actions and had started fighting again for the freedom of Cuba, this time against his much larger and better armed forces in cities and rural areas.

Castro found in communism another key element for the support of his killing machinery and it is well documented how he studied carefully all the details of the campaigns developed by Lenin and Stalin to exterminate millions of people of all the nationalities they oppressed.

There are also many similarities between his concepts and those of Hitler, another of his favorite readings, in regard to the way in which people had to be mobilized to support their systems and how people had to be treated.

By the time Castro had established his version of communist system, tens of thousands of Cubans of all ages, white and black, farmers and workers, professional and illiterate, had been already killed and imprisoned by him. However, incredible as this might be, he found that, despite all his atrocities, there were many people, even among those never before involved in politics, who kept supporting passionately his infamous actions!

Since he could not achieve his dream of killing many millions of people in the United States with a nuclear attack, which had caused for sure the disappearance of the island in reciprocity, he found few years later other ways to keep killing, and he sent his people, under the flags of communism and armed by his new criminal partners in Moscow, to Africa and Latin America, where they killed many tens of thousand people more.

The Soviet Union found in Castro a kind of super mercenary, able to assemble, under the façade of the Cuban army, a huge force of warriors, who were able to go, with short notice, to any corner of the planet, with total impunity, armed to their tooth, with missions designed well to support weak governments sympathetic to the Soviet Union or to enhance otherwise small guerrilla movements, previously created and supported by Moscow in many countries, all this with the clear objective of conquering huge territories, which obviously were passed to the Soviets for control and administration once his forces had achieved their military objectives.

Some authors refer to the existence of discrepancies between the Soviets and Castro in regard to the willingness to spread the armed struggles around the world. To me, these supposed differences were just another show. The Soviets, as a world power, wanted to save their face, in front of the rest of the countries, but they were extremely happy of having Castro conquest for them those huge territories and growing their influence. At the end, however, this may have been the sentence of death of their system, which was not in the conditions to assume such a load.

The case was that tens of thousands of Cubans were enrolled in these almost fantastic operations in distant zones of the world, fighting for causes they had never heard of and many of them died, without knowing exactly why they were there or what they were representing. The only thing they could be sure was that Castro had sent them there.

The only payment all these men received for these military services and for risking their lives for something totally strange to them were the small salaries their families received back in Cuba, in devaluated Cuban pesos, which made them the cheapest mercenaries in the world.

In the meanwhile, as compensation for these valuable services, Castro continue receiving from the Soviet Union huge subsidies to support his increasingly bankrupt system and economy while he also became a key piece in the world chess game, something he enjoyed even more.

The magnitude of those Soviet subsidies to Castro reached enormous proportions, especially considering the size of the island, but they were only a portion of the costs the Soviets assumed, trying to keep under the flag of communism all those countries and territories, which Castro had conquest for them, which they also had to subsidize and eventually, as I mentioned above, this new empire, obtained with Castro's help, became a burden the Soviet Union economy was not in the capacity to carry on its back and ultimately, all this had a tremendous role in the disappearance of the Soviet Union.

Nobody will probably ever know how many hundreds of thousands of people from those countries, together with the mentioned Cubans, died as a result of the support of Castro to all sorts of movements and the military expeditions he sent to Ethiopia, Algeria, Morocco, Somalia, Congo, Angola, Namibia, Zimbabwe, Mozambique, and Guinea Bissau, to mention the most important. Or those who died on the wars he promoted in El Salvador, Guatemala, Nicaragua, and Colombia, and as a result of the movements he supported in Vietnam, Laos, Cambodia, Palestine, Brazil, Venezuela, Dominican Republic, Mexico, Granada, Ecuador, Bolivia, Uruguay, Paraguay, Peru, Argentina, Dominican Republic, and Chile, to mention some of them.

In the middle of all these military international operations, Castro developed other more sophisticated ways to satisfy his unlimited thirst of blood and found that he could also use his secret services for the most complex operations to assassinate other people at all levels of society in those countries which he had included in his list as targets for his crusade of pseudo revolutions.

From the United States to many countries of Europe and from Africa to Latin American, his agents and hit men went to carry out the most audacious missions, killing people who Castro did not like or he considered his enemies, also getting involved in numerous violent conspiracies in many countries.

While all these criminal activities happened, a kind of underground opposition of important sectors of the Cuban society started spontaneously to develop, simultaneously with a growing social ferment, which was created by the deteriorating conditions of the Cuban economy and the worsening conditions of life.

Evidently, all of the above was more than what the Cuban people could afford and this was creating the potential for a huge social explosion of large dimensions, the menace of a huge popular rebellion becoming real, which made Castro feel that he needed to increase even more the level of repression within the island.

Thus, he ordered the construction on permanent basis of a huge network of fortified high security prisons, farms for forced labor, and centers of detention and torture, which soon were operating in practically every corner of the island, this requiring the increase in size of his Ministry of Interior and secret services, following the methods learned from his partners in the Soviet Union.

As a result, many other people found their death at them or were victims of all sorts of abuses. Young and old people, women, homosexuals, people of all races, functionaries in disgrace, deserters among the army recruits, officers who had to be disciplined, those caught at sea trying to abandon Cuba, thieves, children, criminals, and insane people, all went together to those prisons and will live the rest of their lives with the marks of them in their minds and bodies.

Since he could not kill everybody, he decided to find other ways to destroy as many lives as possible and hundreds of thousands of people of all races, sexes, and educational level have been subject to the most inhumane treatments and humiliations at those prisons, while they have fulfilled years and years of sentence, living under the worst conditions, separate from their families and with no possibility of improvement, unless an almost miracle happened and they were allowed to leave for the United States.

For many years, the Castro's regime has been using some wards of the main psychiatric hospitals as centers of torture and has sent thousands of political and common prisoners to live among insane inmates, those who have committed the worst and most horrendous kinds of crimes, and were the most dangerous criminals existing in Cuba, in order to intimidate them and this not being enough, thousands of them have been applied electroshocks, with double electric load than the established limit, and they have been injected drugs to destroy their minds forever.

I could see with my own eyes, when I was also sent there, lines of people thrown on the floors, one beside the other, unconscious for days, after having received these electroshocks and drugs at the Psychiatric Hospital of Havana, which Castro's propaganda presents as a model hospital.

Those who tried to fight against these electroshocks were sent to even worse wards, in which inmates are kept naked, without beds or toilet facilities, being bathed with hoses with cold water and had to eat with their hands, all this for many months or even years, in which they do not have any medical attention or contact with their families.

As I explained before, in January 2010, more than forty people in some of those wards at the Psychiatric Hospital of Havana died of cold and hunger, when the temperatures dropped due to a cold weather front. They were naked, without food, and nobody bothered to protect them. The photos of all this are horrendous.

When, thanks largely to this repression, things became quieter again in Cuba and the opposition had been trimmed, reaching a point in which apparently there was no more justification to keep killing people, Castro found a new possibility to continue with his crimes, when thousands of desperate Cubans started trying to leave the island, going away, one way or another, from his oppressive policies. Soon, the world could see how an almost interminable number of men, women, and children started to die at sea, trying desperately to reach the United States and other countries aboard precarious rafts, even when they knew that their lives where the high price they could pay for it, on top of the cost of abandoning behind all what they had.

Following Castro's barbaric orders, some of his troops have killed many of those people they have found alive at sea, aboard all sorts of rustic and elemental rafts. Thus, Castro could keep counting deaths. Many others of them were "luckier" and were caught and brought to his prisons, to be there separate from their families for many years, all this due to their dreams of freedom.

It is evident that Castro's social order has been based on the most brutal repression, but this repression has included aspects not always understood as such. It is important that I also refer to them.

In every country in which Castro has managed to establish puppet governments formed by a selection of the most corrupt and irrational people he was able to find, these people, whom he trained in Cuba, started reproducing the same conditions that exist in Cuba. This could be observed in Nicaragua, where the Sandinista movement committed many crimes and their corrupt leaders stole many properties and introduced the same kind of system established in Cuba during their first time in power and keep trying to do the same again. It is also happening in Venezuela, where Hugo Chavez and Maduro destroyed the economy and society of that rich country, while they have tried to introduce all the absurd methods of his patrons from Cuba. It happened in Chile, where Salvador Allende accepted that Castro started to introduce large lots of arms and people to support a coup against the military and the opposition. It happened in Bolivia, and in some extent, in Ecuador, and it also happened in other countries in Africa.

When one studies each of these cases in all these mentioned countries, one can see the increase in repression as soon as the disciples of Castro manage to get hold of the government and this always have come accompanied, like in Cuba, by all kind of signs of deterioration of the conditions of life. Newspapers, television, and radio stations are closed or punished after they start receiving all sorts of attacks, and menaces and strange characters, with very low intellectual capacity, are promoted to high positions, and every sign of free enterprise is vilified while a new cast of secret service agents start showing up everywhere, after being trained by Cuban services, which keep a control on them, going above traditional concepts of sovereignty.

When most of the Cuban population was brought by Castro to live under the worst conditions of housing, practically lacking every basic product to satisfy the most elemental needs and with continued deteriorating services of all kinds, all this was also part of the repression he conceived to keep under control the Cuban people. The same was also applied in these other countries.

While Castro and his family enjoyed an abundance of everything, becoming a billionaire himself, and his wife and children have lived a good life, the average people in Cuba have been forced to keep their frustration and miseries for themselves. This is another way of repression.

When all those people Castro enrolled, indoctrinated, and trained in the armed forces and at all the different quasi-military organizations he simultaneously created engaged in all sorts of abuses and crimes against the rest of the Cuban population or when acting on behalf of him and his revolution, they went to kill people in other countries, all of them also became victims of Castro's repression because their lives have been impacted by these actions; they had never been involved in those crimes or had carried out those activities if Castro had not been in control of Cuba.

This is another face of the disaster he has created and when psychologists in Cuba try to explain the enormous surge of violence within the Cuban society, they need to study all of the above if they really want to find out the cause of it.

It is impossible to know how many people have been forced to kill in the name of the Castro's system, people who otherwise would never have committed a crime in their whole lives, under normal conditions. This is a trauma that is going to be present during all their lives and a reason for them to remember Castro.

If one compares the case of Cuba with the situation of many other countries that could be compared with Cuba before Castro took power, one realizes that the people who live at them have never had to live those kind of violent experiences, and in general, they have much better and normal conditions of life than the ones people have in Cuba.

The repression is the spinal cord of the political system created and implemented by Fidel Castro in Cuba and it exists and is organized at all levels and within all aspects of the Cuban society in all detail. From the politburo to the people on the streets, absolutely everybody must be scared of even thinking of opposing anything that is part of Castro's system.

The repression is designed in a way in which the people who have the highest level of education, those who one should expect could understand better the absurd reality in which they are forced to live, are frightened to their bones and their minds become paralyzed and cannot challenge any concept or idea imposed to them, while those with the lowest level of education are also afraid of everything around them and prefer to accept as real the myth of the almost magic presence of Castro's agents listening and observing all what they do than to have all sorts of problems, ending in one of the prisons existing everywhere.

All those in high positions of the party and the government, like the high-ranking officers within the army, are afraid of being taped in their conversations, even if they are with their closest relatives, or of being photographed by the secret services in any activity outside their ordinary ones. They feel that they cannot share with anybody their ideas and even less any concerns they may have about the situations they have to deal with.

All these people in charge of so many levels of the numerous organizations conforming the Cuban government are as anxious as the rest of the population to feel free of the burden that Castro's repression means in their lives, and all wish, like any average citizen, to be able one day of enjoying some new products and properties of their own, which they know may be considered privileges in Cuba now, but are something normal everywhere else.

They have seen Castro and other top leaders regularly enjoy these privileges, but everybody is frightened about what could happen to them if they talk about this. One sees the hypocrisy of all these people referring to Castro, and more recently his brother Raúl, as examples of all the virtues, as if they were the architects of all the right policies in the world. They have become scared to death of showing their individuality and their own character and they have lost their capacity for decision making.

Cuba has become a paranoiac society and hypocrisy has become the main practical value at all levels of it. It is the key element for many people to survive.

The hypocrisy is so much that it involves all the policies and orders of the party and the government; every activity that is carried on, once it is bisected, shows its core putrid by the infection caused by the corruption of the system and the lack of scruples Castro has induced into it.

There is no way that a society as ill as the Cuban society can advance while the people have to live immersed in a cloud of omnipresent terror caused by the repression instituted by Castro and within the level of the immorality they have to accept, if they want to avoid getting in trouble.

Castro considers corruption, terror, and repression his most powerful tools and this is why he has tried to introduce a different fashion of these elements in many countries in which he would like to be able to introduce his political system. Through the many faces of his secret services, he has given support and has acted as intermediary and ultimately promoter of the drug traffic and the development of gangs in Mexico, Peru, Central America, Colombia, and the United States and has managed to establish links with numerous corrupt political figures and other authorities of those countries.

All of the above could seem a huge burden for most people in the world, used to live in more open societies, in which democratic institutions rule, but unfortunately, what I have described so far in this chapter is only part of Castro's repression.

Since the early years of his revolution, Castro established a network to keep control and vigilance of every citizen in every rural corner or city block of the island, which has operated under the name of "Committees for the Defense of the Revolution," which are overseen by the Ministry of Interior.

These committees are formed by common citizens, including the most furious supporters of Castro and other more normal ones who are afraid of being considered "worms," which is the term created by Castro to classify his opponents. These people must carry on a permanent vigilance on every neighbor living around them, from their homes, passing the results of their surveillance to the different levels of the Ministry of Interior.

I think that anybody reading this chapter can visualize what it would mean for them to have somebody looking into your private life twenty-four hours a day the whole year, year after year. This is just part of what the Cuban people have to endure, living under the Castro's system rule.

The lack of privacy and the violation of individual rights are just common day atrocities featured by Castro's model of government and repression.

The people of the Ministry of Interior are used to come at any time and assign missions of vigilance to these mentioned committees, which may include, among others, the installation of electronic means, to tape conversations of other neighbors at their homes or the use of hidden cameras to see with whom they relate or even to keep control on their personal family matters.

Another task of these people include the keeping of records about the participation of their neighbors in the activities and events promoted by the regime, as well as in the vigilance shifts established to check at night the activities of people in each neighborhood.

The surveillance of everybody's lives extends to their working places, in which there are always a number of people, who have the secret mission of keeping vigilance on all the others and inform the result of their observation to people of the Ministry of Interior assigned to each work center, at all levels of the infrastructure of the country.

Every school and educational institution of the country, from primary to the universities, has a similar system of vigilance established, to keep control on every student and teacher; when something irregular to them is detected, there are good chances that the student or the teacher is removed from the school.

The members of the military are not exempt of this absolute control either. On the contrary, there is an even stricter parallel machinery of vigilance for them, which exists beside the own structure of the forces and is established in every unit of the different bodies of the armed forces, to keep under close surveillance every soldier, from the recruits of the forced military service established by Castro since the beginning of the revolution to the high ranks.

One example of this, was the case of General Arnaldo Ochoa and several other high ranking officers of the Armed Forces and the Ministry of Interior, all with a long record within the regime, who were sentenced to death in 1989 after a well advertised trial accused of a number of activities that were, according to Castro, contradictory with their functions and their level of responsibility, like drug smuggling and many other crimes. In reality, both Castro brothers have been involved in these and many other similar activities for many years and this should not have been a motif for such a violent reprisal and the real reason for the execution of them seems to have been that they were the most visible personalities within many others who were expressing their frustrations for the total failure of the system instituted by Castro.

Everybody within the army, the navy, and the air force, as well as those in the many other quasi-military bodies adscript to them, is permanently observed in secret and detailed records are kept on every aspect of their lives, to ensure that the slightest sign of opposition to the government is immediately detected and measures are taken to eliminate it.

It is frequent that those in high positions have their wives and girlfriends recruited by the secret services, especially if they are married in second nuptials with young women. This way, all the personal aspects of their lives are controlled and the regime does with them whatever it likes.

There are military prisons in every province and the conditions of them are even worse, in most of the cases, than in other common prisons existing in the island. What happens at them is kept secret from the rest of the population, but the rumors that filtrate from them indicate that the people who are sent to them experience an even more violent repression because they must become an example to others in the military of how serious the consequences of any activity contrary to the system can be.

The people at the different levels of the government, as well as those belonging to the communist party and the communist youth, are not exempt either of the continuing vigilance of Castro's system, which is designed and organized in a way that keeps everybody under permanent control.

All these people must live under the permanent stress of knowing that their lives are scrutinized continually, without any notion of privacy or limit regarding what can be considered their personal life. The political aspect of their lives oversees every other aspect and they must accept this or risk punishment and separation of their functions.

They must know that, if they deviate an inch from their script, within the scope of their functions, they are going to be removed from their positions, and most likely, they will be sent to the most conspicuous activities, usually in enterprises located at remote places, after suffering all sorts of humiliations, which may include the loss of the houses assigned to them, their cars, the possible special school for their children, and any other pseudo privileges they may have due to their positions, all of which could mean, for them and their families, a total disaster in their lives and a very dark future.

Cuba has become a land of repression, in which nobody literally can feel safe. The possibilities of any citizen of achieving practically anything in life, depend largely on the way their activities and ideas, and basically all their background, are scrutinized and evaluated by people they do not know, located in some obscure places, who are dedicated full time to do this kind of work on people that work at all the different levels of society.

Obviously, a system like this creates a constraint of all individual liberties and limits to unimaginable levels the freedom of expression, forcing the individual to act in very strange ways. Cuba has become a country where simulation is a permanent act of living and it becomes an essential part of the character of people since their early years until they die.

There are people in the world that illusorily pretend to transplant Castro's system to other countries, this is, to apply it in their own countries, wrongly thinking that this could be a solution for the problems those countries may have. They do not realize that, contrary to their expectations, the one thing they will obtain from these attempts will be to bring their countries to a state of permanent disaster, which is going to contradict the advance of civilization at them, by annihilating most of the most valuable liberties that the human beings have achieved through centuries of social and intellectual development.

A system based on repression can be an invaluable tool for a dictator to keep a country subjugated, but it will never be a proper mechanism to allow the development of free societies and the whole potential of human beings.

It is recommended that those who, stupidly, still look at Cuba as a potential political model, which should be applied in other countries, try to become better informed about the real conditions in the island and learn to look at the real facts behind the curtain of propaganda Castro has created.

CHAPTER XV

~

Castro's interpretation of foreign policy

The Cuban revolution was followed with extraordinary interest in all parts of the world since its early days, mainly because of the symbolic implications of having a small and powerless country confronting the most powerful nation on earth and it continued being a focus of attention after it transformed in a brutal dictatorship, something that has lasted to our days and Fidel Castro, being the main leader of this curious phenomenom, has received the attention not only of all levels of world politics, but also of those common people in many countries, who usually live their existence far from the great decisions and without involving at all in politics.

Castro's image and ideas, as well as his actions, have been followed, and in some extent magnified, by the international press, which has brought them to every corner of the world and this facilitated that he became a sensation of world politics, a sort of idol for friends and a demon for enemies, but always a connoted figure, with a very unique image.

Castro tried hard to keep that status by doing eccentric political movements to attract attention and also by using his large propaganda machinery to this end. The result has been that, even now, after so many of his criminal actions have been exposed in detail by some of his former close allies, there are still many people around the world who feel an enormous fascination for him, no matter their political or ideological affiliation.

It is not simple to explain how a small island in the Caribbean, and the dictator running it, could reach such a level of publicity, but the fact is that, for half a century, Cuba has been somehow a relatively important piece of world politics, and Castro enjoyed a status that very few people, with similar responsibilities in other countries, has had.

Evidently, Castro considered that the more he internationalized his revolution, the more this was going to provide him an effective and quick way to project and enlarge his image, this helping him to keep his status as a well-known and powerful politician, something that also could provide to him some coverage to allow him to do whatever he wished in Cuba.

There are big differences and contradictions between Castro's theoretical slogans of freedom, economic independence, and development for the poor countries in the world, which he used continually as part of his propaganda and the insane repression he has imposed on the Cuban people and the obscure designs of his international policies.

Foreign policy became a key element within Castro's conceptual system and he devoted to it enormous energies and resources, even during those stages in which his regime has been more isolated due to the changing conditions in the world.

The way Castro interpreted foreign policy was radically different from the way most other small nations and their leaders do. In large extent, Castro approached the relationship with the rest of the world in the same way that only some of the most powerful countries have done during their most aggressive historical periods.

During the initial stage of his regime, Castro established the bases of its infrastructure, including its foreign services, which included not only the personnel to carry on diplomatic functions, but also those who were going to become the branch of his secret services devoted to international operations.

This period was characterized by the accelerated training of people whom Castro considered loyal to him to work in his foreign services, including those who were going to work in the branch of his secret services that he specialized in international operations.

Simultaneously, he established links and signed cooperation agreements with the Soviet Union and other European countries, which soon started to provide accelerated training courses for his people, something that soon reflected in the beginning of operations of the Cuban secret services in numerous countries and very specially in Latin America and Africa, the United States and the main countries of Europe.

For many years, Castro used as his foreign minister, a man of intellect and an eloquent speaker, Raul Roa, and he placed above him, as a vice prime minister in charge of the sector of foreign relations and commerce, another communist intellectual, with long ties with the Soviet Union, Carlos Rafael Rodriguez.

Those were the men in charge of the diplomatic side of Castro's foreign policy. Parallel to them and directly under Castro's orders, there were a number of other more obscure characters, like Commander Manuel Piñeiro and Coronel Antonio de la Guardia, in charge of special departments of the secret services, created to operate Castro's espionage network in the different regions and countries of the world. Both sides of this machinery of foreign "relations" worked coordinately.

Even when the secret services of those initial years of his government could not be compared with what his regime has now; they were able to participate very prominently not only in the internal repression of the opposition in Cuba, but also in important and well-elaborated international operations, which were developed with different objectives in mind and included the participation in conspiracies to eliminate foreign leaders, whom Castro considered serious or potential enemies or challengers to his pretended position as leader of the underdeveloped nations.

The main obscure chapter of Castro's operations during those initial years of his regime, which evidently could be considered an advance of what his foreign operations were going to be later, was indeed the assassination of President John F. Kennedy.

Incidentally, those two officers mentioned above had strange deaths. Tony the la Guardia was executed with the mentioned General Arnaldo Ochoa after a well arranged trial, in 1989 and Piñeiro died in an absurd crash going to his home under very strange circumstances, just few days before he started a number of interviews that had been arranged to tell his side of the history in regard to numerous events in which he had a key role related to the frustrated movement of Che Guevara in Bolivia, as well as other many events promoted by Cuba in Latin America and other regions. It is not very difficult to imagine that Castro may have been delighted of eliminating such two witnesses of his crimes.

I have mentioned in the chapter dealing with the Cuban exiled community, that there is a book published in the United States that is based on many declassified documents, recently released by the national archives, which remained secret for almost half a century and are slowly coming to light. Researchers are finding on these documents all sorts of evidences about the resolute will of Kennedy and his brother Robert to overthrow the government of Castro.

There are important elements within the complicated set of events surrounding the assassination of President Kennedy, which could associate Castro to it, even when some authors and researchers have put more emphasis on the idea of the possible existence of a conspiracy between members of the American intelligence community, the mafia, and some important American political figures, including as well some figures of the Cuban exiled community.

It calls my attention that nobody has tried to establish, among those researchers who have published important books and articles on these events, a possible link between Castro's secret services and Santos Traficante and other members of the mafia, who were in Cuba in the early years of Castro's government and have been considered suspects during all these years of having some role in the assassination of the president.

However, despite the mentioned omission, it is important to note, that Traficante and other notorious figures of the mafia, who were also in Cuba at that time and were involved like him in the management of some casinos and gambling places during the government of Batista and the early years of Castro's, could have had reasons to establish some connections with Castro's secret services, despite the fact that Castro had shown his intentions to eliminate most of the casinos in the island.

It is a fact that Traficante was detained in Cuba for several months and he later remained for some more time, almost another year, in the island, which is curious. He was having problems with the law in the United States and he and other mafia people were very concerned about the actions against them by the then attorney general, Robert Kennedy, who was obviously backed by the president. All this presents a scenario that could be a point of contact for mutual interests with Castro, who almost for sure knew or had some indication of one or more imminent new operations against him, which were close to be implemented by the Kennedy brothers in silence and were planned to start just days after Kennedy was assassinated, including the one recently disclosed involving Commander Juan Almeida, one of the key people within Castro's movement and other top officers around Castro.

Also, Castro was closing the casinos in Havana, or so he had shown in the press, but in fact, there were still some casinos operating there several years after he took power, and knowing Castro, he could have the idea of proposing some kind of deal to Traficante and his friends, by which he could offer some protection to him, by merely allowing his stay in Cuba, or even suggesting that he could be allowed to operate some casino under some agreement with Castro and this way he could keep that possibility open for American tourism, which he had to realize was a golden egg.

I had a strange opportunity in my life that I never associated with other events, until I got more documented on things that happened during the Kennedy's years associated with Cuba, of knowing first hand, from people I knew, who had been at the very top levels of Castro's secret services and the Ministry of Interior during the early years of the regime, about some connections between high levels of those services and Santos Traficante, and I could learn that they had meetings with him in Havana, which somehow caused Traficante to give, as a present to one of them, an expensive pistol.

It was evident, according to what the person who talked to me expressed, that the relations between them were somehow friendly, and I keep fresh in my memory the smiling gesture this person had in his face when he told me that. I do not mention his name because he still lives in Cuba.

The fact is that Traficante was detained in Triscornia, an immigration detention center in Havana, and there are accounts indicating that, apparently, he felt that he was enjoying there a good life, according to some recollections of people mentioned in Lamar's book. This is interesting, considering the circumstances in which he was, and it is strange that he was allowed to stay in Cuba another year.

Castro has been all his life a sort of super gangster, who has manipulated very easily terrible people. It may be shocking to some readers, but my perception is that Traficante could be considered a little child compared to Castro, no matter how dangerous he could have looked or been for other people.

I tend to believe that Castro could not lose the opportunity of having such a character detained in Havana, without trying to get some advantage out of it by establishing some connection with this man, with whom, coincidentally, he shared some powerful enemies.

It seems very obvious that Castro's tortuous mind had to visualize very clearly the potential possibilities that establishing some connections with the mafia at a high level could represent for his plans within the United States in the future. After all, it is well known that he has been linked to worse and more elaborate political gangsters or assassins, as well as to other international criminals since then.

One has to question, why the top people of the Ministry of Interior had to deal directly with Traficante and not other lower level officers. There had to be an extremely important motive for this, which is totally contrary to their common practice, and considering the events that happened later and the assassination of the president, one has reasons to be suspicious of this connection, which again, knowing Castro's nature, I do not find strange because it matches perfectly within Castro's and his secret services' style.

If, as I think, Castro established some kind of "cooperation" with Traficante, and through him, probably, with other mafia figures as well, this could become the missing piece in the puzzle of Kennedy's assassination, which could explain how Castro could have been informed about many events that were in process and how he could have indirectly participated in the conspiracy to kill the president.

Following the above links, I would also not be surprised if one day researchers find other track records involving the Cuban secret services in the deaths of Traficante and other mafia figures. Obviously, these are just hypothesis that time will have to confirm or discard.

The fact is that, I am convinced, like many other Cubans who have been involved in the opposition to Castro for a good number of years, that Castro played a key role in the assassination of Kennedy, and one day the real story will be known, even when, for the time being, people will be limited to know only the well-elaborated version of Castro's role, which was created in Havana, by people who are specialists in these kind of work, while the books published in the United States obviously lack the real information from the Cuban side.

There has not been any crisis involving Cuba and the United States of a level even remotely comparable to the ones that occurred during Kennedy's tenure and there is no doubt that the death of Kennedy can be considered the well-defined end of a stage of Cuban-American politics.

Castro emerged from this mentioned stage with considerable more power, because not only was he able to survive the attempts against his regime by Kennedy, but also he established new links with the Soviet Union, which allowed him to expand considerably his activities in practically the whole world.

During the initial stage of his government, which considering all the time he remained in power was relatively short, Castro had been recruiting thousands of people from all Latin America, the United States, Europe, Africa, and Asia, who were brought to Cuba and were trained to promote all sorts of movements. Once he got the support of the Soviet Union, this allowed him to enter into a new stage, in which he actually developed those movements he was planning in many countries while he was also able to increase to incredible levels, with much wider scope, the activities of his secret services.

Castro established a concept of international relations for Cuba, which is basically different from the traditional way small nations have carried on them. While most small nations, as well as other large underdeveloped ones, have limited international links, this due mainly to their financial limitations, and their embassies and foreign offices mainly carry on a reduced number of consular, economic and diplomatic functions, Castro established a vast network of embassies spread in the whole world and many of them carry on very important intelligence activities, separate of the traditional diplomatic ones.

Another aspect of Castro's concept, consists in the establishment of a system by which every Cuban embassy not only has a wide range of diplomatic activities, but also, they can be considered centers for all sorts of intelligence activities, even if this means to interfere in national matters, something his regime has done once and again, without any scruple and with no respect for international rules.

Every nation in which Cuba is diplomatically represented, which is almost the same than saying every nation of the whole world that wishes to have relations with Cuba, must accept that Castro's secret agents use the Cuban embassies as a facade for their operational centers, and that, from these embassies, they collect data, contact, and recruit people at all levels, organize actions, and, if necessary, work to undermine those governments or figures that Castro does not like.

For example, in London alone, Cuba has had for many years more than four hundred people who receive money from the embassy, but are not functionaries of the embassy or diplomats in transit. What all these people who apparently live normally in Britain do is a mystery. The embassy keeps a long list of their data and the only personnel who deals with them are those in an enclosed part of the embassy, with limited access, from which Castro's secret services operate. Apparently, this pattern is also followed in many other Cuban embassies, like the one in Mexico, for example, which seems to be a center for espionage for the whole continent and the one in Spain, a country that Castro considers very important as a pathway to move his illicit fortunes to other European countries and also as his favorite intermediary with the European community, which represents for him a balance of power in his struggle with the United States.

It is not casual that Castro had literally in his pocket numerous politicians and important people of all these mentioned countries, some of whom are in very high positions and I would not be surprised to know that they owe their positions to his "assistance."

The same concept is applied when dealing with international organizations. Every Cuban representation at them includes a large number of people who work for Castro's secret services and they develop their activities with total impunity within each organization. There are numerous people at high positions of them who have contracted debts of gratitude with Castro and his regime and they can be sure that, at one moment, they will have to pay them.

Since the early days of his government, Castro developed a vast international network of espionage, which operated in practically the whole world. While his government official Ministry of Foreign Relations have carried on its version of diplomatic functions, including in first place the task of defending Castro's revolution in every international forum, there is a parallel secret service institution, which operates under its cover, with much more complicated responsibilities.

Under Castro's rule, Cuba established and maintained relationships with more countries than any other small country in the world and has been involved in the most varied scope of activities related to them, at a level that would seem unthinkable, given the limited resources of the island and the poor state of its economy.

From military and intelligence activities to medical and educational services, Cubans have been active participants, for the past six decades, in all sorts of relevant international situations, even in the most distant and remote areas of the world, always following Castro's designs.

Obviously, such a wide range of international activities has required an enormous and expensive infrastructure, but Castro prioritized this sector among most other needs the Cuban people have had, perhaps due to the fact that he considered this side of his political existence the most relevant to promote and preserve his image, something crucial to achieve his unlimited dreams of glory.

One must wonder, how this man could achieve that a small island like Cuba, in a state of permanent economic bankruptcy and social disaster during most of his long dictatorial tenure, could act in such surrealist and varied functions as advisor for educational services of New Zealand or president of the Non-Aligned Movement or as the main provider of international medical assistance to developing nations or, even more incredible, as the military force used to try to impose governments and establish new political systems in Africa, Asia, and Latin America.

One must also wonder how a man able to operate at such a scale and who was able to remain in power against all odds for half a century, a very unusual case, could be so incredibly selfish to ignore the consequences of his brutal actions and the disastrous reality he submerged the Cuban people and how he was so incapable to run the Cuban economy and society in a positive way.

As time passed, Castro assumed a larger international role, thanks to his close relationship with the Soviet Union, which provided guidance and orientation and almost unlimited resources for him, which allowed the Cuban military presence in many countries of the world, something that required an expansion of the machinery of foreign relations. Cuba used its huge network of embassies in every region of the world and increased the size and scope of its representations at numerous organizations, all this obviously including, in the first place, the expansion of its espionage network, which became one of the most notorious in the world.

Following the agreements of the Bandung Conference of 1956, the movement of non-aligned countries was founded by Gamal Abdel Nasser, from Egypt; Jawarharlal Nehru, from India; and Josyf Broz Tito, from the former Yugoslavia, in 1961, with an important role played in its creation also by Kwane Nkrumah, from Ghana; and Sukarno, from Indonesia, as well as by other leaders from a number of new developing countries, which wanted to establish an independent policy in regard to the world's main powers.

Castro saw in this mentioned organization a new possibility to expand his international image and give more value to his services to the Soviet Union and managed to be elected as president of the Non-Aligned Movement in 1979, at a very crucial time, which included the bloody war between Iran and Iraq. This was a paradox because he was in fact the antithesis of that movement due to his communist affiliation and his close ties and dependence of the Soviet Union, but despite this, he was, indeed, able to use this otherwise inefficient and loose organization for some time, even after his presidency, as an instrument to cover up the expansion of his espionage activities in the whole world.

During that time, Castro dedicated almost full time his foreign minister, Isidoro Malmierca Peoli, who had replaced Raul Roa in 1976, to travel to numerous countries and events in his name and especially to act as mediator between Iraq and Iran. Malmierca had had an early important role in the development of his secret services and had been a figure of the former Cuban Socialist Popular Party (communist), so he was ideally suited for this job, even when he was not a diplomat. Curiously, given his high position and functions, his selection seems to have represented a sort of Castro's joke or irony, because his name, in Spanish, closely remind the words toilet, shit and fart!...

The use so openly of people from his secret services for high positions or key roles has been common under Castro's regime. During these past decades, even in the most remote small and poor countries, Cuban agents have been present, in many cases masked under diplomatic functions and always trying to get some advantage, with their traditional modus operandi, which includes the recruiting, blackmailing, corruption and penetration of the societies where they operate.

Castro's concept of international relations includes the use of existing organizations, which he considered useful for his purposes, as well as the creation and ulterior use of all sorts of other new ones in numerous countries, even in those countries in which he has not been allowed to operate freely or those with which Cuba has not had relationships with. Usually, there is a common pattern that is used once and again, by which a new organization is set in a particular country by some people connected to Cuba, who receive funds from an unclear source and it starts recruiting people and creating a resume of actions, promoting some new figures who must have appeal based on ethnic or military factors.

The immediate goal of these new movements is to promote sabotage, crime, and terror within their societies and the use of violent means and corrupt political actions to try to ascend to power, leaving aside the traditional political forces that exist there.

Castro used widely the blackmailing of foreign leaders and functionaries in numerous countries, in order to gather inside information and also to facilitate the positioning of people, who have been previously recruited by his secret services, in different levels of the governments, as well as in the armed forces.

He used extensively the offer of medical and educational services as a way to penetrate the society of many countries. Since most developing nations have limitations in regard to their medical services, when Cuba offers to send to them a large number of people in this field at relatively low cost, this becomes an offer which is difficult to refuse.

By accepting, these governments are intrinsically allowing Cuban secret services, who come disguised among the medical personnel, the access to all levels of their societies. What is presented as a noble purpose is really a carefully elaborated intelligence operation.

Many politicians in poor countries prefer not to consider how it is possible that Cuba, a country with so many limitations, including a poor and decrepit hospital system, can send tens of thousands of doctors, nurses, and other medical assistant personnel to so many countries because they prefer to play the game of presenting these so-called medical services as an achievement of their governments, when in reality what they are doing is precisely to follow Castro's plans of using these services as a way to soften the stand of these societies against communism while using them simultaneously as a way to have access to all kind of matters and people in the countries where they are accepted.

The main intention of these services is not to cure people, but to gain consciousness, something that facilitates the ulterior recruiting of people according to Castro's objectives at all levels of these societies. They allow the penetration of Cuba's secret services almost openly in the countries in which they are admitted. The same can be said of the continuing offers of scholarships in the field of medicine and others, to carry on studies in Cuba, which in reality is an elaborate way to allow the recruitment and training of people to work as informants and agents for Castro's secret services, people who will be planted later in key positions within their countries at a very low cost.

Cuba received considerable material, training, and logistic support for the development of all these complex operations from the Soviet Union and East Germany, countries with which Castro established a close coordination in this field and where he trained his secret service personnel at the highest level existing at them.

For many years, during the decades of the seventies and eighties, Castro developed an enormous effort to try to bring to power in other countries some of the people and organizations he had been promoting, always using any chances that could emerge in local politics, based on national circumstances, personal conditions or deteriorated economic situations or even by trying to impose them by force based on his military will.

Salvador Allende, a socialist with close intelligence links to Cuba, was elected president of Chile in 1970 and Castro tried hard to impose his rule in that country, but the Chilean army deposed Allende and Castro's attempt failed. For many years after that, Castro continued trying to intervene in Chile.

In Granada, he supported Maurice Bishop, but again a military coup deposed Bishop in 1983 and this was followed by an American intervention in the island, which meant that Castro could not carry out his plans either.

Castro's failed attempt to create a communist revolution in Bolivia, where Che Guevara was captured and killed is well known.

We have mentioned already his role in the wars of El Salvador and Nicaragua, which became bloody events of very high intensity.

In general one can say that, during six decades, most Latin American countries have had to fight the attempts that Castro, one way or another, tried to carry on to undermine their democratic course and these countries have had to pay a very serious price to fight him.

Castro also supported a good number of figures in Africa, where he oriented for more than a decade his activities in large extend as a way to reciprocate for all the assistance he was received for the Soviet Union.

One of the earliest figures he supported was Ahmed Ben Bella, who was elected president of Algeria in 1963, a country to which Castro sent a small army, including tanks and artillery, to confront Morocco, its neighboring country, with which that country had a territorial dispute. Ben Bella was deposed by the army in 1965 and Castro had to come to accept this and keep the relationship with his successor, Hoari Boumedienne.

He also supported, among others, Mengistu Haile Marian, an Ethiopian dictator who ruled that country merciless from 1974 to 1991; Agostino Neto and his successor Eduardo Dos Santos, of Angola, a country to which Castro sent a large army in 1976, which was the key to the defeat of the UNITA movement of Jonas Savimbi; Castro also sent important forces to Congo and Guinea Bissau and supported another notorious dictator, Robert Mugave, in Zimbabwe.

His secret services and units of his army also took part in numerous other operations in Yemen, Somalia, South Africa, Morocco, and many other African nations.

He established very close links with Saddam Hussein and even sent to Iraq his best orthopedic doctors to cure him of some illnesses.

In 1973, Castro showed his opportunism and lack of scruples, when he supported the invasion of Czechoslovakia by the Soviet Union and later he did the same with the invasion of Afghanistan in 1979, despite the fact that he was the president of the Non-Aligned Movement at that time.

Castro was involved in the war in Vietnam, a country where he sent people, from his secret services, specialized in tortures and interrogations, together with other specialists.

During this mentioned stage, Castro had a key role in the creation of new international organizations and he organized gigantic anti-American conferences, like the Tri-Continental Conference, which took place in Havana in 1966 and served the purpose of promoting Castro's anti-Americanism in the whole world by creating the World Organization of Solidarity of the Peoples of Asia, Africa, and Latin America, which brought his image to every corner of the world as the antithesis of the United States.

This stage of Castro's foreign policy, characterized by the continuing expansion of Cuban military, intelligence, and diplomatic activities in the whole world, including a very active role in most international organizations, was based in the almost unlimited financial support of the Soviet Union, which also provided Castro with a huge military and intelligence backup.

It was during this stage that Castro's propaganda machinery expanded to become something never before seen in any other small nation and its main clearly defined role was to promote the image of Castro even in the most remote corners of the world, which was emphasized by Castro's well-planned visits to numerous countries of Asia, Africa, and Europe as well as some in Latin America.

Cuba, the small and poor island of the Caribbean, located just ninety miles from the United States, became the base from which several large military expeditions to Africa departed and from where Castro followed, from a newly established command center, not only his African adventures, but also the movements he promoted and organized in different countries of Latin America, including the wars of El Salvador, Colombia, and Nicaragua.

The total lack of scruples shown by Castro in all these wars and movements was absolute and it was in contradiction with the noble objectives his propaganda was announcing. In Somalia, for instance, Cuban forces killed tens of thousands of people and destroyed merciless all the civilian and military infrastructure of a country infinitely weaker than Cuba and this was one of the reasons why that country entered in a long stage of total dismembering which lasts to our days and the same degree of merciless occupation characterized by massive assassinations and destruction was introduced in every country in which Castro decided to intervene in one way or another always in the name of the "liberation" of those countries.

During all this stage, Castro continued using his secret services for his systematic penetration of the societies of most Latin American countries as well as the United States and other European countries, and they operated almost freely within international organizations, recruiting people at all levels of governments and armies and among the most important functionaries in all sorts of fields.

If a president or important leader of one of these nations became ill, Castro immediately offered his medical services and the best Cuban doctors were urgently sent to attend them, that is, if they could not go to Havana to receive "free" treatments at the best Cuban institutions, which all have special areas for foreigners only.

The most prominent writers and artists of the world did not escape Castro's attention, and many of them were invited to Havana and received economic and promotional support from Cuba, in most cases under the cover of some of the international artistic and writers organizations developed there to promote another more "independent" culture. The House of the Americas and the National Union of Artists and Writers became the literary and artistic undercover for Castro's secret services, which arranged an intricate set of relationships between communist Cuba and authors from all over the world.

Based on all of the above, Cuba became a key participant in every world forum or organization and Castro's role was praised by many prominent international figures as a leader of new nations and good causes of the world and even prestigious religious and philosophical international leaders avoided to express their criticism of Castro's actions, apparently because they were not "convinced" of the cruelty of his actions or perhaps because they were afraid of the consequences of having an ideological collision with him.

When the Soviet Union and the European communist bloc of nations disappeared, Castro continued operating and expanding his secret services autonomously and he even procured the recruitment of former agents of those European countries, who had been working with the Cuban services for many years and were well known by his people.

It is surreal that, leaving well behind his excommunication by John XXIII, when Castro visited the Vatican in 1996, he was invited to lunch by five cardinals, after meeting the pope for thirty-five minutes while then Cuban Cardinal, Jaime Lucas Ortega y Alaminos, in Havana, could not receive my wife, the wife of a political prisoner, who risked her freedom by trying to give to him a list of prisoners who were ill at the main Cuban prison and were claiming for some medical treatment.

It is not surprising that Castro and his regime have been able to penetrate even the closed circles of the Catholic Church considering that has had more than enough time in sixty years to plant his secret agents masked as clerics. It is interesting to note the fact of the excellent relations of the present Pope Francisco, who even went to visit Castro at his home before his death!...

When the respected Dalai Lama visited Miami, he elected not to mention Castro'dictatorship over the hopes of all the Cubans who were praising his fight for human rights in Tibet, avoiding any mention about Cuba's situation. One wonder why this happened with such a moral figure.

Important religious leaders of numerous other churches and religions have also visited more discreetly Cuba and shared with Castro and talked normally about the problems of this world, without giving much time to the situation of the Cuban people under his regime.

Practically every director of every important organization of the United Nations has been courted by Castro and his regime and been invited to Havana, where they are usually shown around while visiting some of the crazy plans Castro promoted during these past decades and regularly there is no mention of those in Cuban jails included in any document at the end of their visits.

What does it make that so many prominent leaders have been afraid of expressing openly and without limitations their real feelings when they are in Cuba in front of the Cuban people and obviously of Castro? Quite frankly, I believe that all of them have lacked the courage and the will to defend the Cuban people and they have been afraid of what this man, who they perfectly know was a specialist in blackmailing and a sadist criminal without scruples, can do to them!

Why have so many distinguished personalities been so circumspect in criticizing Castro? Is there anything that makes these people, in many cases powerful moral figures, afraid of doing it, or is there any kind of obscure interest behind so much coward behavior? Or is it that Castro had some kind of special mental power over them? I do not pretend to have an answer for these questions and I believe every case may be different in some extend, but I have the feeling that overall, this is a case of lack of moral, if not also of material corruption within world politics, a territory in which Castro proved to be a real master, and corruption, in this case, is a term with many meanings!

Castro was excommunicated by Pope Juan XXIII in January 1962, based on his communist orientation and all his mentioned actions against the church, but this very important religious leader died few months later and since then, Castro has been playing with numerous Catholic figures of all levels, and has managed to keep his relations with the Vatican at a level acceptable to him.

The fact is that, despite his excommunication, he has managed to place the church in a defensive position, mostly oriented to survive what its main authorities may consider a period of Cuban history which will be followed by something more positive for them.

It is really worrying to see the photos of some smiling prominent cardinals, members of the top circles of the Vatican, visiting Castro and his brother Raúl, shaking effusively their hands, while so many people rot in jail from one corner to the other of the island.

When Pope John Paul II visited Cuba in 1996, he was brought to act within very narrow limits, avoiding any categorical statement about what clearly have been deeply established abusive and discriminatory practices against the Catholic and the faith for fifty years and, no matter the attempts of many honest Catholic to create a higher expectancy of the results of his visit, the fact is that one could not expect that the venerable pope with such a short visit and his limited contacts with the people could remove the heavy burden of fifty years of Castro's animosity and hatred against the church, even when it certainly allowed people to feel the positive fact that many people in Cuba are returning to the faith, after experiencing a deception due to their failed revolution.

The visit of Pope John Paul II caused a tremendous expectancy, especially among exiled Cubans, who have kept attached to their same faith for fifty years, considering the late pope's long record against communism, but the venerable pope's visit could not produce a miracle in such a short time. Castro tried as usual to manipulate and use the visit to give more credibility to his image around the world and to create more internal ideological confusion among the masses.

It is interesting to note that, while some prominent cardinals and other members of the church, all smiles, have acted in Havana in a way that has caused real astonishment to most Cubans who oppose Castro, other ecclesiastical figures of lower ranks have had a much more noble role that deserves applause and have tried, every time they have had a chance, to express their disagreement with Castro's policies.

The above creates an image of the church as an institution that seems to be ambiguous, having several orientations at the same time, like a hydra, which can have several heads.

Another problem with this is that, in general, one notes an unbalance between the hierarchical level of those who, within the faith, have apparently at least being ready to accept Castro in recent years and those who have opposed firmly him.

Castro developed a very special connection with most of the main Soviet leaders during more than twenty-six years and also with the leaders of other communist countries of Europe, and while, for sure, most of these people who were notorious for their cruelty and lack of scruples may have had reserves regarding his role as communist leader, there is no doubt that they supported him with more than what they could, considering the limitations their countries had, and it is another paradox that Castro used this enormous assistance, among other things, to promote his image above the one all of them had.

One can ask a college student, everywhere in the world, who these people were, by name or in terms of their actions, and most likely they will not know. Ask them about Castro and they will almost surely tell you that he was a dictator in Cuba or a great political leader, depending of their views.

While most leaders of the communist countries of Europe limited their functions to the administrative role assigned by the Soviet Union, which was the occupying power behind them, Castro convinced, and in some extend politically forced, the Soviet leaders, to accept that he was useful in another role, as a communist leader of another dimension, who was oriented to the developing world, and they found him their best card for this, in comparison to all the other existing figures of the developing world in his lifetime, whom we have mentioned before, this being also valid in regard to the main figures of other satellite communist countries.

All the main communist leaders, who coexisted with Castro from 1959 to 1986, when the Soviet Union started to change under Mikhail Gorvachev's leadership, had a much less cultivated image and a narrower philosophical scope than him, which somehow limited their world recognition. Mao Tse-Tung, Chou En-lai, and Deng Xiaoping were mainly oriented to try to transform China, a gigantic, violent, and strange cultural task, which made them rather strange to be accepted in the rest of the world. Nikita Khrushev, Leonid Brezhnev, Yuri Andropov, Chernenko, and all the other Soviet leaders were old men who lacked the charisma to be likable to the masses of the world and were all smeared by their role during Stalin's rule. Ho Chi Min was the leader of a remote country in Asia, who was in charge of fighting a war, not pretending to lead the world. Kim Il Sung, the Korean leader, was a sick fanatic. Erich Honecker was a dark sinister figure imposed by the Soviets. Ceausescu was an aberration. Tito was an independent figure and he was one of the leaders behind the creation of the Non-Aligned Movement, but he never could reach the masses of the world, probably because he lacked the material support for this and he had had numerous clashes with the Soviet Union on top of his numerous ethnic crimes. Most main figures in the communist countries of Europe were not real leaders, but just administrators, who had been placed in their positions by the Soviets. Most of these men were also old and many were ill people and they did not last much in the world scene compared with Castro's long stay in power.

The international arena was Castro's natural environment and he got in love with the idea of being acclaimed and recognized as one of the most well-known world figures, like a rock star, but also in terms of influence and power, because even the most powerful people in world politics came to realize that he was not only the leader of a small country, but also a man with influences beyond his position, who had an undisputed talent, as well as the power and resources, to implement the worst schemes and carry on the most determined actions everywhere in the world.

He became well known, but also feared and it is this second aspect that has made him able to reach a level very rarely seen in world politics.

When Mikhail Gorvachev was appointed as the new Soviet leader and started his political reforms, Castro immediately detected in him a formidable enemy and he found that the combination of the new political ideas and the movement that came with them with the obvious enormous power this man had inherited, could become a huge obstacle to his permanence in power in Cuba.

Gorvachev's different views and the new trend he represented in terms of ideology were the opposite of Castro's system, but also, he realized that any change or disruption of the established order in the Soviet Union and the rest of the European communist bloc was going to affect substantially the way his regime was supported and also the way in which he had got already used to operate.

The main public events that happened during Gorvachev's presidency are well known because they were covered by the world media, but this is not so in regard to all the obvious events that happened behind closed doors during those few years in which the Soviet Union was dismantled and Russia and all the other nations that were part of it became independent states.

There are clear indications and rumors in the sense that Castro not only expressed his disagreement with Gorvachev's policies and the new orientation of Soviet politics, but also that he started to plot against the new Soviet government presided by him, trying to contact people among the many Soviet authorities he had met in previous decades, who he considered disagreed with Gorvachev's policies.

There is a notable coincidence in the fact that, when a group of officers and other people of the old guard tried to produce a coup in Moscow against Gorvachev and the policy of perestroika in 1991, which failed among other things due to the intervention of Boris Yeltzin, many of the people who participated in it had been in Cuba in recent months.

As time passes, the role of Castro in these and other events that happened during those years in Russia will be better known, but nobody can be surprised if these rumors are true.

The disappearance of the Soviet Union and the new political trends that Russia and the other former communist countries of Europe followed represented the end of the second stage of Castro's foreign policy and left him and his regime in a very difficult position, after losing the main source of economic support they had.

China, the other existing communist power that remained in the world after those changes, had never been a full supporter of Castro, because of rivalries with the Soviet Union and ideological and personal differences its leaders had with him, and even when he tried to achieve some improvements in the relationships with the Chinese leaders, including visiting China, he could not relay in any full economic support for his regime from them at that time.

To make things worse for Castro, China's economic policies had started to change and the new policies that were being implemented were based on the introduction of elements and rules of capitalism and free enterprise, which in Castro's views were wrong, and what was more relevant, he did not consider them suitable for Cuba and the existence of his regime.

During the time Castro had been under the patronage of the Soviet Union, he not only engaged in all the military and intelligence actions that we have mentioned before, but he also devoted considerable resources and energies to a number of illicit activities related to the promotion and development of the international drug traffic, which he has considered an important element of his policy to undermine the American society and in general, the Western civilization, as well as the traffic and smuggling of arms and other commodities obtained through a network of corruption around the world.

He and his people also engaged in a vast scope of illegal banking operations and monetary transactions at very high levels, including the laundry of money coming from all of them and the acquisition of properties in many countries, with money stolen from Cuba's resources, as well as the operation of numerous facade enterprises in different countries, including developed and underdeveloped ones.

He also used his considerable resources during those years to promote and position numerous people in key positions in many countries and to establish an international network of espionage with the participation of people from other countries as well as Cubans, all of whom he planted at them for many years. With this scheme, he has been able to penetrate deeply the most closed institutions and has managed to use the information he has obtained as a trade commodity with anybody who shares with him his visceral hatred for the United States and the Western civilization.

When the mentioned changes in the Soviet Union happened, Castro not only found himself in a difficult situation due to his isolation in regard to his former allies, but also Cuba was in a situation of total disaster because, after several decades under his rule, the economy of the island was a total chaos and the conditions of living of the people were extremely poor while all the main sources of supply for the island were gone.

Castro also found that he and his main people, those who had stayed in power with him for many years, were already old and were entrapped by their own irrational policies of terror and corruption, what made any change in internal Cuban policy extremely unfavorable for their stay in power.

At that point, Castro started his third stage of foreign policy, which consisted of putting in line all the above-described activities and the people he controlled, using them the best he could as a network, to try to find the means to survive.

Incredible as this may seem, was been able, by doing that, to extend for another thirty years the stay in power of his regime and the Cuban people have been forced to resist another three more decades of miseries and calamities.

During these past three decades, despite the extremely bad conditions of the Cuban economy and the lack of external economic support for his regime, the Castro's regime has not stopped recruiting people in numerous countries and bringing them to Cuba to "study" at Cuban schools. The regime has not stopped sending more and more professionals, especially doctors, to those countries either.

Maybe some people in the world may consider these activities something that does not produce any harm or just a lenient way to carry on Castro's political objectives. Those who think this way should better reconsider their approach.

There are clear records and evidence showing that a number of these people, who have taken power in several countries of Latin America in recent years, received training in Havana and established close links with Castro's secret services. There are also well-supported accounts indicating that relatives of some of the terrorists behind the attacks of September 11, 2002, were studying in Cuba before that date. Is this a coincidence? I don't think so.

Some people, among those involved in international terrorist activities, consider Cuba a very safe heaven because they know that they can go there and during their stay they will be protected by the Castro's regime.

This has been the well-documented case of the members of ETA, the terrorist Spanish organization, who have lived in Cuba and used that country as their base of operations, but there have been many other leaders and members of terrorist groups like the Irish IRA, who similarly got important intelligence support, assistance and protection from Castro.

The same has happened and has been well documented, with the most notorious leaders of the main drug traffic organizations, who have been many times in Cuba and have had full access to the top level of the government, an example of this being the late Pablo Escobar and other important Mexican drug capos. It is impossible that those people could live in Cuba and get together with people like Commander of the Revolution Guillermo Garcia without establishing some level of coordination of their activities with Castro.

The same is the case of a good number of high-profile politicians and corrupt business people from many countries, who have lived in Havana for long periods of time, establishing links with Castro's secret services to obtain some protection for their activities.

Castro used his secret services to obtain gains from all of the former, but he also used them to collect classified information of numerous countries and specially the United States and Europe, which has been sold or bartered to other regimes interested in it. The case is that the regime has been able to plant its agents within very high levels of numerous governments, including the United States and Europe and also within numerous international organizations and the sensitive information they collect has become a precious item not only for Cuba but also for other regimes, among them some of the worst regimes in the world.

There is another key element of Castro's foreign operations, which is the procurement of access to important financial sources, something that has given to him the possibility of collecting an unprecedented amount of money and other resources during his long stay in power, which in most cases his government has not paid back.

As a matter of fact, Castro used the existence of this huge international debt, which I describe later in this chapter, to create a concern, in other countries and institutions, for whatever drastic change that could occur in Cuba that could imperil the collection of this money.

The United States broke its relationships with Castro's government in 1961, but prior to that, under President Eisenhower, the United States started an economic embargo against Castro, which was widened during President Kennedy's administration prohibiting most commerce with the island. This embargo has had ups and downs, but in general, it has been maintained until present days. President Carter removed some travel restrictions to the island, keeping most of the embargo measures in place, while President Reagan reinforced again the measures limiting travels and the embargo as such. During President Obama's years there was a huge increase in business and relations with Cuba.

In recent years, under President Trump, relations with Cuba have been restricted even when the island has been buying increasing quantities of food and other products from the United States. There have also been some recent restrictions in travel regulations that had been eased under the Obama administration as well as in the items that Cubans living in the United States are allowed to send to their relatives in Cuba.

The Castro's regime has used the existence of the American embargo as an instrument of foreign policy, and after sixty years of existence, it has become a pretext used by its propaganda to cover the state of permanent disaster in which the Cuban economy has been under the bad administration of its government.

People tend to forget, but Castro used every opportunity he had, during so many years, to get large loans from numerous countries, which are separate of those huge ones received from the Soviet Union. Castro's government failed to pay most of them plus all the interests they should have generated.

An example of the above happened when President Peron had his short comeback to the Argentinean presidency in 1973-74. Peron returned to power after an unusual process, in which one of his closest followers, his Secretary Hector Campora, ran for president, while Peron was in exile, and once he won the election, he allowed the return of Peron, renounced to the presidency, after few months, and ordered new elections, in which Peron was elected.

Curiously, in the middle of such a volatile situation, which lasted only few months, one of the things that the good Campora did was to sign a decree, ratified later by Peron himself, opening a very large line of credit to Castro, who immediately used the credit, getting into a huge debt of close to two billion dollars with that country, a debt that, to this day, has never been paid despite many discussions, offers, and counteroffers. Why was it so important for Campora and Peron to give such a priority to this credit to Castro is a good question.

Similar situations have happened with Mexico, Venezuela, Spain, Brazil, Panama, and many other European countries and even Japan, in which different governments have agreed to give large credits to Castro without any support, this being in most of the cases in contradiction with the own difficult economic situations they have had. Why something so strange has happened would need a research work that is above the limits of this book.

There are some real facts and statistics that reflect that Castro's regime has received several times more money during the past sixty years than during the whole previous existence of the island.

Castro, obviously, was not interested in talking about the real crude facts, but there is wide economic evidence of the enormous amount of subsidies he received from the Soviet bloc for more than twenty-five years as well as the huge debt Cuba has accumulated with a large number of countries.

It is precisely here that one can find another important element of what the foreign policy has meant for Castro and his regime, because they have used every chance they have had to take money from every source available in the world, which they have in general never bothered to pay, bringing Cuba to be the worst country in the world in regard to security of investments.

How those countries and their institutions, which one must assume have some degree of seriousness and responsibility, have agreed to such monumental idiotic loan decisions in regard to Cuba, can only be explained by going into the dark side of Castro's foreign policy, where the role of his secret services have prevailed.

Castro got most of this almost unbelievable amount of money, which I describe in the coming paragraphs, thanks to his schemes of corruption, which have been implemented once and again for the case of different countries and institutions, and this has become, thanks to that, a delicate matter very rarely mentioned outside closed circles of international finance.

Castro has used his well-elaborated blackmailing techniques and the use of bribery as his favorite tools and has provided very valuable services to numerous corrupt politicians in many countries, to assist in, or facilitate, their access to power, and the opening of those unjustified credit lines may have been their payment.

According to the University of Miami, Cuba facts, Cuba owed, in 2008, approximately 24 billion dollars to a wide range of countries, including Venezuela, Spain, Japan, Argentina, Mexico, France, United Kingdom, Italy, Russia (post-Soviet era), China, Iran, Panama, and many others while it also owed approximately another 22 billion to the Soviet Union and other former socialist countries of Europe, which makes a total of 46 billion dollar of debt for a small country of 11 million people. There is no doubt that Castro pretended to be the pimp of the world.

Every debt Castro contracted, with each of the countries in the long list of Cuba's debtors, has a story of strange dealings behind it, and these stories are much more complicated than the normal financial procedures for regular loans between two countries. It is here that Castro's lack of scruples and intrinsic corruption found another role.

What Castro did with such a monster amount of money is a question that probably will never be fully answered, but the case is that it becomes almost incomprehensible how this man and his followers managed to keep Cuba under such a state of poverty and disgrace having had free access to so many resources, which evidently are more than what any other small or large developing nation in the world received during the time it lasted.

Considering the above, one wonders what the real effect of the American embargo on the economy of Cuba could be after all these years, but apparently Castro considered that he was entitled to receive even more money, to support his regime, from the United States and other countries, on top of all the money he got from all these mentioned countries and many others, and this is why, he claimed for the end of the embargo as if it was a scratched record that repeats and repeats.

Evidently, if Castro's model was to be applied in other countries, even if they were only few of them, the whole world would need to dedicate its work just to keep those few countries afloat.

I mentioned in previous paragraphs the resources and conditions that Castro had when he lost the support he received from the Soviet Union, once it disappeared, which forced him to define a new policy of foreign relations. The fact is that soon, after the dissolution of the Soviet Union, he started collecting some results from some of his previous movements, when, due to very curious changes in the situation of some countries, unexpectedly, some of these people he had been recruiting, training and promoting found their way to the top positions of their countries.

During the past decades, the world has seen with incredulity how this same Castro's regime, the connoted violator of human rights, the assassin of so many people, the thief of enormous proportions, the drug, commodities and arm trafficker, the smuggler and money laundry washer and international criminal mastermind, has become an idol and respected master for a number of new presidents, elected in different countries, all of which belonged to movements that had received its support for many years and most of whom have even been connected personally with its secret services, during earlier stages of their lives.

Hugo Chavez, a repulsive and very primitive character, came to power in Venezuela, after following a path that seems a kind of replica of Castro's actions in Cuba, curiously including some of the same "ingredients" that helped to create the image of Castro, that is, a rebellion and attack to a guard barrack, a number of deaths, some short time of prison, his amnesty by the country's president and then, a new element, his participation and success in free elections. He considered that his success qualified him to change the constitution and the electoral laws to be reelected once and again, in manipulated and fraudulent elections, which obviously represent a big laugh of democratic institutions.

Since Castro had always been allergic to free elections, this obviously was a new element within his revolutionary methodology.

Chavez acted openly as a subordinate of Castro and gave to him huge credits and opened without prejudice his country to the penetration of Castro's secret services, allowing him to take control of most of the main activities.

The level of corruption established by Chavez's regime in Venezuela menaces to break the records established by Castro and this is also the case in regard to the destruction of every aspect of the economy and the society. Chavez and his follower Maduro created a disaster in Venezuela that probably will be even larger than the one Castro has created in Cuba, if this is possible to exist.

Chavez's case is very interesting because most Cuban officers and functionaries always openly considered him a primitive and crazy character and they used to make jokes about him and what more important, all of them realized the stupid role he was playing, by giving all kind of resources to Castro, who everybody knew was not going to pay to Venezuela for this.

It looks that most people, within the circles of power in Cuba, may have found difficult to understand how a character like Chavez could come to power in Venezuela, a country with so many entrepreneur and educated leaders, but they had to accept the enormous convenience of this almost "miracle" to allow them to survive, thanks to their avid exploitation of Venezuela's richness.

Some people considered that Hugo Chavez was going to be the real heir of Castro, given the role he pretended to assume, but this was far from being true. A careful and detailed look shows that the government of both Castros did not allow Chavez to have much, if any, participation in Cuban matters, even when Chavez has opened Venezuela for them. They were suspicious about the real thoughts and objectives of Chavez, given the strange circumstances of his ascension to power and the too much exaggerated fervor with which he got involved in the strangest causes and with the most sinister characters.

There is no doubt that, with the support of all the money that started coming from Venezuela's oil, the erratic Chavez became a very good interlocutor with some of the worst characters the world have had.

However, even if Chavez was giving money to Cuba the way he did and facilitating access to numerous other things, it is very unlikely that both Castro trusted him because they did not like his increasing presence in world politics and maybe this explains his strange death and his quick replacement with an even more idiotic Nicolas Maduro, a man basically formed in Cuba and controlled by Cuban intelligence.

In Brazil, Luiz Inácio da Silva, known as Lula, a corrupt socialist coming from the Workers' Party, with long and deep intelligence connections with Cuba, won consecutive elections and has been the President of that important emerging nation.

Perhaps due to the fact that that Brazil was already much more politically and economically structured than other counties in the region, he was forced to act more moderately in regard to internal politics, but this does not mean that he did not give to Castro huge credits, which most likely will never be paid, as it is a regular pattern for him. It was not, after all, Lula's money, so he was be very happy of having paid this way his debt of gratitude to Castro, after so many years enjoying his support.

The support of Lula to Iran and numerous other regimes, which are among the most dangerous in the world due to their links with terrorism and their animosity to the United States, made him very valuable to Castro and this was specially so considering his aspiration to become General Secretary of the United Nations, once he finished his presidency period.

In Nicaragua, incredible as this may be, Daniel Ortega, a Sandinista and communist leader, trained in Havana by the Cuban intelligence, who everybody in his country and outside it knows is a thief who stole all kinds of properties and money during his previous stay in power, was elected again, and he found only natural to commit fraud to remain in power and become reelected once and again.

Ortega was recruited and trained by Castro's secret services many decades ago and he has been so used to act as a puppet of Castro that sometimes he looks more like the secretary of the party in a province than the president of an independent nation. He has developed a system of corruption and immorality, which obviously is not going to improve Nicaragua's status as a poor country.

In Bolivia, another leader with old links with Castro's secret services, Evo Morales, who came from the movement of the coca growers, also came to power and among his most brilliant ideas, he decided to force the Bolivian army to reproduce Castro's well-known cry of "Motherland or Death" at the end of every event. This is the same army who defeated and captured Che Guevara and they decided to remove him from power after his attempt to get reelected once again.

Argentina, the large and formerly powerful South American country, also decided to go back to General Peron's diffused ideology and elected a corrupt couple, the Kirchners, Nestor and Cristina, as consecutive presidents, and they immediately moved to establish close links with Castro and Chavez, as well as with other left wing leaders of the continent, obviously, without this moving Castro to even attempt to pay the huge debt to that country for all the money that Peron and his secretary Campora gave so "candidly" to him decades ago.

The corruption established by the Kitchners and their acceptance of money from Chavez during their campaigns was a sad stage of Peronism.

In Ecuador, Rafael Correa, who loves to go to Havana, where he has had close ties for many years, won also the presidency, until he was replaced in elections by Lenin Moreno, his until then close associate who later decided to change curse and denounce him. In Uruguay, Jose Mujica, a former urban guerrilla man of the Tupamaru, a movement that was promoted and assisted by Castro several decades ago, also took power for some years.

A former president of Panama, Martin Torrijos, the son of the late General Omar Torrijos, who had died mysteriously in a plane accident years ago, went to Cuba almost ten times during his tenure. Nobody knew exactly what he was doing there, not being precisely a communist himself, embraced with Castro and his brother and in close talks at late hours of the night. Cuba has all sorts of facade enterprises established in the Panama

Free Zone and Castro's secret services have been using that country openly for many years to engage in all sorts of dubious trades and espionage, but this does not justify such a closeness.

There is also the illustrative case of another notorious thief, the former Mexican president Carlos Salinas, who like other former presidents of Latin America, established his dubious operations from Havana, where apparently he felt more protected.

Castro kept close connections with other important figures, not necessarily presidents, but also with considerable influence, who years ago started their careers under his auspice and have remained connected to his regime even when, because of their achievements, they have assumed very discreet roles.

A good example of this was Castro's intimate friend, the Colombian Nobel Prize winner Gabriel Garcia Marquez, a brilliant writer, whose figure has reached legendary dimensions thanks to his works, but who started his career working for Castro's press services, Prensa Latina, a suspicious job for a non-Cuban. Reading his books, one would think that he was a good candidate to be a democrat, not a follower of a decrepit communist leader like Castro, but inexplicably, there was something that kept him attached to his former mentor and brought him to avoid any expression of condemn to what happened in Cuba.

There is something very clear, that perhaps many people do not realize, when considering all these leaders and figures who have been connected to Castro and his regime for many years. They have come to power or have reached fame and fortune in other ways, but they all know that this does not mean that they are allowed to be independent in regard to their ties to Cuba.

If any of these people, by any chance, decides to change course in regard to Castro and his regime, because they may get convinced that their former course is obsolete and anachronistic, and they try to separate from Castro's links, this would mean the end of their political careers and most likely of their lives and they and their families would be exposed to many bad things because Castro, following the mafia methods he has studied and applied so well, will make sure that this does not go away without consequences.

There are other countries of the region following the same trend and friends of Castro have become presidents everywhere. This has given so much confidence to these mentioned Castro's followers that, when other candidates with democratic ideologies win free and open elections in Panama or Chile, they complain, as if the world was going to fall, and they accuse them of being puppets of the United States.

In their minds, however, all these disciples of Castro may be thinking what they will do once Castro and his brother are no longer in power. Are they going to keep their subordination to whoever comes after them? And what would happen if Castro's system fails? Would they be able to survive without Castro's secret services' support? There is no doubt that they have a lot in which to entertain their minds.

In the meantime, while all these astonishing events were happening, a sick and old Castro saw how his time in this world was passing and every minute of his life he felt was more valuable, and he was disturbed because he still could find time and energies to receive and give advice to all these legion of new figures, he kept in his mind that all of them were a bunch of crooks that he had recruited, who went there to receive his blessing while they looked at him with candor and appreciation.

He knew that, while they visited him and his brother Raúl, in other places in Havana, others of his people were arranging with their counterparts of those countries the final details of as many agreements as they could sign, to give more access to their resources to Castro's people and to facilitate his secret services could penetrate their societies as much as they liked.

All these new figures realized that Castro's time was finishing, but they were so afraid of him, that probably, even after he died, they were going to be scared of him.

They could not accept, however, that they had become an inconvenience for his limited time, because he still had to check, to be sure once more, that all his legacy and his image was going to be alive for many years to come and also that those properties and money he accumulated, thanks to so many "noble" causes in which he was engaged, which he intends to pass to his children as a good father and grandfather, are safe.

CHAPTER XVI

~

Castro and his brother Raúl:
The agony of a disaster

Almost four years ago, on July 31, 2006, Raúl Castro assumed temporarily the position of president of Cuba from his brother Fidel Castro and he was ratified officially for this position by the Cuban National Assembly, on February 19, 2008, once it became obvious that Castro was not physically able to assume back his former functions due to his delicate health condition.

Even when Fidel Castro kept initially his other key position, as first secretary of the Communist Party, which, according to the traditional communist interpretation, is the highest position in the country, it soon became evident that, due to his health conditions, he was considerably limited to fully develop his leadership functions, and as a result, his role, in large extent, became ceremonial or behind-the-scene advisor, if certainly his figure still frightened his close followers as well as his enemies, given his criminal background and his tortuous mind.

The real ailment Castro suffered has been considered a state secret and was never explained in full detail, but according to the own explanations of the government and himself, it was some kind of intestinal problem. Whether he had cancer or not was the subject of considerable speculation. The fact is that every image of Castro that was shown since then showed a weak convalescent old man with considerable physical and also mental limitations.

For a whole decade, however, Castro tried to develop a number of activities to show that he was still a valid figure within the country, including the periodical publishing of articles dealing with a wide variety of issues and his photos and videos periodically appeared in the press, usually showing his meetings with a number of foreign leaders who visited Havana during those years, but it was obvious that he was already an old and ill man, who had entered the last stage of his long political life.

He finally passed away on November 25th, 2016. By that time his brother Raul Castro had assumed all his former positions and duties.

I have not devoted much space in this book to the role of Raúl Castro within the Cuban revolution and I have avoided also to get into much detail about a number of other figures of Castro's revolution, who have been also relatively well known and have played important functions, at least during some stages of it, because I believe that their main role has consisted in being unconditional followers of Castro, who no doubt has been the creator and by far the main figure of this monstrous regime, being the one that gave to all of them the chance to participate in so many extraordinary events of Cuban history.

It is enough to say that Raúl Castro followed his brother during all the different stages of his political career, being a participant in all the main events of it, including the attack to the Moncada barracks, their short stay in prison, the exile stage, the Granma expedition, and the fight at the Sierra Maestra, as well as all the main events that have happened during the past six decades.

During all these years, he has played a key role backing and supporting his brother and, very importantly, keeping away all other figures, who may have wished to play a more predominant role, if he had not been there to keep them away. His physical presence allowed a confident Castro to travel the world and devote time to engage in all sorts of activities, inside and outside the country in his role as a leader of the government and party.

There have been many references to Raúl Castro's shortcomings during the fourteen years he has acted as the main leader of the regime established by his brother and there have also been many other references associated to other personal characteristics of him for many years.

It is well known by those who follow Cuban matters that he has been a heavy drinker and a man with very little, if any, scruples, who has been involved in all the same crimes and illegal activities of his brother Fidel, being in this regard a consummated accomplice.

The main reason why he stayed in that important position, as second in command of everything in Cuba for sixty years, is not due to any special talent or capacity, but because Castro found in him a sort of bodyguard, who he put in charge of the military, avoiding the permanence in such a powerful position of other figure, who could have challenged his power.

Practically, no other figure of the revolution has been able to stay right at the top of the regime continually during all these five decades. Some of them, like Ramiro Valdes, Guillermo Garcia, and the late Juan Almeida, euphemistically called Commanders of the Revolution, have been or were in charge of key positions during some long stages, but they were separated from power also during long periods of time. Others, like Jose Machado Ventura, who recently was appointed as a second in command at Raúl Castro's government, have stayed close to the top most of the time, but have had a more obscure role than the former and have been less identified by the people.

It is interesting to observe how Castro protected his brother Raúl during the early stage of the revolution, when he was appointed as chief of what was called the second front of his revolutionary army, which operated in an area that was considered much secure than other regions of the country to which he sent Che Guevara and Camilo Cienfuegos, who had to take, due to this, much more risks.

When Castro's forces entered Havana in 1959, Raúl used a ponytail and had very little hair in his face and had a sort of funny voice, which he changed somehow years later to a crisper one, and his enemies used this image to spread all sorts of rumors about his character, but in reality and most importantly, what he was since those days was a violent character, whose hands have never trembled when he has done atrocious acts.

If one takes, one by one, all the main characters of Castro's revolution, one arrives at the conclusion that practically all the main figures who have been in charge of the main responsibilities assigned by Castro to them, well at the Communist Party or at the government and the armed forces, are mediocre characters, full of imperfections, who absolutely lack all kinds of moral principles and scruples, having a low level of education and sensibility.

There have been other relatively secondary figures within the regime who have played important roles at one stage or another and have had much higher educational standards than these mentioned main people around Castro, but he used the other more primitive ones around him as a barrier to avoid the slightest competition to his leadership.

At the end, all these more qualified figures must have felt the discrimination imposed to their talent and only their opportunism and cowardice could justify their unconditional presence in Castro's ranks.

Leaving the myths created by the propaganda aside, one finds that those few main characters around Castro have been a bunch of incompetent and uneducated men, if certainly they have proven to have the same sadist and corrupt personality of their undisputed boss, a characteristic that has made them valuable for Castro, who picked and used them for the most varied functions.

There are a number of people who have tried to introduce a new imaginative concept, showing Raúl Castro as a better administrator than Castro and a man with more "realism" than his brother, indicating that his permanency in all the high positions he has held for so many years reflects that is a competent person.

Apparently, for these people, there are no more people to govern in Cuba than a Castro!...

I believe that the lack of moral of this concept and what it implies is so overwhelming that this can be considered offensive for the Cuban people.

Raúl Castro is a criminal and a delinquent, like his brother, and the people who try to validate the above concept should be more concerned about the disaster both have created than in justifying a smooth transition within the same system, which at the end kept the same absurd conditions in place.

More than anything else, Raúl Castro represents the attempt of his brother Fidel to preserve for his family and for himself, until his last minute of life and even after his death, the enormous power he has accumulated and the wealth he and some among his main followers have illicitly acquired.

Raúl Castro also represents, for many concerned interests in this world, the illusory possibility of collecting at least part of the accumulated debt originated under his brother's regime, which they accurately consider will not be paid otherwise. For others among them, he also represents the possibility of keeping the same status quo in Cuba, which results in a benefit for the most varied foreign interests in numerous fields, from tourism to commerce.

A newly free Cuba would bring with it an explosion of many currently dormant potential business possibilities as well as productive capacities and talents of the Cuban people and would represent a huge competition to other neighbor countries in numerous political, economic, and social aspects and there are obviously many people who do not want this and prefer to support the continuity of Castro.

There are people in the world also, who, after sixty years without much concern about the sacrifices the Cuban people have been forced to endure, are currently very concerned about a possible violent change in Cuba, if the Castro's system falls.

Those are the ones who hypocritically see Raúl Castro as their best chance of achieving a stable evolution to some kind of softer regime, diminishing the real potential for a fully democratic Cuba, which could be governed by decent, competent and qualified people.

In October 10, 2019, an already very old Raul Castro appointed Miguel Diaz-Canel, a younger communist cadre who had been previously occupying the position of President of the Council of State for one year and had also been First Vice President from 2103-18 as the new Cuban President, keeping the position of First Secretary of the Communist Party. Nothing significant has come so far from this and the fact is that the essence of the regime is the same established by Fidel Castro.

In reality, one must consider what the real status of the hypertrophic system currently in power in Cuba is, in order to make a proper evaluation of the situation before establishing what should be the best alternative for the future.

I have described, in the different chapters of this book, many of the key elements within the complex situation that currently exists in the island, as well as the background of historical events that have accumulated behind every aspect of its life. I feel that it is only logical that I try to add and integrate all of them to get a complete picture of the status of the current system, which can allow me to give a forecast of the future.

After sixty years of Castro, Cuba is currently a country in bankruptcy, in terms both of financing and moral conditions. It is a country immersed in its worst historical crisis in practically every aspect of its life, with a dictatorship that has oppressed even the most elemental aspirations of the people, with a brutality rarely seen in the whole American continent during the whole history of all their countries.

The Cuban economy, which could have received all the benefits of the many privileged human and geographical conditions the island has, has been brought to a state of permanent disaster by the idiotic and fanatical policies introduced by Castro and his followers.

The Cuban society has been oppressed for sixty years and all the natural virtuosities of freedom have been consequently kept away by Castro and his followers, something that no doubt has produced severe damage to the people in general and their customs and institutions.

The conditions of living in the island have gone backward the equivalent to many decades and have brought Cuba to primitive conditions in numerous main aspects and the whole infrastructure of housing, services, transport and communications, commerce and administration is in a state of such deterioration that in most aspects it can only be compared with those of the poorest countries on Earth.

The tourism industry, one of the most important sources of income all these past years, is based on the criteria of discrimination for the Cuban people and is limited by the repression existing under Castro and the lack of efficiency of the administration provided by his government, which is incompatible with the international standards for the industry and its own significance.

The educational and health services both suffer the same conditions of abandonment of the physical infrastructure of their installations and the poor and corrupt administration of the government, the lack of modern means, as well as the continuing drainage of human resources to satisfy irrational international services, which are contradictory with the state of those services in Cuba and the low degree of functioning they currently have.

The conditions for women and for the Cuban youth cannot be worse than those currently existing in the island and the population is oppressed to unthinkable levels and forced to live in the poorest conditions, without any hope for improvement.

The Cuban workers are exploited to unimaginable levels, suffering incredibly low salaries and bad working conditions, and they lack any possibility of improvement of their economic and social conditions.

The population has been forced to live under a permanent state of repression, which includes a permanent surveillance by the secret services of even their most private acts of living and they have been immersed in a backward and irrational system, where there is a lack of practically all the most common products existing in other countries, including food and proper clothes and they are living in the worst housing conditions, with no chance of enjoying any free expression of art nor travel rights.

The environmental conditions in the island are so deplorable that have become a real danger for the health of the population, and due to this, numerous epidemics and illnesses have developed, which are not addressed properly by the government, which is more interested in hiding their existence in order to avoid their inclusion in the manipulated statistics presented by Castro.

Cuba has a penal population, which is thousand times larger than the one it had before Castro or the ones of other much larger countries, and there are numerous Cuban families suffering due to this. The conditions in which all these prisoners live are against all the most basic principles of human rights.

Every attempt to express a new positive idea or protest against the situation in the island is immediately repressed with hatred by Castro's police and secret services who are full of torturers and assassins.

All intellectual activities and every branch of art have their potential achievements crushed by the ideological repression of the system and the lack of freedom characteristic of all its administrative levels.

Most sports practiced in the island have seen every day poorer and poorer results and the athletes find more difficulties to freely practice and advance their lives due to the system of exploitation established by Castro, which is oriented to satisfy his propaganda more than to encourage those athletes.

Cuba's foreign commerce and international financing and banking are in a state of permanent bankruptcy and strictly limited of funds due to the huge international debts contracted under Castro and it does not exist any possibility of any improvement in any aspect of them under the current conditions.

Practically every branch of the current Cuban government is badly administered and all of them present a state of abandonment and depreciation of their infrastructures and a lack of clear objectives of development.

The armed forces have been brought to a state of abandonment of their moral values and converted in a mechanism of exploitation for their members and it represents another gross instrument of oppression for the people.

The attempt of some people to create the image that the armed forces have some more prestige among other institutions and that Raúl Castro has been an effective administrator of them is false. Most of the main figures of the armed forces are among the most corrupt figures of the country, and they have been involved in all sorts of crimes and abuses, and the way this military machinery has been administered and operated shows considerably deficiencies and has become an enormous source of waste.

Most of the high-ranking officers of the armed forces who have been sent to other high civilian positions of the government, have caused numerous disasters at them, proving to be completely incompetent for their functions and absolutely corrupt.

Every industry in the country is in conditions of deterioration and they have extremely backward technological standards and they are unable to satisfy, even remotely, the basic needs of the people or the potential access to foreign markets.

The full administration of the country, from the top levels to the base, is absolutely corrupt and there is a lack of moral and honest values, and it needs the introduction of modern principles and technologies of administration, which allow the establishment of proper controls.

There is a whole vacuum of new ideas that could promote some kind of improvement in the situation the country is living as a result of the lack of incentives and the terrible conditions in which people are. Simultaneously, the anchylosed structure of the government and the communist system do not allow the promotion of new competent younger figures who could start a transformation of the country and bring it to a more rational system.

The main symbols of the country have been altered and the whole traditional concepts of love and respect for the motherland have been destroyed in the name of a fanatical approach, which does not have any kind of connection with the real historical values of the Cuban people.

Foreign relationships have been converted in a mechanism of secret services which have nothing to do with the real concepts of diplomacy, friendships and respect toward other countries and this reduces the possibilities of Cuba as a nation and it has been the source of a gigantic waste of resources and the dilapidation of Cuban richness.

The position of Cuba in world politics has been based more on corruption, blackmailing, and traffic of influences as well as on the unreal propaganda of Castro than in prestigious political, moral and economic values and in the real progress of the Cuban people.

The real position of the Cuban people in regard to numerous international events and modern political principles and ideas has been kidnapped and converted by both Castro in a monstrous engender of irrational interpretations, oriented to support their own personal interests and ambitions, as well as their homophobic political views and this has only served the interests of those who have committed all sorts of illegal activities in the name of the revolution.

There is a total impunity established for all sorts of illegal activities, which have been practiced continually by both Castro and their main followers and relatives, in violation of national and international laws and the degree of corruption and delinquency this represents cannot be compared with anything that happened in Cuba before, even during the worst governments Cuba had.

All the system of law and the Cuban constitution, among the most advanced in the world before Castro, have been dismantled and they have been replaced by an absurd and repressive set of primitive laws and a corrupt and maniac structure, which is used to keep the Cuban people in the worst conditions of their history.

Cuba has become a safe haven for all the wrong causes and characters and its territory has been used for a vast scope of illegal activities, and the Cuban authorities have been involved in the most reproachable actions while simultaneously they have proved incapable of administering properly the island and to devote the required attention to the advancement of its people.

Based on all the above facts that I have described, and given the enormity of the disaster in which Cuba has been immersed by Castro and his system, one reaches the conclusion that it is impossible that Raúl Castro and the same main top people, who have been following his brother and him all these years, can transform democratically and improve economically and socially Cuba, because they have used all their chances to do so for sixty years and have failed.

CHAPTER XVII

~

Cuba: The alternatives for the future

Most people in the world, including the Cuban people, realize that the era of Fidel Castro and his followers is ending, but nobody is sure about how long the process of disappearance of his regime will last, because the regime has managed to stay in power and keep the system operating for almost fourteen years after Castro's death, despite its numerous and obvious shortcomings, but there are also many indications that some of the other people at the top of the regime could attempt to give continuity to this monstrous engender of regime, once he, also a very old and sick man, can not continue with his functions.

It is becoming evident that the capacity of Raúl Castro, a much less outspoken personality, to replace his brother, has been limited and he may actually be bringing Cuba to an even worse situation, if this is possible to conceive, than the disastrous one his brother Fidel has created.

Whether Raúl Castro manages to keep the system alive and under control or not, will depend of numerous factors, some of which, like his own health, are difficult to predict in the short run, but it is becoming obvious that a number of conditions capable of producing a change in the system are growing.

Not only the whole economy of the island is in state of bankruptcy and the social problems and terrible living conditions are every day more serious, but there are signs of desperation of the people, who evidently are fed off with so much repression and misery and the lack of individual rights imposed on them.

The level of corruption of the regime has become incontrollable and everybody inside and outside Cuba realize that something has to be done to end the brutal and demoralized order established by Castro and his gang of corrupt, abusive, and depraved followers.

The alternatives for the Cuban people are relatively clear in broad terms, these being as follows: to continue with the same communist system, to reform the system by trying to introduce some flexibility within its ideological and economic orientation, also maybe trying to diminish the repression, even when this seems to be very difficult or a third much better path to change the whole system and leave behind this horrendous communist era, starting a new path of democracy and modern economics for the good of all the Cubans.

After sixty years of disaster, one should expect that these mentioned possibilities bring to a no-brainer and very clear decision, but unfortunately, there are so many interests in play and so many attachments to the current situation that the most likely way this third alternative is taken is if some kind of violent movement takes place.

Since Castro's illness was announced almost fourteen years ago, there have been all sorts of speculations about who could be the figure or figures that could govern Cuba after Castro's era finishes, and many people, including experts who follow Cuban events regularly, have given their opinions and have made their analysis on this situation, which implicates that a change of figures within the same system may be the most possible alternative that occurs at least in the short term.

Most of the above-mentioned analyses tend to use the method of going through the ranks of the top levels of the Communist Party, the Councils of Ministers and State, and the National Assembly, as well as the armed forces and the Ministry of Interior, trying to define those people who are in key positions of power and, therefore, have the best chances to assume the main leadership, after Raul Castro is gone, also trying to establish links among the different figures that could result in tactical alliances of them to try to prevail over others.

There is no doubt that a very important factor that comes out from these analysis is that most of the main figures of the politburo of the Communist Party, who also belong to the Council of State, are extremely old. There are a good number of other younger people in these bodies, but most of them seem mainly to be innocuous decorative figures, similar to others before them, who have been appointed and later kicked off by Castro according to his capricious will, leaving very little if any imprint in the people.

In the case of the Ministry of the Armed Forces, as well as in the Ministry of Interior, there are also a number of high-ranking relatively younger figures, a decade or more younger than the elder generation, who have important positions and could have a chance to assume key roles, depending on the way a transition or a more drastic kind of change takes place. The fact that they have the power to give orders within the military, not necessarily gives to them a special chance because even when the Cubans tend to give a somehow special connotation to the military, due to our historical background, something that cannot be ignored, there are many other people in other entities of the party and the government who also could have considerable weight at the right moment.

Unless a military coup occur, a possibility that increases as the current main people get older and the anxiety of the younger generation grows, the value of the positions of these officers in a stage of transition may not be substantially more than those of other figures, who operate outside the military, in other functions of the regime, some of whom even have accumulated important illegal fortunes that they keep abroad as well as contacts with other interests outside Cuba.

Despite the above, it is obvious that, whoever assumes control of the regime, will have to establish immediately his rule over the military and it may not be easy to keep them under control, once these officers absorb the idea that they are free of the control of Castro and his brother and must compete with the others to get their piece of the government pie.

The present regime seems to have contingency secret plans to deal with the eventual case in which Raul Castro can no longer function as a leader of it, if certainly, as I have analyzed before in this book, I have no doubt that Castro has also other kind of plans, for his children and his family, which almost surely will try to give to them, at least, some participation within the structure of power and, if this is not achievable, will allow them to continue their lives comfortably in other countries.

I would not be surprised if, at the moment of change, many of the people who have accumulated important fortunes abroad decide to leave the country with their relatives, as has happened in other countries including Cuba, when dictatorships have fallen, to avoid any confrontation that could create a risk for them. Probably, each of these people and their families have established his own contingency plans for such a possible situation.

A careful look at the people who are included in each of the main entities of the power structure of Castro shows that only very few of them are represented simultaneously in all of them, or even in the main ones, this is the politburo, secretariat, central committee, the Council of State, the Council of Ministries and the Armed Forces. Whether this can be considered a factor of some decisive weight or not is arguable, but there is no doubt that this should mean something, because of the inside knowledge and the connections these positions represent.

It is important to note that since Raúl Castro assumed the functions of president of the Council of State and the Council of Ministers, there have been numerous movements of people and new appointments at the top levels of the party and the government, which have increased the power of figures like Jose Ramon Machado, a hard-line octogenarian, who, after years of being at top positions of the party with relatively lower exposure than other figures, is now the second figure of these two bodies plus member of the politburo, and Ramiro Valdes, a commander of the revolution and a figure associated with the worst stages of repression of the regime, who is now again after years of being separated from the top positions, a powerful figure. Evidently the appointment of these hard-line figures indicates that Raul Castro is trying to intimidate all those people who could be thinking that changes are necessary, well if they are opponents or if they currently are within the ranks of the regime.

It is obvious that, in a regime as violent, corrupt, and capricious as the one Castro established in Cuba, all the main people at the top must be extremely fanatic and opportunistic and they must have an almost total lack of scruples in order to remain in their positions. It is extremely unlikely that anybody who does not have those characteristics could have survived for so many years under Castro.

There may be some myths regarding the bravery and courage of many of these people around Castro, including those at the top levels of the party and the military, who, after all, have accepted to be puppets of Castro during most of their lives in order to receive in retribution good and privileged positions. But most of these people have practiced all sorts of abuses, something that apparently they enjoy, and this means that they can be dangerous at some moment, especially if they are trying to survive a situation of change within the regime structures.

The Cuban people have been intimidated so much for so many years by all these people in uniforms and the sophisticated methods of abuse and repression, as well as by the weight of the structure of power imposed on their heads, that they may find difficult to react under some conditions of change; however, as recent hunger strikes by groups of pacific dissidents in the island indicate, there may be a subjacent tremor of liberty growing, which may indicate that more and more people are no longer intimidated by the repression and this can produce a social explosion and uprising that gets out of the control of the regime and under those conditions, evidently, nobody can be sure of what will happen.

Considering the overall situation, it seems that, unless something out of the established contingency plans happens suddenly, like a military coup or a popular uprising as we mentioned, which may provoke an alteration of the current positions and the relative influence of individual people at the different entities, the regime seems to have its options to create a state of continuity in the short term and, if this happens, it may take a while for people from younger generations, who may have different ideas, to be able to assume real control.

The fact remains, however, that the situation created by Castro and his regime in the island is, to me, insoluble under the current system, and no matter the interest that a group of people at the top may have in preserving it, it will be only a matter of time that a real change will have to come in the island.

I consider that the longer the arrival of this process of change takes, the more violent it may be, and it may be advisable for many of these people within the government and the party now to leave aside their ambitions and make more flexible their position in order to facilitate a change.

If they keep forcing their cards, it may be that one of these days, they and their families end up receiving a well-deserved punishment for all the abuses and crimes they have committed or have been accomplices of during these years and all the illicit activities they have practiced.

It is important to note that the size of the current structures of the party and the government of Cuba, which are designed for a centralized concept of government, according to the communist vision, can be considered very large for a country of its size and this represents a heavy burden, especially given their low level of efficiency and productivity.

There are so many people involved at the top levels of the present regime, that things may get very confusing in a stage of transition and even more so if what happens is a more drastic change.

If one considers the number of political and administrative organizations, the numerous ministries and other institutions, most of them with provincial and even international branches and dependencies, plus the different bodies of the armed forces and the secret services, the number of people under this huge structure of power is very large.

Considering that there is no way that the country can achieve any progress if it continues operating under this unproductive apparatus, it is almost certain that it will take a total transformation of the main elements of the political system to change this; therefore, this brings one to the conclusion that there may not be any other alternative available for Cuba than a democratic revolution.

I believe that in order to be able to advance, Cuba needs a radical change, which alters deeply its political and economic orientation and its government structure, its system of laws and the main figures who govern the country.

In Cuba, there is a need for something radically new that could bring freedom, democracy, and progress to the Cuban people, which translates in the establishment of a different political and economic order and most especially within this, in a climate of respect for individual human rights.

I understand that many of the people who are currently involved in the different levels of the Cuban government and have not been involved in crimes, should be able to participate in the political future of the island, without any kind of limitations.

One would think that, given the current structure of power in Cuba, which is immensely larger than any other Cuban political and economic power that could exist abroad, and given the lack of any well-structured movement of opposition that could be strong enough to represent a real and valid alternative of government, the most likely scenario for the immediate future of the island would be some kind of transition within the system, but things not necessarily have to be that way.

The conditions in which Cuba is at this moment, with a marked degree of social failure, a bankrupt state, and the violation of all the rules of good government, plus a repressive policy that ignores all human rights, may force whoever takes power in Cuba to follow a different path and start dismantling the current system almost immediately, introducing measures of political democratization and economic common sense, allowing more qualified and decent people to manage their country.

If certainly most of what happens in a situation of change in the island will largely depend on what the main people, who become the new key figures of it, have in their minds, the above are factors of weight that may influence them to take a new course.

If a sudden social explosion takes places in Cuba and a wave of spontaneous rebellion sweeps the structures of power, this may reach a point in which the intervention of foreign forces under the United Nations may be required to avoid a blood bath, and the same can happen if a military coup by some younger officers, whether with new democratic ideas or not, takes place.

It may be advisable, given the state of things in the island, that many people start thinking about what to do if this occurs because there is a very real possibility that our generation sees those changes happening.

If none of the above possibilities occur, the participation of people from the Cuban exiled community in any future government of the island, as well as the presence of new investing capital to promote the development of the economy, will probably have to wait some more time, until sooner or later changes are implemented in the policies of the island, including the ideological reorientation of its system or until a new overwhelming democratic revolution takes place at a later day.

One way or another, any new government Cuba will have will be forced to start introducing changes and most of those changes that are required contradict the own nature of the current regime; therefore, there it won't be possible that anybody can avoid to change somehow it.

There may be people who can try to delay this mentioned changes, but this will only last until they are swept by the historical trends because, evidently, the wave of changes will come one way or another, because this is the only way to put Cuba in the track of progress and prosperity.

One of the main problems Cuba will have in the future is the need to enforce a system of laws and administration to eradicate corruption and impunity and to control the personal behavior of people in positions of power, which have been so deeply and widely established in the island, at all levels and forms, that they represent a real plague.

The above has become a problem of mentality for many Cubans, which is probably influenced by the apparent easiness with which many people, politicians, and businessmen, for more than a century have accumulated undue richness, thanks to their illegal practices and their association with government positions.

Like in many other countries, there are Cubans, who see the government as the source of all kind of chances and opportunities for their easy enrichment and a life of ostentation and do not care much about moral and honest values.

Unless the future Cuban government establishes much more strict rules in regard to this and a more stringent system of laws is established in the island, which prevail above individualities and positions, the chances of having a good government there would remain slim and this would have serious consequences, one of them that the possibilities of bringing the country and its people for a new path of prosperity and administrative success will not be possible.

Another problem many Cubans will have to deal with is their enormous ego, which affects people at all levels and inhibit an objective vision of their role and their disciplined participation in any political movement.

There seems to be a condition among many Cubans that every time people assume a leadership role, they are considered to be irreplaceable and do not want to accept any democratic rules to transfer their positions after some time, ignoring the need for periodical elections to allow new figures to govern.

After sixty years of Castro's dictatorship and another previous seven years of Batista's, plus several other shorter attempts of dictatorship during the years of the republic, I believe that it is time for the introduction in Cuba of an equilibrated system, which includes the possibility of periodical elections, under a well-established and seriously enforced system of laws.

I believe that most of the success of Cubans in the United States and other countries has come from having found in them an established system of laws and regulations, which has made impossible to them to enforce their own capricious will.

Apparently, we are a courageous race of entrepreneurial and hardworking people, but we have lacked other capacities to govern our own country properly.

It is also worrying to me to realize that many of the current entrepreneurial people that exist in Cuba and outside of it, who think, no doubt, of the future of the island, do not see it through the prism of patriotism and virtue, or as a source of honest possibilities created by a new development orientation, but simply as the opening of all sorts of dubious opportunities. If this is not realistically controlled, the future of Cuba will remain somber, even if Castro's clan is gone.

A sense of reality, even when one always leaves room for optimism, indicates that, given the most likely narrow timeframe established by the advanced age of all the main key figures of the current system, the chances that a completely new movement can suddenly appear and almost spontaneously grow to represent a force able to effectively challenge the current structure of power are limited. Usually, this kind of movements takes some time to materialize; however this is not impossible.

The above analysis of alternatives leaves a middle ground option, in which some people of more recent generations can assume control of the country, perhaps after someone among the older figures who can physically last longer tries to take control of it for a short time.

Most likely, as I said before, any figure who can assume a position of leadership will be forced by reality to introduce changes that allow the gradual growth of new democratic political forces and new economic policies.

If the above does not happen, and the new leaders decide to continue the same path established by Castro, there will most likely be a huge violent social conflict in Cuba. In my view, we must avoid this situation because we cannot continue within the vicious circle of violence to which Castro malevolently is trying to drag the Cuban people after he is no longer in power.

I believe that the most intelligent approach that Cubans could take, considering those who live inside and outside the island, consists of adopting a more flexible and rational approach in order to deal with the future in a civilized way, trying to leave behind the terrible era of Castro.

There are moral and legal imperatives, however, that must be allowed to prevail and must serve as the basis for the development of the Cuban society.

I think that a good deal of effort will be required to control the confronting emotions that currently exist, which were artificially stimulated by Castro, to gradually eliminate the hatred and division planted during half a century by him and allow a process of healing.

Cuba will need the establishment of totally new economic policies, as a basic requirement to achieve an accelerated development, that translates in progress and the improvement of living condition for the people and this will only be possible if the system is changed and there is a drastic change of ideology and all the repressed economic and social forces are liberated by a process of democratization.

There is a need for foreign capital and the introduction of modern technologies and systems in the island, as well as for the opening of new markets for Cuban products and the development to its full potential of the tourism industry, which can become one of the largest in the world, once the current regime disappears.

The United States represents the natural market for many Cuban products and it is the main potential source for its tourism, and Cuba represents, at the same time, a good market for numerous products of the United States while the island has also all the potential conditions to become an important center of manufacture and for the development of sophisticated technological industries, as well as for other industries associated with the processing of raw materials, refining of oil, production of cement, and many other products for the world markets.

Once the Castro's regime and his system are gone, Cuba can become, in a very few years, an important place for numerous economic activities, and its people can improve substantially its standards of living and income per capita, which will reflect in the transformation of the island, and it is likely that Cuba may become a better example for the rest of the developing world for these and other achievements than the kind of example Castro has pretended it to be.

Every analysis on the potential that Cuba has indicates that practically every sector of its economy and society could receive an enormous impulse as a result of a change of system, with many positive implications for the Cuban people.

In my view, the real alternatives for the immediate future of Cuba after Castro must be considered in a different way from the one that has become more frequent, which I described above.

In reality, the alternatives the people who take control of the government will have are simply two: not to allow a process of liberation, which has the "incentive" only for those in charge of trying to become a Castro imitator, or allow this process and liberate all the whole potential of the country.

As I explain in the prologue of this book, I went to prison in Cuba for trying to create a new political party in the island, which was based on the ideas of Jose Marti, our national hero. It was 1988, and at that time, it was almost impossible to even think about doing something like that;

however, thirty two years later, I still think that the ideas and principles of that new party, which was censored by Castro brutally, are still valid.

This is why I include in this book as an addendum those basic principles of the Cuban Revolutionary Party, which also serve to illustrate more comprehensibly my views about what the future should be for the Cuban people.

I believe that, even in the middle of the catastrophe Castro is going to leave behind, there will be people who can rationalize and will be able to take the proper decisions to bring Cuba to a new path of progress and freedom.

Addendum

~

Some of the Basic Principles of the Cuban Revolutionary Party

Some of the Basic Principles of the Cuban Revolutionary Party

- Development of a fully democratic society oriented to the national unity and based on the rule of law and the moral, spiritual, and patriotic values of the Cuban people, with equal rights for all and inspired by the ideas and concepts of Jose Marti.
- Promotion of a real development for the Cuban society, which can materialize in the improvement of living conditions for all its members.
- Development of an accelerated plan of construction of houses and new infrastructure to satisfy the accumulated needs of the population.
- Establishment without limitations of all the principles of the Universal Declaration of Human Rights of UNO.
- Assistance for the development of new store networks of foods, appliances and clothes.
- In regard to foreign policy, full support to the movements for peace and the development of all nations.
- In regard to interior policy, establishment of principles that allow the most absolute freedom of expression and association, on the basis of ethical and moral principles, this including the freedom to exist, with full rights, of all political parties, religious

institutions, trade unions, professional and cultural associations, sport associations as well as newspapers, internet services and every press media.

- Absolute equal rights for people from all races and development of a policy oriented to eliminate any remains of racial discrimination.
- The same absolute equal rights will be applied in regard to political, religious, and sexual orientation.
- Establishment of free elections, with secret ballots, on regular periodical basis, for all the positions of government, at all levels of the society, ensuring a proper balanced regional representation and allowing the open participation of all the candidates that wish to be elected and free access to all communication and news means.
- Promotion of a balanced development for the whole country and the different sectors of the Cuban economy and society, including the assistance for the development of national firms.
- Promotion and development of an efficient and modern economy, with the participation of public and private companies, as well as mixed enterprises and cooperatives and establishment of a proper and balanced taxation system.
- Development of a policy oriented to attract foreign capital and the participation of foreign firms, under an adequate set of rules that can allow the orderly development of all branches of the Cuban economy and foreign trade and an adequate taxation system that contributes to the national development.
- Promotion of links between foreign and national firms.
- Promotion and assistance to Cuban firms interested in foreign markets.
- Implementation of an educational reform that removes political indoctrination from the school curriculum
- Development of adequate and rational economic and financing national policies, including the development of private banks and the promotion of financing plans oriented to develop all the different branches of the economy.
- Development of plans oriented to promote the individual initiative.

BIBLIOGRAPHY

- A Background and Chronology of Castro-Vatican Relations, American Atheist #377, Jan 19, 1997.

- Amnesty International, Yearbook 1987-to present.

- Anuario Estadistico de Cuba, 1957-to present

- Castro's Speech to the Intellectuals, June 30, 1961.

- Castro, the Blacks and Africa, by Carlos Moore.

- Castro's War on religion, Puebla Institute, May 1991.

- Che Guevara and the Latin American Revolution, By Manuel Piñeiro.

- Church and State in Cuba's Revolution by Silvia Pedraza, University of Michigan, May 2009.

- Cómo Terminan las Democracias by Jean Françoise Revel

- Conflicting Missions, Havana, Washington and Africa, by Piero Gleijeses, 2002.

- Corruption in Cuba, Castro and Beyond, by Sergio Diaz and Jorge Perez.

- Constituciones de la República de Cuba, Academia de la Historia de Cuba, 1952.

- Cuba, Siglo XX, by Ines Segura Bustamante

- Cuba in the Twenty First Century. Conference by Carlos Saladrigas and Julia E. Sweig, Council of Foreign Relations.

- Cuba: Nickel on the Line, Time Magazine, September 29, 1952.

- Cuba's Economy, Global Security.

- Cuba. The World Fact Book.-Central Intelligence Agency.

- Cuba's Foreign Debt Fact Sheet, Bureau of Western Hemisphere Affairs, July 24, 2003.

- Cuba's Hard Currency Debt, by Gabriel Fernandez.

- Cuba: Mito y Realidad, by Juan Clark.

- Cuba's Mortgaged Future: Castro Regime Foreign Debt 2007. Cuba Facts, Issue 37, March 2008.

- Cuba's Youth: The New Opposition, by Dr. Andy Gomez.

- Cuban Communism, edited by I. Horowitz and Jaime Suchlicki.

- Cuban Leadership Overview, April 2009. Open Source Center Report.

- Desarrollo Agrícola de Cuba, I and II, Colegio de Ingenieros Agrónomos y Azucareros, 1992 and 1994.

- Demand to return to the Nickel Market in 2010, by Roskill Information Services, Jan 11,2010.

- El Banco de Fomento Agrícola e Industrial de Cuba, by Ing. Casto Ferragut.

- El Estado del Medio Ambiente en Cuba, Asociación Medio Ambiental Cubana, 1992 and 1997.

- Escambray: La Guerra Olvidada, by Enrique Encinosa.

- Estrategia Ambiental Nacional, Ministerio de Ciencia y Tecnología, June 1997.

- Fidel Castro: My Life, A Spoken Autobiography by Ignacio Ramonet.

- Historia Herética de la Revolución Fidelista, by Servando Gonzalez.

- History of Cuba and its Relationships with the United States, Phillip Foner.

- Human Rights in Cuba: An America's Watch Report.

- Impresiones, by Pepin Rivero, 1914-44, Diario de la Marina, 1964.

- Informe Nacional a la Conferencia de Naciones Unidas sobre Medio Ambiente y Desarrollo, Brasil 1992, Comarna.

- Inside the Cuban revolution, Fidel Castro and the Urban Underground, by Julia E. Sweig, Council of Foreign Relations, May 2002.

- JFK: The Cuba Files, by Fabian Escalante.

- La Nueva Historia de la República de Cuba, by Herminio Portel Vilá.

- La Población de Cuba, by Center of Demographic Studies, 1976.

- La Situación del Medio Ambiente en Cuba, XII Conference Cuban Patriotic Board and by Andres J. Solares,1992.

- Let's Talk About the Cuban Economy, by M.B.Roque.

- List of the Richest Communists of Cuba, by Kennetth Rijock, Complinet.

- Los Propietarios de Cuba, 1958, by Guillermo Jimenez.

- Some photos come from the site www.SkyscraperCity, while others came from friends who travel to Cuba or have connections in the island.

- Race and the Cuban Revolution, by Lisa Brock and Otis Cunningham, Center for Latin American Studies, Pittsburgh University.

- Cuba says nickel now top foreign exchange earner. Reuter, Jan 15,2008.

- The Autobiography of Fidel Castro, by Norberto Fuentes.

- The Cuban Economy After Castro, by Raj M. Desai, Brookings Institution, March 28, 2010.

- The Cuban Economy: After the Smoke Clears. Business Week, February 2, 2008.

- The Cuban Economy is Up . . . in Flames, by Oscar Espinosa Chepe, March 8, 2010.

- The Cuban Economy at the Stat of the 21st Century, by Jorge I. Dominguez and Lorena Barberia, David Rockefeller Center for Latin American Studies, 2004.

- The Cuban Economy: Amid Economic Stagnation and Reversal of reforms, by Mauricio de Miranda, Canadian Foundation for the Americas.

- The Cuban Economy as Seen Through Its Trading Partners, by Jorge Salazar Carrillo and David Ebro, Brooking Institution.

- The Cuban Revolution, A Critical Perspective, by Sam Dolgoff.

- The Cuban revolution, by Marifely Perez Stable, 1999.

- The Cuban revolution, by Teo Babun and Victor A. Triay

- The Destruction of the Environment in Cuba, United Nations Conference on the Environment, Brazil, by Andres Solares, 1992.

- The Fall and Recovery of the Cuban Economy on the 1990's: Mirage or reality, by Ernesto Hernandez Cata, IMF Working Paper.

- The Mineral Industry of Cuba, by Ivette Torres, 1998.

- The Politics of Psychiatry in Revolutionary Cuba, by Charles Brown and Armando Lago.

- The Pope opposes Communism, but how does he see Castro?, by Juan O. Tamayo, November 19,1996.

- The Problems of Pollution in Cuba, Interamerican Engineering Conference, by Andres Solares, 1990.

- Ultimate Sacrifice, by Lamar Waldron and Tom Hartmann.

- Vilma Espin: The First Lady of the Cuban Revolution, by Alejandro Guevara.

- What the Cuban Revolution Means to Older Cubans, by David L. Strug, PhD.

- Where is the Cuban Economy Heading, by Remy Herrera, Centre d'Economie de la Sorbonne, 2006.

- Wikipedia.

- Wild Cuba, Smithsonian, May 2003.

- Women and the Cuban Revolution, by Fidel Castro, Vilma Espin and others.

[1] Cuban Statistic Yearbook of 1957 published by Cuba's Ministerio de Hacienda

Lightning Source UK Ltd.
Milton Keynes UK
UKHW011412030720
365982UK00001B/71